*Erotic Liberation*

# Erotic Liberation

*Selected Lectures on Thelema: 2019-2023*

## Entelecheia

LAPIS MERCURII PRODUCTIONS
Seattle, Washington
2023

ISBN 979-8-89121-595-5



Designed and produced by
Lapis Mercurii Productions
Seattle, Washington
lapis-mercurii.org

Contents

# Foreword by IAO131

Aleister Crowley once wrote, "The price of existence is eternal warfare." It is also the price of engaging in the online community of Thelema. As with several of my friendships, my first memories of interacting with Entelecheia are almost entirely of arguing with him a lot through online forums. While I've always loved viciously arguing the finer details of religious philosophy, it admittedly takes a rather hard-headed person to endure these conversations. Entelecheia not only survived but also challenged me and my assumptions in a way that feels rare in our community. I left several debates feeling annoyed and perturbed as he would reject points I felt were obviously true. I would be left with nagging doubts around long-held beliefs; other times I would be frustrated or confused.

To me, these conversational discomforts were actually very precious: rather than feeling satisfied and complacent I knew that something was happening with my understanding of Thelema. The discomfort meant I was being challenged. Like many others, I was tired of the same rehashing of the same Thelemic material in the same way. The ongoing interactions with Entelecheia spurred me to return to the source material and to rethink things I thought were settled. We know that a pathway is opened to the Light, not through already knowing everything but through trials and troubles, through the strife of contending forces. Entelecheia's incisive wit can be quite a contending force, yet he has helped me reorient my understanding of Thelema: remembering I came to Thelema not to be an "expert", "writer", or "leader" but to learn and grow. Through the trials of debate and discussion, I found new insights and a deepening of my understanding. It is these kinds of intellectual and spiritual trials that I hope you as the reader can experience in reading this book—not necessarily to agree with every single proposition, but being open enough to be challenged and changed.

This book is a collection of Entelecheia's various essays and lectures on the subject of Thelema, but I believe it represents much more than that. It represents the possibility of taking Thelema seriously. It shows an understanding of Thelema beyond being merely an edgy or spooky flavor of occultism. Entelecheia really does take Thelema seriously, and in reading his material it becomes obvious that Thelema has so much more potential than just being encouraging self-help for occultists. These essays and lectures reveal a Thelema that is much more than an excuse for bad behavior. They show the possibility of Thelema as a real tradition: something substantial, encompassing, and relevant. They reveal a Thelema worth studying, worth being part of, and worth dedicating oneself to as an expression of that timeless Light of the Gnosis passed down through the aeons.

It is undoubtedly not easy being a torchbearer of an obscure and opaque religious tradition in these times, but I have no doubts that the flame is alive in Entelecheia's hands. He has a characteristic sharp, almost harsh intellect, an unflinching confidence, and unshakeable resilience in his approach. (Of course, he can also be very kind, caring, and funny but I do not hold that against him too much.) I have no doubt that he is contributing to the spiritual health of Thelema as a tradition and will continue to help the Thelemic community flourish. I give my curmudgeonly benedictions to him and to all those who wish to deepen their understanding of Thelema and themselves through grappling with these writings.

# Introduction

*Do what thou wilt shall be the whole of the Law.*

It is rare that I give a lecture on a subject I am not in the process of learning something about, and so the essays collected herein represent a process of discovery about Thelema I underwent from 2019 to 2023.

These lectures cover a variety of topics: the nature of the universe and the individual, liberation, vulnerability and embodiment, the will, magick, theology, and the religious significance of beauty and art. While these lectures do not represent a systematic treatment of Thelema, they are united by several themes.

The most important of these themes is that Thelema is at minimum about *two*, not *one*. The ultimate principle in Thelemic philosophy is the Qabalistic Zero, what Crowley refers to as "nothingness extended in no categories," but this principle necessarily expresses itself through the dynamic interplay of opposites. When Crowley summarized Thelema, it was always with *two* statements—"Do what thou wilt shall be the whole of the Law" and "Love is the law, love under will"—not just one. This means that any *monistic* interpretation of Thelema has to be highly qualified, and any *reductionistic* interpretation must be avoided.

The most important of these opposed pairs is Nuit and Hadit. Nuit is the principle of form or appearance; Hadit is the principle of change. These principles always only ever occur together. They unite to form gods or souls, which *The Book of the Law* refers to as *stars*. Stars are manifest individuals or unities undergoing constant change.

This leads to the second important theme in these lectures: the *evolution-*

*ary* framing of Thelema. Hadit is that which drives change in the individual. It is an inchoate will-to-be or to become. Nuit is the particular form or appearance change is constrained to express itself through. Hadit is analogous to variation, while Nuit is analogous to selection. While Darwinian evolution explains the dynamic change of *species* over time, Thelema explains the dynamic change of the *individual* over time.

A third idea is that what we normally take to be the essence of ourselves is actually the product of the complex, ongoing "play" between Nuit and Hadit. We are complex systems that have the ability to reflect upon and work with their own complexity so as to generate a closer "fit" between the unfathomable depths of ourselves and the incomprehensible vastness of nature. Through appropriate self-discipline, we can discover and amplify our moral, intellectual, and spiritual powers. We are not merely subject to change; we can also *grow*. This is what Crowley refers to as *love under will* or *magick*.

Since the drive to become must always take some form, and since no form exists in isolation from the rest of nature, *relationality* is a fourth theme central to the interpretation of Thelema presented in these lectures. At a bare minimum, in order to have any awareness of itself, the will must experience opposition between itself and some state of affairs. Overcoming duality can only mean something if there is a real opposition to be overcome. But for embodied beings, duality is never once and for all overcome. So the question naturally arises of how to build relations with ourselves, our world, and the people in it so as to sustain growth and power over the course of a life. This requires the type of practical wisdom embodied in the Four Powers of the Sphinx. While Thelema rules out *a priori* moral truths or prohibitions, ethics is nevertheless essential in order to live a happy life.

Along with relationality, *embodiment* is central to Thelema. This is the fifth theme. We are restricted to a particular perspective on the universe, and our interaction with it—whether it be outside ourselves or inside ourselves—is always mediated. Since the body is necessary, *vulnerability* is an inescapable dimension of human experience. Bodies get sick. They can be harmed. They age and die. Rather than limiting the expression of our wills, however, bodies serve as the conditions of their realization. Without a body, there is no power, influence, or will. The conditions of our liberation and the conditions of our enslavement are two edges of the same knife. If we are to master life, we must turn to face and embrace that which undermines and limits our mastery of the same. This is not just true of our physicality. We must also embrace those "lower" parts of our psyche: our selfishness, our pettiness, our envy, our pride, and all the other aspects of ourselves we would rather not admit we have. The point of embracing them is not to *surrender* to them but rather to *subordinate* them to the will through self-discipline.

The centrality of the body to Thelema leads naturally to the consideration of aesthetic appreciation and eroticism, the final two themes.

Beauty is an image of all our powers reconciled with one another. Beauty presents internal feeling reconciled with objective reality and form reconciled with content. Whether we are speaking of natural beauty or a work of art, beauty is an image of the unity we must bring to ourselves if we are to consistently do our wills and experience lives of meaning and purpose. Beauty is not *identical* with the accomplishment of the Great Work, but it presents it as a stimulus for the imagination. For this reason beauty adumbrates eternal spiritual truths.

Meanwhile, perhaps the most important implication of Thelema being about the interplay of *two* principles is that experience is fundamentally *erotic* in nature. Our reality is constructed from the yearning of the unfathomable depths of ourselves for the incomprehensible vastness of nature. Because this occurs through the medium of the body—which itself is a product of this erotic relationship—sensation, metabolism, and intercourse must bear the weight of cosmological and theological significance. That these are also markers of our finitude and sites of the potential loss of our dignity and even our sanity means that the Thelemic path of liberation is a knife's edge. The committed Thelemite plays a game with the highest stakes imaginable.

At its extreme, eroticism is the mutual annihilation of the two through fusion. It is the complete transcendence of duality which we find in mystical experience. We do not come to possess nature or the other through eroticism; rather, we lose ourselves through it. This is what Manon Hedenborg White has referred to as the "erotic destruction of self".[1] It is the transcendence of the sense of a limited, separate self through erotic unbinding. The spirit of this process is the Holy Guardian Angel or Apophis. Paradoxically, the self-possession and self-control of the earlier parts of the Thelemic path culminate in complete surrender to the other. One's subjectivity is turned inside-out. It is *exploded*, an accomplishment symbolized by one's exsanguination into the chalice of the Goddess Babalon. The nature of Babalon and her relationship with other figures such as Baphomet, Chaos, and the Phallus are touched upon in the theological lectures in this volume. It is my hope to

---

1  Manon Hedenborg White, *The Eloquent Blood* (New York: Oxford University Press, 2020), 54.

deliver a more systematic treatment of these subjects in the near future. In the meantime I have presented an outline in my lecture on the Creed of the Gnostic Mass.

As most of Crowley's works have been available online for awhile, I have chosen not to reference print copies but rather titles, chapters, and sections as appropriate. Hopefully this will help any researcher quickly look up the relevant passage as needed. Other works have been cited in the footnotes, and a full bibliography is included at the end.

Most of these lectures were delivered through Ordo Templi Orientis, an organization I have had the pleasure of being a member of since 2014. I always try to write with empathy for my audience, and so the form of these lectures is inconceivable without those who have patiently attended and listened to them in person at Horizon Lodge in Seattle, in other locations, and online these last several years. In particular I would like to thank Scott Wilde and Kellen Barber, both of whom have offered encouragement and helpful feedback. "Uncle" Tau Omphalos provides an almost bottomless source of inspiration, both for my reflections upon Thelema and for my continuing involvement in OTO. Finally, writing and presenting under the lidless, disapproving eye of IAO131 keeps me on my toes. We have some of the most heated disagreements I have with anyone about spirituality and philosophy. The fact that they remain productive, friendly, and funny means a great deal to me.

It is my hope that these lectures provide new ways of understanding Thelema and applying it to the present moment. It is also my hope that they offer new frames that create the possibility of asking previously unasked questions of the spiritual philosophy Aleister Crowley created over a century ago.

*Love is the law, love under will.*

Entelecheia
Seattle, WA
Summer Solstice 2023

# 1

# What Is Thelema?

Thelema is the Greek word for *will*.

*Do what thou wilt shall be the whole of the Law* is widely regarded as a summary statement of Thelema. Adherents to Thelema are called *Thelemites*. They typically greet one another in written and verbal communications by saying *Do what thou wilt shall be the whole of the Law*. Sometimes they abbreviate this as 93. 93 is the enumeration of the Greek word *Thelema* when we represent each letter with a number by a system of counting called isopsephy.

93 is also the enumeration of another Greek word, *agape*, which means *love*. Along with *Do what thou wilt*, a second, complementary summary statement of Thelema is *Love is the law, love under will*. So in response to hearing *Do what thou wilt shall be the whole of the Law*, Thelemites will often reply with *Love is the law, love under will* or with 93 93/93 or just 93s. It's a typical Thelemic form of greeting.

Thelema can be tricky to define or even to categorize. There were times when Crowley described it as a religion, and then there were times he emphatically said it was not a religion. This is not as contradictory as it sounds. Even in Crowley's time, religion had come to represent the ossified accretions of superstition. By contrast, writing in the wake of Nietzsche's declaration of the death of God, Crowley's intentions were modernistic and iconoclastic.

On the other hand, consider the etymology of *religion*. It derives from the Latin *religio*, which means *obligation*, *bond*, or *reverence*, and the verb *religare*, which means *to bind*. As we will see, binding and hence religion are apt to describe Thelema.

Especially in the context of Ordo Templi Orientis (O.T.O.), Thelema shows itself also to be a philosophy. The emphasis of O.T.O.'s teachings is on cosmology, ethics, and how they inform our path through life. This is not philosophy as a detached, academic subject of interest solely to intellectual specialists. It is closer to what Pierre Hadot has called *philosophy as a way of life*. By this measure, Thelema is more like ancient Stoicism or Neoplatonism than it is like contemporary academic philosophy.

At the risk of oversimplifying, the core subject matter of Thelema is identical with the core subject matter of religion in its deepest sense; however, Thelemic creeds or doctrines are not the essence of Thelema. Our Holy Texts—one of which I will discuss tonight—are not sets of factually true propositions or beliefs about the world. We don't read our Holy Books to get the kind of information we'd get from reading the New York Times or a textbook on quantum mechanics. By contrast, our doctrines are meant to provoke us into awareness of the sacred depths of ourselves and of the world we live in.

This implies that the depths of Thelema are esoteric. Thelema is intended to lead you to an experience of self-transcendence which shatters illusions about self and world. The goal of Thelema isn't to give you more information about the world or yourself, although in some ways it does that. The point of Thelema is to radically transform your relationship with yourself and the world. That makes it more like Gnosticism than, for example, mainstream Protestantism.

Instead of pretending to explain the entirety of Thelema to you tonight— which I doubt anyone could do—I'll instead drill down into one aspect of Thelema which I think is central to it, which I think is relatively easy to understanding, which pulls together lots of aspects of Thelema, and which has a large number of implications for the cultivation of meaning and spiritual practice. This is the idea of what Aleister Crowley thought the human being is.

## Every man and every woman is a star

In order to understand how Crowley understood the human being, let's consider the foundational text of Thelema, *The Book of the Law*. *The Book of the Law*, also known by its Latin title, *Liber AL vel Legis sub figura 220*, is a short book of 220 verses. Crowley claimed it was dictated to him in Cairo, Egypt in 1904 by a disembodied spiritual being that called itself *Aiwass*. *The Book of the Law* is the source of the phrases *Do what thou wilt shall be the whole of the Law* and *Love is the law, love under will.*

In his 1938 Introduction to *The Book of the Law*, Aleister Crowley said that *The Book of the Law* explains the universe. It describes how the reality we live in is organized. He said the world is composed of two elements. There is space and the matter occupying it—what we might call nature or the sum total of all possibilities—and any conscious viewpoint on nature. These two principles are symbolized in the book by two deities that appear on the funerary stele of Ankh-f-n-khonsu, a priest of the Egyptian god Mentu who lived in Thebes around 725 BCE. The first is symbolized by the Egyptian sky goddess, Nuit, and the second by the winged solar disk, Hadit. There is also a third deity prominent in *The Book of the Law*, Ra-Hoor-Khuit, who I will talk about at the end.

In his Introduction, Crowley described these Egyptian deities as literary conveniences. He describes Shiva and Shakti as roughly equivalent terms, and he often describes them using non-theological language. So while these ideas are represented in *The Book of the Law* as Egyptian deities, it is important not to reduce Thelema to a revival of Egyptian polytheism.

Crowley goes on to say that every event—in other words, every change—is a uniting of Hadit with one of the experiences possible to Him (in other words, some aspect of Nuit). Each person is defined as an aggregate of such experiences, constantly changing with each fresh event, which affects him or her either consciously or subconsciously. This aggregate of experiences which makes up the essence of each person is what Crowley called the *star*, after the third verse of the first chapter of *The Book of the Law* which reads, "Every man and every woman is a star."

According to Crowley, the human being is not a simple entity. Nor would it be appropriate to describe the human being as an animal with a spirit added to it. A human being is the *product* of the interaction between two fundamental, divine principles or forces. There is the active, masculine principle, Hadit. Hadit is both the subjective point of view as well as the "force of energy" and "fire of motion" that animates living beings. An otherwise healthy, thriving, living being doesn't just decide one day that they've had enough of living and experiencing and just sit down and wait for death to set in. Our will-to-be is open-ended and has no final purpose.

The ecstatic coupling of Hadit with Nuit generates our experience of a constantly changing universe. Unlike Hadit, who is the concealed force driving change, Nuit is form or manifest existence. She is all that exists and the condition of all that exists. Hadit's interactions with Her drive changes in appearances or what Crowley refers to as the "events" that constitute the star. But changes do not just occur randomly. An apple will not suddenly turn into a double-decker bus. So while Hadit's actions bring about events, Nuit sets conditions to those changes.

We can understand this interaction on analogy with Darwinian evolution. Darwinian evolution operates on the basis of two principles: variation and selection. Even within a species, not all individuals look the same. They are all at least slightly different in appearance from one another. Some variations (such as cancer or certain deformities) are deleterious, while others allow an orgasm to exploit hitherto unavailable niches in the environment. In the latter case, they *increase* the options available to an organism. The counterbalancing principle, selection, *reduces* options for an organism. Scarcity of resources and competition place selective pressures on a species. The interaction between these two principles—variation and selection—drives the dynamic change of species over time.

The interaction between Hadit and Nuit that creates the individual human being is analogous to Darwinian evolution. Instead of driving the dynamic change of species over time, the coupling of Hadit with Nuit drives the change of the *individual* over time. The core drive of the individual to be, to thrive in its environment, is what Crowley calls *will*. The participation between the individual and the environment which results is what Crowley calls *love*. Conceived this way, will and love are general principles constituting the universe. But to consciously work with that relationship so as to optimize the "fittedness" between the Hadit within and Nuit without, so that there is continual development and constant growth, is what Crowley calls *love under will* or *magick*.

Deep inside of you, below the level of your conscious self, below the level of your freedom of choice and your sense of who you are, there is a primordial impulse or urge *to be*, *to become*, or *to go*. In and of itself, it has no particular reason, aim, or purpose. This is what Crowley calls *Hadit*. The action of Hadit is called the *will*. The Greek word for will is *Thelema*.

But Hadit expresses Himself in an environment which constrains His going in various ways. That environment—which is space and the matter in it—is called *Nuit*. Nuit constrains the activities of Hadit. Constraints don't just restrict us; they create possibilities. For instance, a bird flying through a strong headwind might be led to believe (were it capable of complex thought) that its flight would be faster if it encountered no air resistance. But if that were the case, it would just fall to the ground. This is how Nuit functions as the condition of possibilities. In contrast with Hadit, who makes events or changes occur, Nuit makes things *possible* by constraining events in various ways.

Who and what you are as an individual is the product of the interaction between these two principles. Your physical body, your personality, your mind, your intellect, your memory, your imagination, and your sense of agency are all the results of the constant, passionate, ongoing interactions between Hadit and Nuit, an interaction which Crowley calls *love*.

You are not Nuit. You are not Hadit. You are Nuit and Hadit conjoined. Every conjunction between the two is called a *star*. As *The Book of the Law* says, "Every man and every woman is a star."

When we self-consciously work to affect a more optimal relationship between Hadit within and Nuit without—in other words when we are affecting a stronger connection between the depths of ourselves and the depths of reality—that is called *love under will* or *magick*.

Hadit represents the core drive to become. Love is the result of that drive expressing itself in an environment. Love under will is when we consciously optimize the relationship between the core of ourselves and our environment. The result is that we experience constant, dynamic, continual, open-ended growth. Our moral and spiritual powers increase. We experience more joy and meaning in life.

Having established the nature of the individual human being as the conjunction of Hadit and Nuit, let us consider some of the implications that follow.

## Implications

### Flow States

First, the deepest part of yourself strives to have contact with the deepest part of reality. Many of the most satisfying experiences in life confirm this. For instance, when you are acquiring a new skill or are challenging yourself to develop an existing skill, it is necessary to direct all of your attention and effort to the task right in front of you. Your consciousness and your will become deeply coupled with your environment. This leads to a diminution of your sense of self and self-management. The resulting state of mind is called "flow" or being "in the zone". This is a universal, cross-cultural, intrinsically satisfying state.

The experience of profound natural beauty also confirms this. Think about a time you were hiking or on a road trip, and rounding a bend you are suddenly confronted with a stunning view of a mountain range or a coast. We often describe these views as "picture perfect". At those moments we instinctively think of natural beauty as though it were artistic beauty: in other words we start to treat nature as though it were created *by* a mind like ours *for* a mind like ours. A coupling occurs between the depths of ourselves and the depths of the world, and we feel at home in the universe.

This sort of deep coupling also occurs when we become absorbed in a compelling novel or film. It also occurs when we are lost in painting, writing, or making music.

Think about what it's like to fall in love. You are revealing depths of yourself to another person while they are doing the same with you. There is mutual, accelerating disclosure. It's not an accident that Crowley used the term *love* to describe the relationship I'm talking about.

## Connectedness

Second, notice how this emphasis on connection or what Crowley calls *love* harkens back to the original meaning of religion as binding or connecting, especially connecting with the sacred. The goal of Thelema is the deepening of a kind of connection which we're already familiar with in our everyday lives. When this connection is profound—when our sense of oneness with reality is pushed to the extreme—that's generally how people describe religious or mystical experiences.

## Open-Ended Growth and Development

Third, notice how the focus of Thelema is not on a particular object or outcome but rather on a process: love under will. Love relationships don't have a particular object. They are open-ended and adaptive. To stop working on a love relationship is the end of the relationship. Love does not have any final form.

Crowley said, "The joy of life consists in the exercise of one's energies, continual growth, constant change, the enjoyment of every new experience. To stop means simply to die. The eternal mistake of mankind is to set up an attainable ideal."

This isn't simply romanticism. Other religions set up a narrative ideal of what a person should be like. We've all heard the expression "What would Jesus do?" There's a Jesus-like figure in Thelema, and that is Ra-Hoor-Khuit, the third figure after Nuit and Hadit who figures in *The Book of the Law*.

At the risk of oversimplifying, Ra-Hoor-Khuit is to Thelema what Christ is to Christianity. This is not an invitation to grow a beak and pluck out your eye. The ideal represented by Ra-Hoor-Khuit is that of continual growth and open-ended development. There is no such thing as a finished form of an alligator or even a human being. Species are constantly changing as a result of the dynamic interaction between variation and selection. Thelema is the same outlook applied to the individual in their spiritual development.

## Ecstatic Participation

Fourth, it is wrong to think of ourselves as detached observers of experience. We're not disembodied minds looking out at the world from behind our eyes. Our fundamental way of relating to the world is participatory.

Sometimes when congregants show up for Gnostic Mass the first time, we show them the steps and signs and words they have to say, and we explain that the Gnostic Mass is a *participatory ritual*.

*Life is a participatory ritual.*

We're caught up in things in a way which is engaged, engaging, and recip-rocal. We're not standing outside the world looking in and thinking about it. We're *in* the world—spatially, but more importantly, we're in the world in the way someone is in college or in the army or in love. We're *caught up in it*. The conscious, intellectual mind does not create that relationship or connection with the world, although it can get clearer about it.

## Freedom

Fifth, it's equally wrong to think of ourselves as detached *doers*. We're not making decisions or initiating courses of action from a place outside of the universe. We're not simply imposing our wills on reality. Our sense of agency or freedom of choice depends upon a more basic coupling within us of di-vine forces which is self-organizing and self-driven. It's the *fittedness*—or lack thereof—between these two principles which is responsible for our sense of choice and opportunity in life. One of the functions of ceremonial magick is to allow us to interact with these underlying processes by means of symbols.

## Magick and Mysticism

This leads into the sixth implication, which has to do with the self-conscious working with the relationship between these two divine principles by means of love under will or magick.

Magick in the Thelemic sense includes ceremonial magick, but it more generally involves conditioning the body and the mind so that they more adequately enable the loving interaction between Hadit within and Nuit without. Because this is an ongoing, developing process in which the conditions are constantly changing, Thelema tends to reject rigid moral and ethical codes of conduct. Instead Crowley encouraged Thelemites to develop discretion, truthfulness, courage, independence, skepticism, and other virtues that would better help them transform the conditions of life into conditions of growth and empowerment. The initiation rituals of Ordo Templi Orientis teach these virtues using the idiom of Masonic-style initiatory drama.

We saw how the coupling of Hadit with Nuit explains flow states, the experience of "being in the zone," being bowled over by natural or artistic beauty, creating art, or falling in love. A mystical experience is the extreme version of this. This is the seventh implication of our thesis. A mystical experience is not the acquisition of a new skill or a new piece of information about the world. It's more like a thunder clap as our mind and body align in such a way that these two divine principles of Nuit and Hadit rush together in a life-changing experience.

Mystical experiences heighten our sense of participation in the depths of reality. There is a sudden, deep, direct, non-intellectual understanding of reality which drastically changes the significance of self. It is the mutual, accelerating disclosure characteristic of falling in love, but now with the whole universe.

Mystical experiences also decenter us. They humiliate us. They make us realize we're not the center of things. They give us insight into our nature—and nature generally—so that we see that what we call ourselves is part of, and dependent upon, something much larger. This is the deep meaning of *true* will.

## Conclusion

Crowley's teachings, like the world they describe, are interrelated in complex ways. It is difficult to point out any one teaching underlying everything else, as all the teachings are mutually dependent. Even if we choose a teaching like *doing one's will* as our starting place, we still have to explain what it means to will, and there are a few possible points of entry. In this lecture I have taken as my point of departure the idea that every man and every woman is a *star*, that is, a product of the ecstatic coupling of the two most fundamental principles or "elements" of the Thelemic universe: Hadit and Nuit.

By beginning this way, I have chosen to emphasize the *dynamic* nature, both of the human being and the Thelemic philosophy that serves to make the human being transparent to his or herself for the purposes of self-empowerment.

Beginning this way also allows us immediately to relate Thelema to experiences all human beings are familiar with: skill-acquisition, flow states, aesthetic appreciation, artistic creation, and falling in love. This allows us to interpret the more "exotic" aspects of Thelema—mysticism and magick—as more extreme versions of experiences we are all already familiar with.

# 2

# The Path of Erotic Liberation

The term *liberation* implies that we are in a state of captivity or enslavement which Thelema is intended to free us from. If you adequately understand the problem, then you should be able to tell how and to what extent Thelema offers a solution. If you understand how and to what extent Thelema offers a solution, then you will have deep insight into what Thelema is for and why someone would want to walk the Thelemic spiritual path. Furthermore, if you recognize the problem I am about to describe as your own, and if you understand how Thelema might solve that problem, then you will understand how Thelema could potentially help you.

Crowley was attempting to solve the problem of human dissatisfaction generally, what in Buddhism is called the *First Noble Truth*. The solution offered by Thelema is the radical acceptance or affirmation of existence, which Crowley saw as identical with *doing one's will*. And the path to the achievement of this solution involved progressive overcoming of opposition between the will and things external to it, which ultimately results in the erotic unbinding of individuality and of one's own sense of separateness from things. Crowley called this method *love under will*.

## The Problem

The problem Thelema is intended to solve is the deepest problem there is: we are born into a world in which we are subject to influences and conditions beyond our control, many of which cause us stress and pain. By virtue of having bodies, we are subject to injury, sickness, aging, infirmity, and ultimately death. People and things we love go away, are unreliable, or die. Things which annoy or harm us make themselves present unbidden. In short, we suffer stress and dissatisfaction. If you are not currently suffering, you will. At the very least you probably know someone who is right now.

The solution one proposes to the problem of suffering will depend in large part on what one thinks the ultimate cause of suffering is. Christianity locates the problem in the Original Sin of Adam and Eve, who having disobeyed God and eaten the fruit of the Tree of the Knowledge of Good and Evil were stricken with the curses of self-awareness, labor, pain in childbirth, and death. According to Christianity, liberation is to be sought in the cleansing of this Original Sin through the blood shed by the sacrifice of Jesus Christ. Placing one's faith in Jesus ensures a second birth in this life and avoidance of a second death in the fires of hell.

Alternatively, one can decide that life is a bitch. There is no salvation, and it doesn't matter what you do, say, think, or feel. This is the response of nihilism, which many of us find naturally when we're about 15 or 16 years old.

By contrast the Buddha's approach was more optimistic than the nihilist approach but more DIY than the Christian approach. He believed the cause of suffering was to be found in the way the individual human being related to existence. The problem, he said, is that human beings crave or desire that things should be a certain way. We want to hold on to pleasant things, push away painful things, and ignore boring things. The problem is that we can only ever achieve so much control over things outside of us and even within ourselves. The universe is in a state of ceaseless change, and those changes occur because of conditions entirely outside our control. However, if we come to a thorough and complete understanding of the true nature of things—in other words, if we can learn at a deep level that reality is necessarily bound to disappoint us—we will become disillusioned with the universe and cease attempting to get any joy out of it. At that moment our minds will abandon the unreliable universe and instead embrace that which does not change, which in Buddhism is called *nibbana* or *nirvana*.

Aleister Crowley agreed with the Buddha on a few points, and as such, Thelema can be understood to some extent through the points of agreement and disagreement with Buddhism. Crowley was sensitive to the fact that life can be quite terrible when you get right down to it. He understood well the temptation of nihilism. Search as one may, you will find no toxic positivity in Crowley's writings. And like the Buddha, he agreed that the problem arose primarily from craving, in particular, by expecting that a constantly changing universe was bound to meet our expectations for it. Like the Buddha, Crowley recognized that disillusionment and a clear understanding of the nature of reality were important motivators of liberation.

Yet while the Buddha's solution required the progressive renunciation of the universe, Crowley's proposed path went 180 degrees in the opposite direction.

## The Solution

From both the Buddha's and Crowley's perspectives, reality is like a violent, turbulent hurricane. But while the Buddha taught a path of retreat from the storm and from reality, Crowley's proposed path to freedom goes directly into the storm itself. If the Buddhist path to liberation required the unconditional renunciation of conditioned reality, the Thelemic path, according to Crowley, entails the unconditional *acceptance* of conditioned reality: an open-hearted embrace of every change whatsoever.

It's a journey straight into the eye of the hurricane.

Crowley accepted the Buddha's premises and his conclusion; he just realized there was another way to accomplish the same thing. Paradoxically it went in the exact opposite direction the Buddha proposed, but it arrived at a similar or near-identical end state of total liberation from conditions.

In other words, you're either all in, or you're all out. Be a Thelemite, be a Buddhist. Either one works. Just whatever you do, don't try to stand in the middle!

If you try to stand in the middle, you're now in the position of trying to cut a course through life that seeks pleasure and avoids pain. You're necessarily in a position of attempting to control outcomes which, in principle, can never be fully guaranteed. This requires the subjugation of life to reason, which Crowley insisted was a no-no. It means erecting a wall around oneself that lets in pleasure and keeps out pain. It means imposing one's will on reality.

Crowley had a word he used to describe this attitude toward life. He called it *evil*. As far as I can tell, he never used that word except in this very precise, technical sense. Everything I'm about to teach you about the Thelemic path of liberation is about *destroying evil* in one form or another. And whenever I talk about evil, there's nothing inherently moral attached to it. I mean it in this precise, technical sense of opposing one thing to another, of walling things off from one another or restricting them.

Crowley also had a name for those who adhered to this path in life. He called them *Black Brothers* or *Left-Hand Path* adherents. When we talk about left-hand path these days, we mean Satanists or people who practice Tantra. That is not what Crowley meant at all. He meant those who attempt to have it both ways and who as a result wall themselves off from the flow of life, from what Crowley taught was the cosmic feminine, and as a result they have to constantly impose their will on things to preserve their individuality.

The opposite of being a Black Brother—and therefore the personification of goodness or holiness in Thelema—is to be a *Saint*. But these aren't your parents' Saints. Crowley meant something very different from a goody-good.

Rather than imposing their wills on reality, rather than trying to control how much life or joy accrues to them, the Saints have turned that control over to the universe itself. Rather than asserting their individuality over and against reality, the Saint has sacrificed that individuality in erotic union with the divine feminine, which Crowley calls *Babalon*. Their sense of separateness has been undone through love, and as a result, they are now free. That is why I call this a path of erotic liberation or even erotic destruction.

The personification of evil in Thelema is the person who insists upon their separation from life. They observe and control nature from an outside point of view. They assert their individuality against time. The personification of goodness or holiness is the Saint. They have sacrificed their individuality, meaning, there is no longer anything standing between them and the universe. Their hearts are open, and they unconditionally affirm existence. Regardless of whatever misfortune befalls them, they no longer experience resentment. While they may not be free of physical pain, they are free of existential despair.

In Ordo Templi Orientis, we do a beautiful ritual called *Liber XV* which celebrates this spiritual achievement. In it, a Priest devotes his will solely and exclusively to Babalon, who is represented by a Priestess. He ceremonially relinquishes control over his own life, and he relinquishes control over his own joy. He offers these up to the universe, essentially declaring them no longer to be his own. At the climax of the ritual, they are ecstatically ripped from him through a sublimated act of coitus.

But then something quite remarkable happens. Kneeling before the Priestess, who in this case represents the universe itself, the Priest receives all of it back. Only this time it is the life of the Sun and the joy of the Earth that are given back to him—by the Priestess. His small pleasures have been returned to him as the bounties of heaven and earth themselves. Having released the stranglehold he once had over life, he experiences life and joy almost as if for the first time—one might say, almost like a child. He is finally and truly free.

## The Path to Liberation

Crowley called the process by means of which the ordinary human being achieves liberation through ecstatic union with the divine the *Great Work*. The term *Great Work* originally comes from the alchemical tradition, where it is used to describe the creation of the Philosophers Stone. The Philosophers Stone was a mythical substance capable of turning base metals such as mercury into gold. The process of the Great Work describes the exaltation of the first matter into something divine. From a Thelemic point of view, the first matter which must be transformed is the individual human being. This exaltation occurs when the microcosm (the individual) models him or herself on the structure of the macrocosm or the universe. The universe as a whole is divine. If you want to become divine, you need to become like the universe.

Until relatively recently, people thought the Earth was the center of the universe, and they thought the planets, the Sun, and the stars all moved around it. They viewed the universe as a living, organic whole, as an animal in its own right. This is not the view of the universe Crowley took. He thought such views were outdated and unscientific, and he wanted to replace them with a more objective take on things.

Crowley's own view of the universe is expressed in a short book called *Liber AL vel Legis sub figura CCXX*, otherwise known as *The Book of the Law*. *The Book of the Law* is the foundational text of Thelema.

*The Book of the Law* describes the world as being composed of two divinities. On the one hand, there is the sum total of all possibilities, represented by the Egyptian sky goddess Nuit; and on the other hand there is the subjective point of view on any of those possibilities—in other words the first-person perspective which each of you is acquainted with right now—represented by the Egyptian solar god, Hadit. It is the combination of Nuit and Hadit which gives rise to experience.

Anything you are aware of or could be aware of is Nuit, and therefore from a magical point of view is cosmically feminine. From your perspective right now, I am Nuit, even though I am male. The sound of my voice is Nuit. The sensation of your body on the chair is Nuit. Whether you are male or female, your physical body is Nuit. Even your thoughts and feelings are Nuit, because they are experienced by you.

The one doing the experiencing is Hadit. Whether you are male or female, your consciousness is Hadit. If you reflect on your consciousness—if you turn it into an object of awareness—the thing you are aware of is not Hadit. It's Nuit! Anything you are aware of is Nuit. The thing which is aware is Hadit. Hadit can never know himself. He can only ever know Nuit. Conversely, if Hadit is aware of anything, it is always Nuit.

In addition to explaining the universe, Crowley also said *The Book of the Law* directed each person to realize one's own God-head in each and every experience. By that he meant that *The Book of the Law* teaches us that we should seek to be or identify with Hadit.

Now you might think to yourself, "How could I help being anything other than Hadit?" The answer is, you can't, you just don't know it. It's human nature to confuse ourselves with the things we're aware of. So we tend to identify with our bodies. We identify with our desires. We identify with our aspirations. We identify with things that have happened to us. We identify with our emotions. We identify with our thoughts.

Notice how your sense of self constantly shifts and moves all over the place. Sometimes it's near the center of your chest. Sometimes it's behind your eyes. Sometimes it's off in some other world. There's almost nothing less clear to you than the nature of your self. A big part of Thelema is coming to realize who you really are, and who you really are is *Hadit*.

So what does it mean to be Hadit exactly? If you read *The Book of the Law*, you see Hadit doing and saying quite a few things, but much of it boils down to him loving or adoring Nuit. He is constantly going toward her, constantly uniting with her, constantly and ecstatically penetrating her. Each moment is orgasmic union with her.

You think you live in a world of tables, chairs, subatomic particles, Wednesdays, and climbing gas prices. You're wrong. You live in a world of *orgasms*. You can't see that, because your ego with its constant worries about potential losses and what someone said about you is in the way.

As Crowley says, "Hadit knows Nuit by virtue of his 'Going' or 'Love'. It is therefore wrong to worship Hadit; one is to be Hadit, and worship Her."[1]

Keeping in mind that Nuit is whatever could possibly be experienced, to be Hadit means to embrace each and every experience—every change from one thing into another—as just another manifestation of one's beloved. Whether it's a bouquet of roses, a stack of hundred dollar bills, a stomach virus, or an exchange of intercontinental ballistic missiles, to be Hadit means to *affirm* it. Being Hadit means *to accept, to affirm All.*

---

[1] New Comment on AL II.8

But how exactly does one begin the journey?

There are many ways to divide up the Thelemic spiritual path. I'm going to use the simplified path that Crowley describes in an essay called *Liber CL*. *Liber CL* divides the path up into four stages: Liberty, Love, Life, and Light. This can be a little confusing, because while one part of the path is called "Liberty," the whole thing is about achieving liberty. While one part is called "Love," the whole thing is the method of love under will. The whole thing is about achieving liberation in this life, even though only one part of the path is called "Life," and the whole thing is about divine illumination, even though that's only described as one stage of it. So try not to get too hung up on the individual words. Think more in terms of a single process leading to the pinnacle I just described in which one achieves liberation through an acceptance brought about by erotic abandonment to the universe. That's the key idea motivating all of this.

Each of these four stages involves overcoming a particular form of "evil". Remember, Crowley uses "evil" in a purely technical sense to mean arbitrary limitation between one thing and any other thing. At this point we can also say that evil arises from the false identification of ourselves with some aspect of Nuit. We take some set of sensations—for example the thoughts happening in my head, the desire for a sandwich, the sensation just behind my eyes—we slap the term "self" on them, and oppose them to another set of sensations over there that we call "other". This is the basic mechanism giving rise to "evil" in the Thelemic sense. As you can see, there is no moral connotation to it.

But this means that overcoming evil in any instance is going to involve two moves. There has to be disidentification from some aspect of experience, by which I mean we no longer confuse some aspect of Nuit with ourselves. This inherently involves surrender and letting go, since part of what it means to identify with something is to assert ownership or control over it. But then each time we do this, we are moving one step toward properly identifying ourselves with Hadit. This is going to occur in stages, so that every time we see through some false duality, a new, more profound false duality comes in to take its place. This happens until the ultimate duality is seen through. At that moment there is no longer anything standing between Hadit and the All, and they ecstatically collide.

# Liberty

The first stage is called *Liberty*. This stage is largely concerned with ridding ourselves of arbitrary expectations of our conduct and how we ought to spend our time. This stage is about overcoming "evil" or restriction within oneself, which tends to manifest itself as ambivalence or desiring two outcomes simultaneously. For instance, you agree to your wife's request to clean the garage after work, but you conveniently forget and watch TV instead. That's a classic example of ambivalence, specifically passive-aggression. Or you experience a conflict between your desire to be a poet and your family's expectation that you become an engineer. This internal conflict or "evil" is overcome when thought, feeling, speech, and action are in perfect alignment and accord with your nature as an individual human being. This is the state that Crowley refers to as *doing one's will.*

Doing your will is first and foremost about having internal consistency or what we might call *integrity*. You can find out the strength of your will in the Thelemic sense by entering into situations that tempt you to abandon it, for example, those situations where you are tempted to be dishonest or inauthentic.

Paths in life are necessarily dependent upon external circumstances, and external circumstances are constantly changing. What doesn't change is the law governing exactly who and what you are, and that's what your will is. It's primarily internal, secondarily external. This is important, because being confused about which way to go in life doesn't necessarily mean you don't know your will. It means you're confused about how to apply knowledge of your will to the situation you're faced with. That's different from not knowing who or what you are or what you stand for. Of course you may be completely ignorant of that, too, in which case you're in a lot of trouble! And so your first order of business as a human being—whether you intend to walk the Thelemic spiritual path or not—is to "pull it together" as they say and get yourself in the habit of living a life full of integrity, which has a lot less to do with which way you choose to go in life and more to do with how much character you bring along with you for the journey.

If all you gain from Thelema is this self-possession and stability of character in the face of life, that's quite an accomplishment on its own. Many people never even try to do that let alone succeed. This is obviously a life-long task, one which is complete only with death. However, this does not mean you have to have perfect character or wait for death to progress along the spiritual path. From the perspective of the path of erotic liberation, what's important is that you learn how to gather your internal resources and direct them exclusively toward one object. In other words, from the perspective of mysticism—which is what the rest of this path is about—all we need to concern ourselves with from an ethical point of view is what aids or hinders concentration.

In this first stage, everything you are—or more accurately, everything you *think* you are—is gradually becoming subordinated to the Hadit within you. Your physical body, your emotions, your thoughts, your desires, your path through the universe: all of this is just a vehicle for the divine part of you, Hadit, to experience the universe, who is Nuit. The problem, as we saw, is that this vehicle also has a tendency to get in the way. It's like a vehicle that hasn't had its wheels aligned in awhile, which makes a lot of noise under the hood, and which has a tailpipe that drags along the ground. It's kind of a drag for Hadit. So the first order of business is to get the wheels aligned, tighten the screws, get the muffler attached properly, and maybe clean the windshield and fix the air conditioner while we're at it.

At this point in the game, we think we're doing this for ourselves. And we are, but we think we're the car rather than the person driving the car. Or more accurately, sometimes we think we're the car, sometimes we think we're the steering wheel, sometimes we think we're the front driver side tire, and sometimes we think we're the alternator. We're really confused. So the first order of business is to get our act together, to become one car with one driver, not a car about to burst into flame and have its wheels fly off.

So now the question is: *where exactly is the car supposed to go?* This brings us to the second stage of the path, which is called *Love*.

## Love

In the ritual I mentioned earlier, *Liber XV*, which we perform regularly in O.T.O., there is a part at the beginning where the Priestess—who, again, represents the cosmic feminine, the sum total of all that is or could be— kneels before the Priest and strokes his lance eleven times. Shortly thereafter, he raises the lance. The symbolism isn't exactly subtle. She's gotten him ready to love. But to love what exactly?

To love *her*. To love *everything*. To love *All*.

Among other things, the lance is the Priest's will. When the lance is down at the beginning, it's not unlike our example of the car with the wheels about to fly off. But when she strokes the lance, she is consecrating it. She is devoting it to its true object, the only thing in the universe which it really, truly, deeply desires: *Her.* From that point on in the ritual, there's only one place that lance can possibly end up—and that's in her cup, the chalice, the Holy Grail. The Priest's will is now on a one-way trip which ends in erotic dissolution in the divine feminine.

The love which leads to erotic liberation is not sentimental. Sentimentality arises from attachment. The kind of love Crowley was interested in was not an attachment to any one thing. It was a drive toward union with nothing less than everything. That includes coronavirus as much as it includes daisies. No one has ever gotten sentimental over coronavirus, and no one ever will.

While the path of erotic liberation leads to the transcendence of ego and separation, it is not catastrophic. You sometimes hear mystics talk about the death of the ego or something like that. Crowley himself used this kind of language and even freaked himself out a bit over it. Sometimes you also hear people talk about the difference between the small-s self versus the big-s Self, and that the small-s self has to die and so forth. So let's be crystal clear about our terms and what they mean.

There is no small-s self versus a big-s Self. Everything you take to be your self is not your self at all. It's Nuit. This seems like a nit-picky distinction, but it's not. It's a piece of theory which is very useful and demolishes a lot of misunderstanding at the start.

When you're driving your car, do you really ever think your car is a person, let alone you? No, of course not. Sometimes we get sentimental about vehicles and imagine they have personalities, but hardly anyone really believes their car is conscious. This path is in large part about getting clear about that distinction, realizing there is only one self, and it is not what we thought it was. In other words, it is about gaining clarity, and once the thoughts, feelings, sensations, and other things are seen clearly, they're also clearly seen *through.* It is that transparency of the "ego," so to speak, which allows the ecstatic union between Hadit and Nuit or Babalon (I'll use the names interchangeably) to occur.

There are two ways in which this union between consciousness and the world can be carried out, and this is where we start to get into the techniques of practice.

The first, probably more familiar way, is through meditation. If you sit down and practice quieting your mind, perhaps by focusing on the breath, on a colored disk, on a candle flame, or upon a word, you will after some time enter into a state of meditative absorption which is called *samadhi* or concentration. This state of concentration will initially be accompanied by intense joy and rapture, but eventually it will become a calmer, more neutral state. From there, different qualities of mind can be accurately investigated and understood as being devoid of self. Buddhists are connoisseurs of these meditative states. It's very easy nowadays to find someone who can teach you samadhi. One hundred twenty years ago that was not the case, and so Crowley had to go to India to learn. That made him an early pioneer in the west of these techniques.

The second way to achieve union is by doing magick. In fact one of Crowley's original insights was that ceremonial magick is a kind of yoga of the west, and done a certain way it leads to samadhi.

He didn't mean the kind of magick where you just draw shapes in the air while mispronouncing Hebrew. He meant working yourself up into a frenzy that carries you out and away from yourself and into union with God. Crowley rediscovered a way of doing ceremonial magick that was much more like what we might call shamanism. He said the "secret" to this kind of magick is to "enflame oneself in praying."[2]

This could be done by chanting the spirit's name like a mantra. It could be done by rocking back and forth. It could be done by singing. It could be aided greatly by hashish and other mind-altering drugs. And eventually he realized it could be done by fucking. Once he did, that became his preferred method for the rest of his life.

So you have two paths, both of which lead to the same destination. There is the path of stillness leading to eternity. That's the path of meditation, which we might also call the reflective path, the path of making the mind like still water. And there is the path of ecstasy leading to eternity. That's the path of ecstatic magick, which Crowley at one point attributes to the gnostic god, IAO.

But whichever way one chooses to affect the union, the first time it occurs, it is an experience of the oneness and beauty of all things which is accompanied by bliss and rapture. Crowley referred to this as the beatific vision or the Knowledge and Conversation of the Holy Guardian Angel.

The Holy Guardian Angel is one of the most sacred mysteries in Thelema. I cannot really do it justice in this short talk. If you wish to understand what the Holy Guardian Angel is and what its influence in your life could mean to you, read *Liber Cordis Cincti Serpente sub figura* אדני, the English translation

---

2   New Comment on AL II.34

of which is *The Book of the Heart Girt with a Serpent under the figure Adonai.* It's also called Book 65, since the Hebrew letters that spell Adonai add up to 65.

As the title of the book suggests, the Holy Guardian Angel is like a serpent which wraps itself around your heart. This suggests a reversal or inversion of the meaning given to the serpent in Christianity. The serpent with its poisonous bite and tendency to conceal itself in the grass or by hanging dangerously from trees is a symbol of deception and of evil. Yet in the context of Thelema, it is a symbol of the Holy Guardian Angel or the spirit of erotic liberation.

This inversion of the symbol of the serpent—its transformation from a symbol of evil into a symbol of liberation—reflects one of the core, distinctive features of Thelemic spirituality: its tendency toward inversion or subversion of meaning. But this deification of the serpent does not transform it into a force for "good". It does not make it a friend. The characteristic mode of behavior of the serpent is still to slither, to shed its skin, and, importantly, to poison and devour. So the turn toward the divine in the stage of Love, while initially beautiful and joyful, eventually reveals itself as a turn toward darkness.

This is far and away one of the most difficult aspects of Thelema to grasp. It's paradoxical in the extreme. The idea is that the greatest healing power is to be found in the most destructive poison, that the greatest light is to be found in the most profound darkness, and that God is to be found in total surrender to something that might be experienced as potently demonic.

The illusion that we really have control over our lives is potent. The abandonment of that sense of control through surrender to a reality which is in ceaseless change is bound to be experienced as frightening, at least at first. From the perspective of the ego, what's coming can only look like death.

Thus we arrive at the third stage of our journey, that of Life properly understood.

## Life

In the stage of Love, the will turned toward its one, true object, which is the All, and it united with it in a peak experience of beauty and rapture. But peak experiences are just that: singular experiences. And even an experience as holy as the beatific vision fades away, and we are once again deposited back down into our ordinary lives. "After the ecstasy, the laundry," as the

Buddhist teacher Jack Kornfield titled one of his books. Now the will is faced with a new delusion, a new duality, a new form of evil. It's the dualism that arises between the rapturous religious experience on the one hand—which is exceedingly pleasant—and the rest of life on the other.

The temptation here will be to try to return to the beatific vision, to re-create peak unitary experiences. There could be a strong temptation here to renounce ordinary life, to quit liquor and sex, to take monastic vows, to say to hell with it to the ordinary world. This is a result of one having gotten a glimpse, if only for a moment, of an unconditioned reality which can offer real peace and bliss. And indeed, monastic communities exist to support such seekers in their quests, if that quest is a renunciate one. But from a Thelemic point of view, the task now is to see that all things—not just ecstatic peak religious experiences—are divine.

This means deliberately exposing oneself to things which cause fear, pain, disgust, shame and the like. As Crowley says, one must learn to endure them, then to become indifferent to them, then to analyze them until they give pleasure and instruction, and finally to appreciate them for their own sake, as aspects of Truth.[3] Crowley's own experiments in this regard—documented in his diaries and his poetry as an obsession with deviant sex acts, especially coprophagy—are legendary. But it is wrong to see them as mere kinks. They were deliberate attempts on his part to shatter his reflexive belief in the difference between pleasure and disgust or pain.

The idea isn't to do things that cause harm to yourself. For instance you shouldn't drink a vial of acid or jump in front of a speeding bus in order to unite yourself mystically with it. Instead you're trying to understand everything on its own terms, to see things from a detached, dispassionate point of view, and to elevate yourself to something akin to a God's eye perspective on things.

In the stage of love, it was all about gathering the consciousness together and launching it, one-pointed, at a single thing so as to unite with it. The attention had to remain narrow and focused. In this stage, the stage of Life, the attention has to widen. One's awareness must become broad, embracing, and comprehensive of the entire universe of phenomena.

At this point there is a more acute confrontation with death. One must come to terms with the fact that one's own death is just another phase of phenomena, no more or less important than any other change in the universe. It's only the attachment to ego that makes one's own death seem some-

---

3   See *Liber V vel Reguli*.

how of more concern than anything else. One must take up a more universal, more detached, more objective perspective on things, as the awareness itself becomes disentangled from the particularities of the personality. Hadit more clearly than ever sees the ego as a mere vehicle of its journey through the universe and begins to appreciate more its independence from all conditioned phenomena.

It might be difficult to see how one could go any higher than this, but there is one more stage, that of Light, which is, again paradoxically, an initiation into darkness or night which Crowley calls the ordeal of the Abyss.

## Light

This is where one is given the choice to become a Left-Hand Path adherent. That would mean maintaining one's attachment to personality, to the illusion of ego. It means walling oneself off from change and attempting to preserve one's personality in the face of change. Or one can let go, and through a final act of erotic abandon, relinquish all attachment and forfeit one's life and joy into the cup of the goddess Babalon. This latter path results in one emptying their blood into the cup of Babalon and becoming a Saint.

The left-hand path is ostensibly a path toward union, toward self-possession in the face of change. But the rule of time is universal. There is no way to hide from death. As Crowley describes it, the means by which the Black Brother attempts to preserve themselves is their very undoing.[4] What I take him to mean is that the strategy of self-preservation is ultimately self-defeating. The unity they seek is ultimately based upon a confusion of Nuit with Hadit. So that with which they identify—thoughts, feelings, even the power of willing itself—is ultimately subject to change, no matter what. So what initially appeared as a path toward union is in reality a path toward dissolution and the ravages of time.

The path toward Babalon is ostensibly a path toward night, toward destruction. It is symbolized by emptying out one's blood in the Cup of Our Lady, the cup of her fornications. One relinquishes control over one's life, what one considers to be one's self, which can only be seen from the perspective of the ego as death, a casting of oneself to the four winds. This is described as becoming like a pile of dust in the City of the Pyramids.[5] But by relinquishing this false sense of self and by surrendering to universal life, one is able to embrace true life and true joy. One achieves real unity, which is

---

4   *Magick Without Tears*, ch 12
5   *The Vision and the Voice*, The Cry of the 14th Aethyr

the continual, ongoing unity or unification between the self and the universe, which is experienced as joy. So what initially appeared as a path toward destruction is in reality a path toward unification, a path toward the recognition of eternity in time.

This is different from the kind of mystical unification we looked at earlier in the stage of love. That was a peak experience in which the sense of separateness was overcome in an instant of bliss. By contrast this experience of Light is a fundamental shift in how one experiences oneself in relationship to the universe and to time. There's no longer any confusion between Hadit and Nuit in any experience. It's no longer possible to take one part of Nuit, call it "self," and oppose it to another part of Nuit and call it "world" or "other". There is no longer any difference made between one thing and another. This doesn't mean everything blends into a gray mush. It means all experiences are seen clearly *as* experiences. Their true nature is understood, which is similar to what in Buddhism is called *suññata* or *emptiness*. This doesn't make the experience worthless. On the contrary, it means—paradoxically—that each can be appreciated on its own terms without expecting the impossible from them. Craving is done with, and in its place is acceptance and affirmation of what is. One is delivered from lust of result.

The problem with which we began—the suffering that arises from wanting things to be other than what they are—has been overcome. Something akin to nirvana has been achieved, but it has been done through ecstatic abandonment or erotic reunion with the universe rather than through a renunciation of the universe.

## Conclusion

Crowley thought one could be free of the perennial spiritual problems of human existence by cultivating ecstatic union with reality. The main method by which this is accomplished he called *love under will* or *magick*. His method addressed the same problem the Buddha saw, but he went in the exact opposite direction to seek the solution. Rather than the ascetic abandonment of becoming, Crowley's resolution entails ecstatically uniting oneself with reality through a process of erotic liberation.

3

# A Path With Heart

Magick has a unique relationship with sensuality and with sensation. The trappings of magick—incense, candles, the magical weapons—are part of the enjoyment intrinsic to it. At a deep level, magick speaks to the relationship that we have with sensuality and with our bodies.

If you compare the magical path with a renunciate spiritual path, such as classical Buddhism, the renunciate spiritual paths tend to reject or pull away from the what are called gross forms of sensuality. "Gross" does not mean disgusting; it refers to obvious sources of trouble. One of the key ones in Buddhism is money. Buddhist monks don't handle money, and they don't engage in commerce. They collect alms. They live on charity, and as inconvenient as that may seem, it's easy to see why they do it. If you personally aren't having any money problems right now, you know somebody who is. Money is a common source of stress and distress in life. So it's perfectly logical and consistent, in the interest of minimizing stress, just not to have anything to do with money if at all possible.

The same logic applies to sexuality, romantic love, and even intimacy. We get a lot of joy out of sexuality, romantic love, and intimacy. They're incredibly powerful and enjoyable, but everybody knows the dangers. Even if you have a wonderful relationship with someone, one or the other of you is probably going to die first. There is always the specter of loss. And so again, simply renouncing those sources of pleasure—what are called gross pleasures—is a logical response.

In addition to gross pleasures, there are also fine forms of sensuality and enjoyment. Renunciate traditions have developed meditative techniques to deal with them. The purpose of such practices is to bring an end to becoming all together. The goal of such practices is to end generation and to "get off the ride" of existence completely. Anything that exists is impermanent and unreliable, and so for the renunciate, the goal is to embrace something which does not change at all. It is to unite with something which is independent of the material universe and which brings lasting peace, stability, and happiness. In Buddhism this unconditioned and unconditional source of happiness is called *nibbana.*

By contrast the magical path goes in the exact opposite direction. Magical practitioners do not recoil from sensuality. Different modes of sensation and sensuality are divine. For example, different colors are associated with different planets and different zodiacal signs. Different smells, different kinds of perfume or incense, are beloved by different gods, goddesses, and spirits. Different sounds, different kinds of music, are important to ritual. Even taste and touch are potentially sacred. All of the different modes of sensuality have divine aspects to them. We can activate a divine quality in them. They are integral parts of this path. Of course, you could do magic entirely in your head, but most people don't. Instead we bring in all of these different modes of sensuality. And so for most magical practitioners, sensuality tends to be at the heart of their practice.

## The Role of the Body in Magick

To put sensuality and sensations at the heart of a spiritual practice is unavoidably to put the *body* at the center of the practice. On the face of it, this is an odd choice. Most forms of suffering and distress relate in some way back to the body. They have their source in the body. Through the body we are impinged upon by reality and by other people. The body is a source of vulnerability and weakness. To place something at the center of our spiritual lives is to assert its power and importance. And yet at the center of magical practice is our ultimate source of weakness.

One finds a similar paradox in Christianity. God is an unlimited, all-powerful, all-knowing being. He is free of matter, space, time, and all condtions. This is a being so powerful that He can create an entire universe. He is impervious to all things. Now take this concept and put it in a single human individual capable of illness, suffering, torture, and death. How the hell is that supposed to work? Even after all the ecumenical councils, there was and has been substantial disagreement over exactly how God and humanity are supposed to have been united in the figure of Jesus Christ. The idea is paradoxical in the extreme.

For the time in which the Gospels were written, Jesus was supposed to be the best kind of person a human could be. And to this best of all possible people, the worst punishments are inflicted. He is treated as unfairly as you could imagine: he is betrayed by his friend, he suffers an unfair verdict in court, he is tortured, and his execution is cruel and barbaric. Yet rather than his being overcome by his suffering, his goodness transcends it. The story is a union of extremes to the point of almost being paradoxical.

When a story does not make any sense on the face of it and yet still has this kind of motivating power, that is the sign of an archetypal myth. It pushes our sense of meaning-making to its limit. As a result, an entirely new way of making sense of the world and our place in it emerges.

The Hebrew word for *Messiah* (מָשִׁיחַ) has the same numerical value as the Hebrew word for *serpent* (נָחָשׁ) by a system of counting called Gematria. According to occult doctrine, when two words have an identical numerical value (in this case 358), especially if they seem to have absolutely nothing to do with one another and even contradict one another, there has to be some kind of underlying hidden occult connection between these two things. In the case of the Messiah, you already have a completely bonkers story about an individual who went so deeply into suffering that he somehow passed through to the other side. On the other hand, you have the story about the serpent in the Garden of Eden who manages to trick Eve and then Adam into eating the fruit of the Tree of the Knowledge of Good and Evil. The serpent tricked them by saying that if they ate of the tree, they would be like gods. No sooner did they eat it, what happened? *They felt ashamed.* They experienced the pain of the knowledge of their own existence.

When God found out, he was cross. Adam blamed it on Eve. Eve blamed it on the serpent. God kicked them out of the garden, and they were ejected into the state of sorrow and suffering we know as the human condition and which Buddhists call *samsara*.

The Messiah penetrated so deeply into this suffering that he ultimately transcended it. The serpent invited Adam and Eve to participate so deeply in divine knowledge that they were ejected into a world of suffering. One path leads up, from Earth into Heaven; the other path goes down from Heaven into Hell. Snakes and Ladders!

Judging by the legends surrounding them, humans have always been fascinated by snakes. Snakes live in nearly every environment human beings inhabit. They shed their skins, and so they are symbols of rebirth or regeneration to many people. Snakes also have the ability to bite their own tails, symbolically capturing or completing themselves as in the figure of the ouroboros. This makes them natural symbols of wholeness, completion, and transcendence of death.

On the other hand, snakes can be incredibly dangerous. The bite of some can kill a person almost instantly, and they have a habit of concealing themselves under rocks or hanging from trees. Any person wandering out in search of food had better keep an eye out for them. The mere possibility of encountering one invokes a heightened sense of awareness. Perhaps for that reason, snakes are associated with the quality of being awake.

The serpent is a paradoxical symbol in its own right, similar to the Messiah, except now we have combined in one being rebirth and destruction. This makes the serpent an apt symbol of life itself and the inherent danger of being alive in this world.

If we are going to reject the renunciate path and instead base our spirituality on the body, if we are going to put sensuousness at the center of what we do, then this requires us to cultivate the same qualities of awareness and attunement to existence that one would require if they were going to approach something as dangerous as a venomous snake with the intention of grabbing it with their bare hand.

On the face of it, the renunciate path is more logical. *Just leave the fucking snake alone.* If you approach non-renunciate spirituality as though it is just simply an excuse for indulgence, it's like approaching a cobra as if it were a golden retriever puppy. The non-renunciate path which leads us more deeply into sensuousness is the path to Heaven that leads you straight through the heart of Hell. You cannot stroll nonchalantly through Hell. This path requires as much self-discipline, consciousness, and attunement as any other spiritual path—perhaps moreso.

The spiritual path I follow is called *Thelema. Thelema* is the Greek word for *will* as in the Lord's prayer when it says, "Thy will be done on earth as it is in heaven". Thelema does not mean arranging the conditions of your life such that you always get what you want. It's not about control and manipulation. It cannot be. Do you think you can control nature? Do you think you can control a snake? All the time?

The most dangerous thing imaginable is to approach a snake like it's a puppy and to let your guard down. Spiritually, that is the equivalent of remaining connected with this constantly changing, shifting world, but allowing yourself to go to sleep in it. It is the equivalent of interacting with this world with mistaken notions about what is possible in it, in particular allowing yourself to think that you can control it to the point of only getting out of it what you want and being able to reject the rest. It's like wanting a snake's tail or body but without the head, fangs, and heart-stopping venom.

The mythology of control stems from the belief that we can be part of this world but not of this world. Everything we know about the brain and personal identity militates against this idea. We are in and of this world, through and through. The illusion of separation and control requires the mobilization of primitive psychological mechanisms which end up causing more trouble than they solve. They require us to engage in myths of autonomy that end up walling our hearts off from life.

## Turning Around

Imagine for a moment that you overhear your spouse or your significant other mocking your sexual performance to another person. Did you feel a sensation in the center of your chest? That was your heart closing like a clamshell. That is the attempt to wall yourself off from life. That attitude in which the heart is closed against reality—out of the mistaken belief it can protect itself—is what Aleister Crowley called the attitude of the Virgin Mary.

The Thelemic spiritual path asks that in those situations where your heart wants to close, you work to keep it open. The expectation is that you remain affirmative, awake, and aware, and that you do not curse yourself, your luck, or being. It's a training in resisting resentment and keeping the heart open. It is a path that leads to Our Lady Babalon. She is a major goddess in Thelema. She is a sacred Whore or Harlot. Why? Because she represents an attitude of acceptance of all things, whatever they are, however repulsive they are, however much they hurt.

The Thelemic path is a path of heart.

The path of heart is not for the faint of heart. It requires massive amounts of courage.

There's a wonderful book you all should read. It's called *A Wizard of Earthsea*. It's by Ursula Le Guin, one of the 20th century's greatest science fiction and fantasy authors. It is about a young magician named Ged. Ged does something pretty stupid, and like so many stupid things we do, he does it out of hubris. He does it out of arrogance and pride. Then he has to spend the rest of the book dealing with the consequences of this arrogant decision that he made.

Toward the end of the second act of the book, after he's gotten his ass kicked up one side of the world and down the other, he runs into his old mentor, a powerful and wise wizard named Ogion. Ogion gives him a piece of advice. It's two words. He says: "Turn around."

Turn around. Face what you fear. Turn around and face what you fear, or else it will control you for as long as you live. *Turn around.*

And so he does. Ged turns around. He faces the darkness. He faces what he fears. And he is not only able to undo the harm that he caused. In the process, he becomes whole. And true to Ogion's advice, Ged can never be controlled by anyone, ever again.

The path of heart is not without risks. It can kill you, because life can kill you, and this path is nothing short of the embrace of life.

The organization I am a part of—Ordo Templi Orientis—offers opportunities for people to practice opening in various ways. Our central rite, the Gnostic Mass, represents the opening of the heart in the form of a religious drama. At the climax of the ritual, the Priest and the Priestess insert the lance into the cup. The significance of the symbolism is difficult to miss. It is the union of lingam and yoni. But one form the yoni takes is the heart. If you look at the O.T.O. lamen, you will notice the dove descending into the cup at the bottom. The cup has some flames coming out of it, and there's a six-petal flower around it. The six-petal flower symbolizes the Anahata chakra, which is the chakra at the center of your chest. Your heart is obviously not in your vagina. It should not be. So there is more going on here than mere sexual symbolism. The lamen symbolizes, among other things, the Holy Spirit descending into an open heart.

Sexuality is important in Thelema because so much of our vulnerability and our joy is concentrated in our sexuality. So many of the joys and perils of the body and of life are wrapped around love.

In addition to the Gnostic Mass, we also offer initiation ceremonies as a means of opening the heart. Initiations offer an opportunity to place trust in yourself as you walk into the unknown and accept whatever may come.

We also provide a community of individuals who are walking the Thelemic spiritual path. Thelema is a highly individualistic religion, and you will find people of all different walks of life involved with it who interpret it and practice it in very different ways. Interacting with individuals with strong opinions that differ from your own is another way to practice acceptance: acceptance of whatever is arising in you and acceptance of whatever is happening outside of you. This happens in a safe, structured environment.

## Conclusion

Unlike classical Buddhism, Thelema is a non-renunciate spiritual path. We do not renounce gross forms of sensuality or pleasure. Yet it is not for this reason a hedonistic path. It is not a path of self-indulgence. Non-renunciate spirituality requires just as much awareness and self-discipline as spirituality of the renunciate kind. This is because of the unique dangers present in sensuality.

Because Thelema is focused on the body, it is also a form of spirituality in which magick is integral. Magick is more than directing the will toward material ends. It implies a particular relationship to sensuality in which sacred potentials of matter—hidden divine energies of creation—are worked with for the purposes of creativity and liberation. It is a form of spirituality which necessarily involves the body and which therefore necessarily requires vulnerability. To successfully walk the Thelemic magical path requires one to work on opening one's heart and to affirm all that exists without discrimination. The culmination of this path is represented by emptying oneself into the cup of Our Lady Babalon.

# 4

# True Will and Magick

Thelema is a recent form of spirituality, but magic is a much older practice. Crowley spells it *magick* with a *k* to differentiate it from stage magic. In order to understand what Crowley means by magick, we have to differentiate it from more than stage magic. But whichever way we spell it, the word *magic* derives from Latin *magica* and Greek *magike tekhne*, which means *art of a magus*. The Magi were Zoroastrian priests from Persia, which is present day Iran; however, magic probably derived from earlier shamanic practices.

Shamanic practices involved soul travel and healing practices. In the year 10,000 BCE, a shaman was the closest thing you could get to a doctor. We know they engaged in techniques of sleep deprivation, singing, dancing, and chanting for hours on end to bring about altered states of consciousness. They used techniques of dressing up like animals. They utilized social isolation and possibly psychedelics. And we know that these techniques worked in some sense—they offered a meaningful survival and reproductive advantage—because they were pervasive throughout hunter-gatherer groups by the time people formed civilizations about 4,000 years ago.[1]

Juensung Kim, a researcher at the University of Toronto, has suggested that different parts of this early shamanic toolkit were taken up and adapted by different civilizations in Eurasia.[2] The Greeks took up observation of the patterns of the natural world. Nature keeps secrets that we can trick it to reveal to us. Through Renaissance esotericism, this had an impact on the formation of the scientific revolution. The Middle Eastern magi took up the

---

1  See John Vervaeke, *Awakening from the Meaning Crisis*, episode 1: https://youtu.be/54l8_ewcOlY

2  See Juensung Kim, *The Science of Magic & Transformation*: https://youtu.be/jlbwdKvS_Zo

shamanic narrative cosmology or the idea of the universe as a living being going through cycles. India took up the skills of manipulating the mind and the imagination and systematized them into meditative and contemplative practices. Magic was established in early Chinese civilization in the concept of *Li*. Originally denoting court rites to sustain social and cosmic order, Li encompassed ritual, proper conduct, or propriety. The Chinese also systematized shamanic healing practices into the art of medicine.

As far as contemporary magical practice goes, I find it useful to sort them into four basic types:

1. Pattern finding/predictive magic: divination, astrology, palmistry, development of psychic abilities—these practices bootstrap the mind's ability to pick up on patterns in the world.

2. Working with magical energy: Most civilizations have some word to denote what we now call energy. The Greeks had pneuma, India had prana, the Chinese had Chi, Arabs had Ruh, the Yoruba emi, the Iroquois orenda.[3] It is often understood as connecting all things, similar to air, and has a special connection with the breath. It can be used to increase psychic abilities, to heal, and to increase perception of various kinds.

3. Communication with spirits: This can run the gamut from seances up through elaborate spirit and angel conjuration and even to petitioning saints and deities. Some people draw a sharp distinction between this practice and more traditional religious practices such as prayer, but they probably exist on a continuum.

All three of these show up in Thelema in various ways. Thelema includes a complex ecology of practices. Especially if you go through the course of training in Aleister Crowley's magical order, A∴A∴, you will learn and be tested in techniques of astral travel, divination, rising on the plains, and talisman consecration, in addition to eastern techniques of asana, pranayama, and control of thoughts.

However, there is a fourth kind of magic. It is not exactly unique to Thelema, although it plays a large, important role in Thelema. To my knowledge, Crowley never mentions it by name, but it's important enough that it de-

---

3  See John Michael Greer's "General Introduction" to Eliphas Levi, *The Doctrine and Ritual of High Magic: A New Translation*, translated by John Michael Greer and Mark Anthony Mikituk (New York: Penguin Random House LLC, 2017), xx.

serves one.

4. Becoming magic itself: This is not the utilization of magical energy or powers or spiritual conjuration for any particular end. This is magic with a deeper existential dimension in the sense that it is more about who you are and who you are becoming as a person in relationship to the world. And while there are lines to be drawn between the other three types of magic and true will, the deepest connection between magick and will is to be found in this fourth type of magic where one becomes magic itself.

I'm not the first person to talk about this idea of becoming magic itself. Donald Michael Kraig invokes a similar idea in his book *Modern Magick*: "I have always found amazing the large number of people who talk magick and the tiny amount of people who practice or live magick."[4]

Lon Duquette echoed a similar sentiment once on social media:

It is one thing to be well-read on a subject; it is quite another to be part of the subject itself. It is an unfortunate fact that there are many individuals who make magick their life without making their life magick.

My intention is to put a fine point on this idea and draw out implications, not just for magick, Thelema, or spiritual practice narrowly construed, but for broader issues we deeply care about, such as our need to live a life full of meaning.

But before I draw these implications, I want to establish for you exactly what I mean by *becoming magick*. (From here on I will spell it *magick* with a *k*.) And to do that, I need to pivot and talk about this concept of will in Thelema.

## True Will and Thelema

Like magick, there are several definitions of *will* in Thelema. The Thelemic writer IAO131 has identified at least three of them.[5]

The first of these is our *will power* or our power of *intention*. This defini-

---

4  Donald Michael Kraig, *Modern Magick, Second Edition, Eleven Lessons in the High Magickal Arts* (St. Paul, Minnesota: Llewellyn Publications, 2001), 165.
5  IAO131, "3 Definitions of True Will in Thelema," https://thelemicunion.com/3-definitions-true-will-thelema/

tion of will is tied up with a lot of harmful romantic notions about asserting our individual wills, either against others or against the world. It invokes the heroic ideal of the lone creative genius climbing mountains, slaying dragons, and asserting values in the face of the mindless mob.

On the other hand, you'll often hear Thelemites say "will is not want". Will is not your desire. It is *your ultimate purpose in life*, the mission you were put on Earth (perhaps by God or your Holy Guardian Angel) to fulfill. But only you can possibly know what your unique path is. No one else—certainly not any priest or guru—can tell you what it is. But that means you can't find it by ordinary means such as taking a personality or career aptitude test. You need to use exotic practices like meditation or ritual to discover it.

This idea is no longer unique to Thelema, even if Crowley deserves some credit for coming up with it. The idea of divine mission or purpose is prevalent now in most forms of spiritual-but-not-religious spirituality. One of the problems with it is that it's not at all clear what counts as success in this endeavor (the yardstick is purely subjective after all), with the result that it can lead to a lot of endless, fruitless self-examination and self-bullshitting.

Both of these ideas of will show up in Crowley's writings. There's no sense trying to escape them. But there's a third idea which also shows up and which connects in a deep way with the idea of becoming magick, of relating to magick in a deep way that promotes positive transformation, enjoyment of meaning in life, and even development of character and the cultivation of wisdom—and that's the idea of *will as our deep nature.*

In order to appreciate this idea of will as nature, we have to understand a little bit about what the human being is from a Thelemic perspective. I don't mean what the human being is in a biological sense as Homo sapiens. I mean what the human being is in a spiritual or existential sense.

## The Thelemic View of the Person

Humans beings are not simple; we're composed of parts. We have physical bodies, which are themselves composed of parts and which exist in causal interaction with their environments. We have thoughts and feelings which are constantly shifting and changing. We have temperaments. For example, some of us are more sensitive than others. We have personality traits. Some of us are more extraverted, more conscientious, more neurotic, more open to experience, or more agreeable. Some of these aspects of ourselves—such as temperament and personality—change a little or not very much at all over the course of life. Others—such as our moods and opinions—change constantly. When we reflect on ourselves and our lives, we construct a unity or an autobiography out of all of this, but the reality is that we are complex and constantly changing.

According to Crowley, the complex, constantly changing individual human being is the result of the interaction between two magical principles or divine forces. One of them is called *Hadit*; the other is called *Nuit*.

Hadit is the core drive of the individual to exist, to be, or to become. This is an open-ended, directionless, purposeless desire to be. All other things being equal, we have a tendency to want to keep going, to keep living. You're probably not going to wake up tomorrow and say, "You know, I've experienced enough of the world. I think I'm going to stop now." Sadly, suicide is a reality, but that usually happens because someone finds themselves in a situation they deem unbearable. But in the absence of unbearable circumstances, there's a sense of open-ended momentum to our existence. We tend to innately hunger for more experiences, for the next thing, for the next thing, for the next thing, etc.

Another term for this core drive to become is *pure will*. In our central holy text, *The Book of the Law*, we read, "For pure will, unassuaged of purpose, delivered from the lust of result, is every way perfect."[6] The pure will does not have a particular result or outcome it is looking for. It exists just for the sake of existing.

As the poet Angelus Silesius, inspired by Meister Eckhart put it:

The rose is without why,
It blooms because it blooms
It cares not for itself
Asks not if it is seen.

*The Book of the Law* echoes a similar sentiment when it says, "If Will stops and cries Why, invoking Because, then Will stops & does nought."[7]

Then we have the other principle, Nuit. If Hadit is going, becoming, changing, and hence time, Nuit is space and matter. Nuit is the environment that Hadit expresses Himself in. So even though Hadit's going is purposeless, that going—that striving or becoming—always occurs in a particular context and acquires definition and specificity from it. It's occurring in the

---

6   AL I.44
7   AL II.30

context of your genetics, your upbringing, how much food and wealth and love you experienced as a child, the education you got, your current life circumstances, your place in history, where you find yourself right this moment, etc.

Nuit *constrains* the actions of Hadit. In other words, at any moment, you do not experience an infinite number of possibilities. Your possibilities are finite. Nuit can do so in two ways. She can set a *selecting constraint*, or she can set an *enabling constraint*. Selecting constraints reduce the ways in which Hadit can become. Right now, none of us are capable of heavier than air flight. That option does not exist for any of us right at this moment. That option could be opened up, but it would require doing other things first, like buying a plane ticket and going to the airport. And even then, certain versions of it, like willing ourselves to levitate, will never be fulfilled. That's a selecting constraint.

But there are also enabling constraints. Enabling constraints create possibilities for us. The fact that we need oxygen to live is an enabling constraint. Oxygen is actually a poison, but it allows us to use energy in a way we couldn't if we were dependent upon carbon dioxide. The fact that we have bodies is an enabling constraint. Bodies are constraints because they limit our actions. We get sick and die. On the other hand, our bodies allow us to solve problems, they allow us to think, and they allow us to enjoy sensuous pleasures.

To return to the flight analogy, a bird flying through a strong headwind might think—if birds could think—that its flight would be faster were it not for the resistance of the air. But what would happen if there were no air? The bird would fall like a stone to the ground. The resistance of the air allows the bird to do things that it wouldn't be able to do otherwise. That's an enabling constraint.

So while Hadit creates change through acting, Nuit creates possibilities by setting constraints.

Don't be fooled into thinking that Hadit is masculine and therefore active, and Nuit is feminine and therefore passive. Nuit is not passive. She is creative. She creates possibilities by constraining the activities of Hadit. Hadit's activity is meaningless without Nuit. Hadit without Nuit is like trying to run a sprint in the vacuum of space. He can't get any traction, so His activity is fruitless.

The interaction between these two principles—the Hadit within you which is your core drive to become and the Nuit which is within and all around you—is responsible for who and what you are as an individual. Their interaction is responsible for who you think you are, where you find yourself, what your current opportunities consist of, what your current trajectory in life is, how much you're enjoying it, and what you currently take to be within your power. In other words their interactions determine the totality of what you take to be real.

Already you can see that there has to be a relationship between the concept of will and the fourth meaning of magick I showed you earlier. Both of them have to do with your being. Both of them have to do with becoming. Both of them have to do with dynamic change over time.

But let's go deeper, and in order to do that, I want to introduce you to a distinction which, if you don't know it already, you're going to find very useful. It's a distinction which comes from the psychologist Erich Fromm, and it's the distinction between having needs and being needs.

## Having Needs vs. Being Needs

*Having needs* are satisfied in the *having mode*; *being needs* are satisfied in the *being mode*. When we're in the having mode, we're categorizing things. We're actively, consciously making distinctions between this and that, between me and the other. We're manipulating and controlling. We're aiming for some particular outcome. We're involved in an I-It relationship as opposed to an I-thou relationship. What do I mean by that? If I say Bill is from Missouri, he's 36 years old, he loves playing golf, he's an architect, his shirt is brown, and his wife's name is Maria—one of these attributes is not like the others. There's a difference between concepts that are appropriate to people and concepts that are appropriate to things. The fact that Bill is wearing a brown shirt refers to an object he has, whereas the other things seem somehow more like they belong to Bill as a *person*.

By contrast, our being needs are met by *becoming something* or *becoming someone*. We don't relate to concepts or ideals as something external in the being mode. We're trying to *internalize* and *express* them. We're engaged in a process of *reciprocal realization*. In other words we impact the environment, the environment is changed as a result, and now the environment is enabling and constraining us in new ways, giving rise to new possibilities, closing off others, soliciting new actions and impacts from us, etc.

Where other people are involved, we're in an I-thou relationship. To illustrate, imagine saying to your partner, "I'm in a relationship with you because you're just attractive enough to satisfy me, but you're not too attractive to make me insecure. You make enough money that you seem realistic as a partner, though if we're being perfectly honest, I wish you'd ask for a promotion at work."

The relationship would be over pretty quickly. It would be over because you would be speaking to your partner from an I-it perspective and from the having mode. We don't look to our partners necessarily to help us strategically overcome concrete problems. We want to be with them hopefully because we value them beyond what they have, and because being with them makes life better. It makes it more meaningful.

Let's apply this distinction between the being mode and the having mode to the four types of magic we looked at earlier.

## Magick, Will, and Needs

The four types of magick were: pattern-finding (as in divination), raising or working with magical energy, spirit conjuration, and being magick itself.

In the case of pattern-finding or prediction, are we in the having mode, or are we in the being mode? Well, we're involved with things, problem-solving, and prediction. We might be involved in meaning cultivation, like when we're interpreting cards for instance. But for the most part we're in a having mode.

What about in the second type where we're working with magical energy? If we're raising energy and directing it toward an end—like when we're doing candle magic for love or money—we're manipulating and controlling something to get something else. While some of this might be directed toward becoming a different type of person, we're mostly in the having mode here as well.

The third type is a little trickier. This should be an I-thou relationship, and hence it should be activating the being mode. And it can, certainly. If you look at Crowley's text, Liber Astarte, he has a really beautiful formula for devotional workings with deities. In the ritual working, the relationship with the deity changes, and as a result, you change and the deity changes. It's a strong example of what I called reciprocal realization a moment ago. That's an I-thou relationship.

And yet undoubtedly there are also types of conjuration which look more like an I-it relationship. Think about interactions with spirits that are purely transactional: if the spirit returns a lost item, you'll sing its praises on Tiktok. Or think about those versions of Goetic magic where the magician is constantly threatening the spirit. It's like smacking a vending machine trying to get candy out. Those interactions would be more in the having mode. So it depends.

The fourth type of magick is unequivocally in the being mode, though. It has nothing to do with getting something. It has nothing to do with solving some discrete problem. It doesn't involve manipulation or control. It's about being or becoming something and ultimately someone.

The three versions of will I've introduced you to also correspond to the having and being modes. The three types of will were will power, your purpose in life, and pure willing or the pure desire to be or become.

The first two of these are in the having mode. I have an outcome that I want. I have a will that I assert to get a promotion. I perform the spell so I can get money. That's having mode. Likewise the idea that I have a unique purpose that was given to me by God or the universe or whatever is also satisfying my having needs.

The having mode isn't necessarily bad, but we can get very caught up in the having mode to the point where we forget about the being mode all together. The idea of will in Thelema—and its associated idea of being magick—is there to help us remember the being mode. It's there to help us remember who and what we truly are, thereby rediscovering the concealed depths of ourselves and of the world and the natural magick in their relations.

## Remembering Who We Are

The word *remember* occurs twice in our central holy text, *The Book of the Law*.

> Remember all ye that existence is pure joy; that all the sorrows are but as shadows; they pass & are done; but there is that which remains.[8]

> But remember, o chosen one, to be me; to follow the love of Nu in the starlit heaven; to look forth upon men, to tell them this glad word.[9]

The first one provokes us to remember something about existence; the second provokes us to remember something about ourselves, namely, to remem-

---

8   AL II.9
9   AL II.76

ber to be Hadit, to remember to be pure willing and to love Nuit.

There is a deep connection between remembering who and what we are in the being mode and waking up to more joy and more meaning in our lives. When we become magick, the world around us becomes magical, too.

Think about the most enjoyable and powerful experiences you've had.

Think about what it's like when you're picking up a new set of skills. Think of a situation where you're being challenged—so there are some constraints in place—but the challenge is just beyond your current ability. In such instances you have to put all you've got into the task at hand. You start to forget yourself a bit; your self-image management fades into the background as your self merges, through your attention and through your body, with the task at hand. You're dynamically changing your relationship with the environment in real time so as to optimize the fit between the two. This is what's called *flow* or *being in the zone*.

Think about what it's like to experience natural beauty. Isn't it a little bit like nature was created by a mind like yours, for a mind like yours? Isn't there a strong sense of fittedness there between your core desire to be and the world you find yourself in? Doesn't the sense of the absurdity of life recede in the face of overwhelming beauty?

What about when we're creating art? Whether you're working with sounds, colors, or words, the artistic medium is constraining your actions in various ways that are inseparable from the opening up of numerous possibilities, so that your desires are finding cascading niches for expression.

What's it like when you fall in love? You're revealing depths of yourself to another person while they're doing the same with you. There is accelerating, reciprocal disclosure. That's why they call it *falling* in love.

Crowley referred to the relationship between Hadit and Nuit as *love*. Why? Because that's what it is. That's exactly the right term for it.

There are different kinds of love, and the Greeks had different terms for them. The proper term for the kind of love between the depths of ourselves and the depths of the world is *eros*. It's where we get the term *erotic* from.

## Magick and Love

Eros is love that seeks to be one with something: one with nature, one with a cookie, one with someone by having sex with them. As they say, love is blind. Depending on what we find ourselves caring about, love can have good or bad results.

Thelema is erotic in multiple senses. In a general sense, both eros and Thelema are about caring about those things that are appropriate to our true natures. Ultimately what the deepest part of ourselves cares about is to enjoy profound contact with the deepest part of reality. Notice how much that sounds like the extreme of religious or mystical experience. But in order to get there, we need to optimize the fittedness between the Hadit within and the Nuit without. This is not a once and for all accomplishment. As we come into contact with the environment, the environment changes, and it changes us. Managing that constant flux and flow to optimize the fittedness between the interior of ourselves and our environments is called *love under will* or *magick*.

Thelemic magick isn't about having something you didn't have before. It's not learning a few extra rituals or worshiping different gods from the ones you worshiped before. Nor is it, appearances to the contrary, about putting yourself before all others.

Thelemic magick is about learning to be magick. It's not about satisfying this or that desire, whether it be for a car, a better job, a sex magick partner, or secrets of the lost continent of Atlantis. It's about satisfying the deepest desire any of us has, which is a desire to feel contact with reality. It's about feeling connected in the deepest part of ourselves to self, world, and others.

And because it has this profound feeling—even tactile—dimension to it, this is why I say this has implications for the question of meaning in life. The idea that we can know something is meaningful without in some sense also feeling that it's meaningful is a contradiction in terms. This idea that we are constituted by a love relationship between Hadit and Nuit is able to capture that.

## The Thelemic Ideal

There's a third figure besides Hadit and Nuit that is important in Thelema, and that is Ra-Hoor-Khuit or the Crowned and Conquering Child. Ra-Hoor-Khuit is referred to as the visible object of worship in Thelema. It is the god that we adore and hold up as an ideal.

Ra-Hoor-Khuit is not a particular individual who we are supposed to emulate. He especially does not represent a particular moral ideal that we have to copy. Ra-Hoor-Khuit is a symbol of ceaseless, open-ended growth: the attitude of the child, the child who plays, the child who is in the being mode. Ra-Hoor-Khuit represents the ideal fittedness or the complete contact between Hadit and Nuit which gives rise to the dynamic growth of the individual over time. In other words, Ra-Hoor-Khuit is love under will or magick itself. *To be Ra-Hoor-Khuit is to be magick.*

And while there might be some similarities, for sure, there are also going to be important differences between how that looks for me versus how it looks for you or your neighbor. The particular outcome or result is not what's important here. What's most important is the *process.*

So how do we do this? How do we remember the being mode? How do we bring the depths of ourselves into contact with the depths of reality so as to become magick?

## Becoming Magick

I keep referring to the *depths* of ourselves and the *depths* of reality as though I know what those depths are. I don't. It's not as though the depths are just sitting there, and we have to pick them up and put them together. Depth is what recedes from us. It is implied by a horizon but not revealed by it. Depths belong to the being mode. We can't *have* depths. We can't hold them in our hands. We can't perceive them or conceptualize them or own them or even really feel them. This means we're physically incapable of profaning them. *Nuit and Hadit are infinitely holy.*

Crowley doesn't expect us to turn directly toward the depths. How could we? We can't actually turn toward darkness, which is what the depths are. But we can turn toward the light, and we can turn toward it with a certain mental attitude. That symbol of light is Ra-Hoor-Khuit, who is an amalgamation of Horus and Ra. He is the Sun. The Sun is the ultimate symbol of light, and in Thelema the Sun is also magick itself, which we are to connect to and ultimately identify with.

Crowley wrote a ritual called Liber Resh vel Helios for the purpose of turning toward the Sun as the source of light and the symbol of union. It's a ritual Thelemites do four times a day: once at dawn, once at midday, once at sunset, and once at midnight. It has three parts. The first part is an invocation, basically a short prayer to the Sun in its current station. The second part is an adoration, a passage from *The Book of the Law* which we recite. And the third part is a silent meditation. So one calls to the Sun, offers adoration to the Sun, and that connection to the Sun being established, one then settles down into simply being in that relationship.

According to Crowley, this ritual had three purposes:

> The object of this practice is firstly to remind the aspirant at regular intervals of the Great Work; secondly, to bring him into conscious personal relations with the centre of our system; and thirdly, for advanced students, to make actual magical contact with the spiritual energy of the Sun and thus to draw actual force from him.[10]

The Great Work is what I've been talking about this entire time: the union of the deepest part of ourselves with the deepest part of reality which is also called love under will. When Crowley talks about conscious personal relations with the center of the solar system, I take that more generally to mean establishing ourselves as part of nature. In other words we share the same being as the rest of nature, and the Sun is the source or center of its vitality. And then to draw actual force from the Sun means to be like a wick that naturally draws up oil. In other words, once we are properly established in the being mode, we are no longer obstacles to magick. Magick moves through us, and we become indistinguishable from it.

This is very close to the idea of Tao.

> The Tao is like a well:
> used but never used up.
> It is like the eternal void:
> filled with infinite possibilities.
>
> It is hidden but always present.
> I don't know who gave birth to it.
> It is older than God.[11]

Here we have the idea of depth that I've been talking about: the void which we can never know but which is also the source of everything we do know, hidden but always present. So Resh is a way of helping us remember the being mode through what manifests—the light of the sun—so that we can drop down into contact with that which never manifests but which is the source of all manifestation. That's the deepest part of what I'm calling being magick.

These moments of flow, of connectedness, of opening to the depths, of

---

10  *The Confessions of Aleister Crowley*, ch 69

11  Lao-Tzu, *Tao Te Ching: A New English Version, with Forward and Notes*, trans. Stephen Mitchell (New York: Harper Perennial Modern Classics, 1988), v4

experiences of awe and wonder that are constitutive of being magick are not Thelemic *per se*. They're human. They can be accessed through many experiences and through many traditions. It can be accessed through beauty, artistic creation, and various kinds of physical activities such as martial arts or climbing.

Stimulating conversations with friends are also a way of accessing it. Many philosophers including Epicurus and Buddha talked about the importance of friendship to the spiritual path. *Philia* or friendship is a different kind of love from eros. You don't consume your friend like a cookie. At least you shouldn't. Magick doesn't necessarily have to be accessed in ecstatic states or in a temple with incense or candles lit. The essence of magick is a quality of connectedness which can manifest in many different settings and in many different ways.

## Conclusion

Just as there are many different ways to understand magick, there are also many different ways to understand will. What I have endeavored to show is that the source of all magick is a profound sense of connectedness between the interior of ourselves and the world around us in which we and everything we perceive become magical and enchanted. Thelema uses magick (narrowly construed) to prime this sense of connection with the goal of leading us toward a religious experience. We considered Liber Resh as one such practice, though Thelema includes many of them, including various forms of meditation and mental and physical discipline.

5

# Thelemic Solar Magick:
# Liber Resh

## What is Liber Resh?

Liber Resh is a short ritual Aleister Crowley first published in 1911 in number six of his journal The Equinox. It is a publication in Class D, meaning it is an official ritual of Crowley's magical order, A∴A∴. He described it in the Appendix of *Book 4* as, "An instruction for adoration of the Sun four times daily, with the object of composing the mind to meditation and of regularizing the practices." The ritual is performed by facing the direction of the Sun four times a day: at dawn, at noon (when the Sun is at its zenith), at sunset, and at nadir (when it is opposite its noon position). One gives what is called a grade sign. Then one offers an invocation to the Sun. This is followed by an adoration and a period of meditation. It can take anywhere from around a minute and a half or longer to do, depending on what type of meditation one does and for how long.

The full title of the ritual is *Liber Resh vel Helios sub figura CC*. *Resh* is a letter in the Hebrew alphabet. Its English meaning is *head*. In the Hermetic Qabalah utilized by Crowley, Resh is associated with the 30th path on the Tree of Life and Atu XIX, the Sun card in the tarot major arcana. Helios is the Greek god of the Sun. In Gematria—which is the practice of assigning numbers to letters of the Hebrew alphabet—Resh has the value of 200. Thus the full title of this ritual in English is *Book Head or Helios (the Greek Sun god) under the figure of 200.*

## Who is it for?

Liber Resh is assigned to Probationers of the A∴A∴. In the A∴A∴ graded system of initiation, the Probationer is the grade immediately after Student and immediately before Neophyte. Even though Liber Resh is an official ritual of the A∴A∴, there are good reasons for all Thelemites to practice it, regardless of their A∴A∴ grade or whether they are in A∴A∴ at all.

Grady Louis McMurtry—also known as Hymenaeus Alpha—was the Outer Head of the Order of O.T.O. from 1971 until his death in 1985. He reported that he once witnessed Aleister Crowley discreetly perform Resh while riding public transit in the 1940s. In a letter from Crowley to McMurtry from the same period, Crowley mentions having shown McMurtry how to do Liber Resh, despite McMurtry not being an aspirant to the A∴A∴. He also mentions having shown McMurtry how to perform Resh using the degree signs of O.T.O. instead of the grade signs of A∴A∴. In *Liber CXXIV: Of Eden and the Sacred Oak*, Crowley says that all residents in O.T.O. Profess-Houses "are formally bound to perform the four daily Salutations to the Sun as prescribed in Liber CC." Residents at the Abbey of Thelema—a Thelemic monastery Crowley maintained in Cefalù, Sicily from 1920 to 1923— were expected to perform Resh, and Crowley mentions the ritual many times and in many contexts throughout the years. All of this points to Crowley having considered Liber Resh to be an essential practice for all Thelemites, not just Probationers to the A∴A∴.

## The Purpose of Resh

But what is it about Liber Resh that makes it so essential?

Crowley gives a somewhat fuller description of Liber Resh and its purpose in his autobiography, *The Confessions of Aleister Crowley*.

The object of this practice is firstly to remind the aspirant at regular intervals of the Great Work; secondly, to bring him into conscious personal relations with the centre of our system; and thirdly, for advanced students, to make actual magical contact with the spiritual energy of the Sun and thus to draw actual force from him.[1]

From this quote we can identify three reasons to practice Resh: (1) as a reminder of the Great Work; (2) consciousness of the center; and (3) magical contact with the Sun. Let's consider each in turn.

---

1  *Confessions*, ch 69

## Purpose One: Reminder of the Great Work

Crowley repeats his assertion that Resh serves to remind one of the Great Work in the "Introduction" to *Magick Without Tears*. There he says:

> ...the first essential is the dedication of all that one is and all that one has to the Great Work, without reservation of any sort. This must be kept constantly in mind; the way to do this is to practice Liber Resh vel Helios, sub figura CC.[2]

But what is the Great Work, and in what way does Liber Resh practice support it by reminding one of it?

In the same chapter of *Magick Without Tears*, Crowley says:

> The Great Work is the uniting of opposites. It may mean the uniting of the soul with God, of the microcosm with the macrocosm, of the female with the male, of the ego with the non-ego—or what not.[3]

In chapter 0 of *Magick in Theory and Practice*, he says:

> The microcosm is an exact image of the Macrocosm; the Great Work is the raising of the whole man in perfect balance to the power of Infinity.[4]

The Great Work is the exaltation of the individual—what Crowley refers to as the microcosm—so as to unite it with what he refers to as God or the macrocosm.

In the context of Thelema, the Sun is the symbol of God in the macrocosm. For example, in *Liber XV*—otherwise known as The Gnostic Mass, the central ritual of O.T.O.—the Priest refers to the Sun as "our Lord in the Universe".[5] The Deacon describes the Sun as the "visible and sensible" Lord, the source of light and life on Earth who makes our labor and enjoyment possible.[6] Later the Priest addresses the Sun as "our Lord and Father [...] that travelleth over the Heavens".[7]

---

2   *Magick Without Tears*, "Introduction"
3   Ibid.
4   *Magick in Theory and Practice*, ch 0
5   *Liber XV*, sec 4
6   Ibid, sec 5
7   Ibid, sec 6

Another phrase Crowley used to describe the Great Work was the Knowledge and Conversation of the Holy Guardian Angel. In the first chapter of *Magick in Theory and Practice*, he says:

There is a single main definition of the object of all magical Ritual. It is the uniting of the Microcosm with the Macrocosm. The Supreme and Complete Ritual is therefore the Invocation of the Holy Guardian Angel; or, in the language of Mysticism, Union with God.[8]

In Crowley's magical teaching order, the A∴A∴, this attainment was attributed to the grade of Adeptus Minor. In his essay, "One Star in Sight," which describes the system of attainment of the A∴A∴, Crowley describes the grade of Adeptus Minor as "the main theme of the instructions of the A∴A∴. It is characterised by the Attainment of the Knowledge and Conversation of the Holy Guardian Angel."

The grade of Adeptus Minor is attributed to the sephira Tiphareth on the Tree of Life, which represents the Sun. In *The Book of Thoth*, Crowley says that Tiphareth

...is in some respects the most important [sephira] of all. It is the centre of the whole system; it is the only Sephira below the Abyss which communicates directly with Kether. It is fed directly from Chokmah and Binah; also from Chesed and Geburah. It is thus admirably fitted to dominate the lower Sephiroth; it is balanced both vertically and horizontally. In the planetary system it represents the Sun; in the system of Tetragrammaton it represents the Son. The entire geometrical complex of the Ruach may be regarded as an expansion from Tiphareth. It represents consciousness in its most harmonized and balanced form; definitely in form, not only in idea, as in the case of the number Two. In other words, the Son is an interpretation of the Father in terms of the mind.[9]

The Sun is a representation of God or the Holy Guardian Angel with whom we unite in the accomplishment of the Great Work. It also represents those qualities of mind—balance and harmony—necessary for the accomplishment of the Great Work. And as the Son of Tetragrammaton, it represents the Adept, the mediator between God and humanity that the individual

---

8  *Magick in Theory and Practice*, ch 1
9  *The Book of Thoth*, "The Four Sixes"

becomes in accomplishing the Great Work. For all of these reasons, physically facing the Sun four times daily and adoring the Sun as we do in Liber Resh serves to remind us of the Great Work.

## Purpose Two: Consciousness of the Center

We will now consider how Liber Resh keeps us conscious of the "centre of our system".

In chapter 3, verse 22 of *The Book of the Law*, we read:

> The other images group around me to support me: let all be worshipped, for they shall cluster to exalt me. I am the visible object of worship; the others are secret; for the Beast & his Bride are they: and for the winners of the Ordeal x. What is this? Thou shalt know.[10]

Commenting on this passage, Crowley says:

> There are to be no regular temples of Nuith and Hadit, for They are in-commensurables and absolutes. Our religion therefore, for the People, is the Cult of the Sun, who is our particular star of the Body of Nuit, from whom, in the strictest scientific sense, come this earth, a chilled spark of Him, and all our Light and Life.[11]

Nuit and Hadit are the two most fundamental deities in the Thelemic universe. They are the personages represented in chapters 1 and 2 of *The Book of the Law* respectively. In his 1938 "Introduction" to *The Book of the Law*, Crowley describes them as the "elements" of the cosmos. "This Book explains the Universe," Crowley says:

> The elements are Nuit—Space—that is, the total of possibilities of every kind—and Hadit, any point which has experience of these possibilities. (This idea is for literary convenience symbolized by the Egyptian Goddess Nuit, a woman bending over like the Arch of the Night Sky. Hadit is symbolized as a Winged Globe at the heart of Nuit.)[12]

At the foundation of the Thelemic universe, we do not find a single Supreme

---

10 AL, III.22
11 New Comment on AL III.22
12 "Introduction" to *The Book of the Law*

Being as in the monotheistic religions, as in Advaita Vedanta, or as in naturalistic monism. Instead we find two deities: Nuit or possibility and Hadit or
the point which experiences or realizes these possibilities.

Yet even though Nuit and Hadit are the two supreme deities in Thelema,
Crowley says it is inappropriate to worship them, because they are "incom-
mensurables and absolutes". To be incommensurable means to have no common measure. Nuit and Hadit may be the most fundamental deities in the
Thelemic universe, but we have no way to relate to them with our intellects
or with our imaginations.

In the Gnostic Mass, the Priest describes Nuit as the "soul of infinite
space, before whom Time is Ashamed, the mind bewildered, and the understanding dark".[13] Quoting from chapter 1 verse 27 of *The Book of the Law*, he
says, "O Nuit, continuous one of Heaven, let it be ever thus; that men speak
not of thee as One but as None; and let them speak not of thee at all, since
thou art continuous!"

Shortly thereafter, he addresses Hadit and indicates an entirely different
reason He may not be directly adored:

O secret of secrets that art hidden in the being of all that lives, not Thee
do we adore, for that which adoreth is also Thou. Thou art That, and
That am I.[14]

Because of her unfathomable immensity, we can form no mental image of
Nuit. She exceeds the imagination. But we also cannot form an image of
Hadit, not because He is so immense, but rather because He is too close to
us. At our deepest level, we are identical with Him. Instead, Crowley says,
we are to orient ourselves toward the Sun and worship Him.

The Sun as the center of our system has at least two meanings in the
context of Thelema. First, the Sun is the center of our solar system. Ancient
religions' notions of immortality and salvation were based upon the observation that God, the Sun, died and was reborn again daily and over the
course of the equinoxes and solstices. The Copernican revolution in astronomy established that the Earth in fact moves around the Sun, not vice versa.
The Sun is not dependent upon our sacrifices for its immortality. Rather
the Earth depends for its existence on the Sun, as it is "but a frozen spark"
of that star. Therefore orienting ourselves toward the Sun as the spiritual

---

13  *Liber XV*, sec 4
14  Ibid.

center, as Crowley says in *Liber Aleph*, affirms our "Place in Nature and her Harmonies," and it is an implicit rejection of the superstitious doctrines of atonement and self-sacrifice of older religions.[15]

But there is a second sense in which the Sun symbolizes the center, and that is as the center of ourselves. In the Gnostic Mass, while giving his speech on the third step of the altar, the Priest says:

> Thou that art One, our Lord in the Universe the Sun, our Lord in ourselves whose name is Mystery of Mystery, uttermost being whose radiance enlightening the worlds is also the breath that maketh every God even and Death to tremble before Thee...[16]

The Sun in the heavens is a symbol of unity. The Sun unifies the solar system by means of the force of gravity. Above and beyond all other celestial beings, we are dependent upon Him for our light and life. For this reason He is uniquely adored by us. But the unity of the Sun is mirrored within ourselves. As the Sun is Lord in the Universe, there is also a Lord within ourselves which Crowley refers to as Mystery of Mystery. And just as the Sun is the symbol of immortality in the heavens, so is this Lord within us connected with our own immortality as spiritual beings. Crowley refers to this interior Lord as the Sun of the Soul or the Silent Self. It is the will of this Silent Self—unconscious and within us—to which we must conform if our magick is going to be effective. Writing in his New Comment on AL I.52, Crowley says:

> He will choose the object of his passion at the nod of his Silent Self. He will not allow the prejudice, either of sense, emotion, or rational judgement, to obscure the Sun of his Soul.[17]

Earlier we looked at a passage in which Crowley said that the exoteric object of religious worship for Thelemites was the Sun. In the same passage he goes on to say:

> [The Sun's] vice-regent and representative in the animal kingdom is His cognate symbol the Phallus, representing Love and Liberty. Ra-Hoor-Khu-

---

15  *Liber Aleph*, "De Cultu"
16  *Liber XV*, sec 4
17  New Comment on AL I.52

it, like all true Gods, is therefore a Solar-Phallic deity. But we regard Him as He is in truth, eternal; the Solar-Phallic deities of the old Aeon, such as Osiris, "Christ", Hiram, Adonis, Hercules, &c., were supposed, through our ignorance of the Cosmos, to 'die' and rise again'. Thus we celebrated rites of 'crucifixion' and so on, which have now become meaningless. Ra-Hoor-Khuit is the Crowned and Conquering Child. This is also a reference to the 'Crowned' and Conquering 'Child' in ourselves, our own personal God. Except ye become as little children, said 'Christ', ye shall not enter into the Kingdom of God. The Kingdom of Malkuth, the Virgin Bride, and the Child is the Dwarf-Self, the Phallic consciousness, which is the true life of Man, beyond his 'veils' of incarnation. We have to thank Freud—and especially Jung—for stating this part of the Magical Doctrine so plainly, as also for their development of the connexion of the Will of this 'child' with the True or Unconscious Will, and so for clarifying our doctrine of the 'Silent Self' or 'Holy Guardian Angel'. They are of course totally ignorant of magical phenomena, and could hardly explain even such terms as Augoeides; and they are seriously to blame for not stating more openly that this True Will is not to be daunted or suppressed; but within their limits they have done excellent work.[18]

When we orient ourselves religiously, magically, and meditatively toward the Sun, we are also orienting ourselves toward that symbolic Sun within ourselves, the Holy Guardian Angel or the true self of our beings. Just as the Earth is a cast-off spark of the physical Sun, we are projections in space and time of immortal beings who transcend all limitations. The Earth's relationship to the Sun is one of dependence. If the light of the Sun ceased for even a moment, most life on Earth would immediately perish. Likewise, the way we appear to ourselves by means of our senses, our imaginations, and our intellects does not represent who we actually are. We are not self-sufficient beings. We are not the centers of ourselves. Our minds and bodies are mere instruments of gods reveling in the joy of existence.

Crowley describes Ra-Hoor-Khuit as a "Solar-Phallic deity." Following the usage of Richard Payne Knight and Hargrave Jennings, the phallus is a term for the generative principle more generally. It is not the male sex organ *tout court*. It is both male and female and is properly represented by Baphomet, Babalon, and the union of the lance and the grail in the Gnostic Mass. It represents the path of love or union by means of which we come into contact

---

18 New Comment on AL III.52

with God Within and unite with our true selves. This brings us to the third purpose Crowley assigned to the practice of Liber Resh: establishing magical contact with the Sun.

## Purpose Three: Magical Contact

While Crowley describes the Great Work as the union of the microcosm with the macrocosm, he sometimes uses the Qabalistic language of Tetragrammaton to do the same. For example in the third chapter of Magick in Theory and Practice, he writes:

> The formation of the "Yod" is the formulation of the first creative force, of that father who is called "self-begotten", and unto whom it is said: "Thou has formulated thy Father, and made fertile thy Mother". The adding of the "He" to the "Yod" is the marriage of that Father to the great co-equal Mother, who is a reflection of Nuit as He is of Hadit. Their union brings forth the son "Vau" who is the heir. Finally the daughter "He" is produced. She is both the twin sister and the daughter of "Vau".

> His mission is to redeem her by making her his bride; the result of this is to set her upon the throne of her mother, and it is only she whose youthful embrace can reawaken the eld of the All-Father. In this complex family relationship is symbolised the whole course of the Universe. It will be seen that (after all) the Climax is at the end. It is the second half of the formula which symbolises the Great Work which we are pledged to accomplish. The first step of this is the attainment of the Knowledge and Conversation of the Holy Guardian Angel, which constitutes the Adept of the Inner Order.[19]

Crowley is referring here to the four-part Tetragrammaton: יהוה. In this formula, the final Heh or the Daughter is the "natural soul" of the individual. In chapter 6 of part 2 of Book 4, he writes:

> In one, the best, system of Magick, the Absolute is called the Crown, God is called the Father, the Pure Soul is called the Mother, the Holy Guardian Angel is called the Son, and the Natural Soul is called the Daughter. The Son purifies the Daughter by wedding her; she thus becomes the Mother,

---

19 *Magick in Theory and Practice*, ch 3

the uniting of whom with the Father absorbs all into the Crown.[20]

By "natural soul," Crowley means those spiritual instincts given to us by nature. Another word for the natural soul is Nephesch. As Crowley says in *Little Essays Toward Truth*, the Nephesch is:

> ...the instrument by which the Mind is brought into contact with the dust of Matter in the Abyss, that it may feel it, judge it, and react to it. This is itself a principle still spiritual, in a sense; the actual body of man is composed of the dust of Matter, temporarily held together by the Principles which inform it, for their own purposes...[21]

In its traffic with matter it:

> ...tends to partake of its incoherence. Its faculties of perceiving pain and pleasure lure it into paying undue attention to one set of phenomena, into shunning another. Hence, for the Nephesch to do its work as it should, it requires to be dominated by the severest discipline.[22]

At the outset of the Gnostic Mass, the Priestess is referred to as "Virgin," thus implicitly identifying her with the Daughter of Tetragrammaton and thus with the natural soul. The lance of the Priest, which he immediately lowers upon issuing forth from the tomb in the Ceremony of the Introit, is equally, perhaps even moreso, to be identified with the Nephesch or natural soul. The discipline the Priestess applies to the Priest allows him to raise his lance. The action of raising the lance symbolizes his attainment to the Knowledge and Conversation of his Holy Guardian Angel and his transformation into an Adept. As we saw earlier, the Adept is the personification both of the Sun and the Son of Tetragrammaton. It is by virtue of his status as an Adept that the Priest is then able to raise the Priestess (now the Daughter) to the altar (the throne of the Mother).

In the context of Thelema, the Mother is called Babalon. Babalon is a goddess Crowley encountered through scrying the Enochian aethyrs, the experience of whom he recorded in his magical record, *The Vision and the Voice*. Describing his vision of the 12th aethyr, he writes:

---

20 *Book 4*, part II, ch 6
21 *Little Essays Toward Truth*, "Man"
22 Ibid.

This is the Mystery of Babylon, the Mother of Abominations, and this is the mystery of her adulteries, for she hath yielded up herself to everything that liveth, and hath become a partaker in its mystery. And because she hath made her self the servant of each, therefore is she become the mistress of all. Not as yet canst thou comprehend her glory.

Beautiful art thou, O Babylon, and desirable, for thou hast given thyself to everything that liveth, and thy weakness hath subdued their strength. For in that union thou didst understand. Therefore art thou called Understanding, O Babylon, Lady of the Night![23]

In *The Vision and the Voice*, Babalon is represented as a goddess, but Crowley also understood Her as a spiritual attainment in which one accepted all experiences without discrimination. For example in the fourth chapter of *The Book of Lies*, titled "Peaches," he wrote:

Soft and hollow, how thou dost overcome the hard
　　and full!
It dies, it gives itself; to Thee is the fruit!
Be thou the Bride; thou shalt be the Mother hereafter.
To all impressions thus.  Let them not overcome thee;
　　yet let them breed within thee.  The least of the
　　impressions, come to its perfection, is Pan.
Receive a thousand lovers; thou shalt bear but One
　　Child.
This child shall be the heir of Fate the Father.[24]

Commenting on this passage he said:

Daleth is the Empress of the Tarot, the letter of Venus, and the title, Peaches, again refers to the Yoni. The chapter is a counsel to accept all impressions; it is the formula of the Scarlet Woman; but no impression must be allowed to dominate you, only to fructify you; just as the artist, seeing an object, does not worship it, but breeds a masterpiece from it.

---

23 *The Vision and the Voice*, 12th aethyr
24 *The Book of Lies*, "Peaches"

This process is exhibited as one aspect of the Great Work.[25]

By "impressions" Crowley presumably means sense impressions. One's mind with its natural impulses is the "Daughter" or Heh Final of Tetragrammaton. As we saw earlier, the connection of the natural soul with matter causes it to be pushed this way and that by pleasurable and painful sense impressions. Part of the Great Work involves training one's natural impulses so as to develop radical acceptance of all changes as they occur. This transformation is symbolized by the exaltation of the Daughter to the throne of the Mother. The natural soul becomes a "Whore," accepting of All. This will "reawaken the eld of the All-Father". The All-Father is Yod of Tetragrammaton or the Secret Self. Once our minds are wide open and accepting, this Secret Self will then be "loosed" on us. Describing this process in his New Comment on AL I.7, Crowley writes:

The Concealed Child becomes the Conquering Child, the armed Horus avenging his father Osiris. So also our own Silent Self, helpless and witless, hidden within us, will spring forth, if we have craft to loose him to the Light, spring lustily forward with his cry of Battle, the Word of our True Wills.

This is the Task of the Adept, to have the Knowledge and Conversation of His Holy Guardian Angel, to become aware of his nature and his purpose, fulfilling them.[26]

Crowley ultimately chose to spell Babalon with an "a" rather than a "y". *Bab* is the Arabic word for *door* or *gate* and *Al* the name for *God*. *On* is the name of the Egyptian city that the Greeks called *Heliopolis*, or the City of the Sun. It is a name by which the Priest refers to the Sun in the Gnostic Mass.[27] Thus the goddess Babalon is the *Gate of the God ON*, or the Sun.

In the 55th verse of the 3rd chapter of *The Book of the Law*, we read:

Let Mary inviolate be torn upon wheels: for her sake let all chaste women be utterly despised among you![28]

---

25 Ibid.
26 New Comment on AL I.7
27 *Liber XV*, sec 6
28 AL III.55

Reflecting upon the symbolism of the Mother, Crowley commenting on this verse says:

> She is Sakti, the Teh, the Magical Door between the Tao and the Manifested World. The great Obstacle then is if that Door be locked up. Therefore Our Lady must be symbolized as an Whore.[29]

We can only establish magical contact with the Sun of our Souls by radically opening ourselves to the outward flow of the divine fire within. We must become "whores" to our personal gods. We must become Babalon.

Crowley gives us yet another metaphor for this process in chapter 15 of *The Book of Lies*, titled "The Gun-Barrel".

> Mighty and erect is this Will of mine, this Pyramid
>   of fire whose summit is lost in Heaven.  Upon it
>   have I burned the corpse of my desires.
> Mighty and erect is this φαλλός of my Will.  The
>   seed thereof is That which I have borne within me
>   from Eternity; and it is lost within the Body of
>   Our Lady of the Stars.
> I am not I; I am but an hollow tube to bring down
>   Fire from Heaven.
> Mighty and marvellous is this Weakness, this
>   Heaven which draweth me into Her Womb, this
>   Dome which hideth, which absorbeth, Me.
> This is The Night wherein I am lost, the Love
>   through which I am no longer I.[30]

In this chapter, the phallus is described as identical with the personal or natural will of the individual, what we have already seen him elsewhere describe as the Daughter or Heh-final of Tetragrammaton. When it is fully erect, it undergoes a polarity shift. It becomes an organ for the reception of "Fire from Heaven," in other words, the power of Our Lord and Father the Sun. The phallus switches from being an organ of penetration to being penetrated. The phallus becomes Babalon.

---

29 New Comment on AL III.55
30 *The Book of Lies*, ch 15

Crowley understood gender fluidity as essential to the accomplishment of the Great Work. Commenting on chapter 2, verse 56 of *Liber LXV*, he wrote:

> Having attained the Knowledge and Conversation of the Holy Guardian Angel (by a male effort so to speak) the Adept becomes receptive, feminine, patient, surrendering his will wholly to that of his Angel.[31]

In his commentary on chapter 5 verse 44 of the same Holy Book, he identifies the refusal to transcend the opposition of sex with the Black Brother.

> The male must have completed himself and become androgyne; the female, and become gynander. This incompleteness imprisons the soul. To think "I am not woman, but man"' or vice versa, is to limit one's self, to set a bar to one's motion. It is the root of the "shutting-up" which culminates in become "Mary inviolate" or a "Black Brother."[32]

In his comment on AL I.8, Crowley describes these self-limitations to the Great Work as "complexes," the dissolution of which transforms oneself from a "dark star" into a passive medium of the light of the Sun within.

> We are not to regard ourselves as base beings, without whose sphere is Light or "God". Our minds and bodies are veils of the Light within. The uninitiate is a "Dark Star", and the Great Work for him is to make his veils transparent by 'purifying' them. This 'purification' is really 'simplification'; it is not that the veil is dirty, but that the complexity of its folds makes it opaque. The Great Work therefore consists principally in the solution of complexes.[33]

Resolving our complexes, making ourselves transparent, making ourselves receptive and affirmative, becoming spiritually androgynous or female, raising our natural souls to the throne of the Mother, and becoming "whores" are all metaphors for the same process in which we become radically open to the divine energies flowing from the unfathomable depths of ourselves outward into the cosmic womb of Nuit. To transform oneself into the passive conduit for this flow of interior sunlight is likely what Crowley had in mind when

---

31 Comment on *Liber LXV*, II.56
32 Comment on *Liber LXV*, V.44
33 New Comment on AL I.8

he said that, for advanced practitioners, Liber Resh offers a way to establish magical contact with the energy of the Sun.

In verse 38 of chapter 3 of *The Book of the Law*, we read:

So that thy light is in me; & its red flame is as a sword in my hand to push thy order. There is a secret door that I shall make to establish thy way in all the quarters, (these are the adorations, as thou hast written), as it is said:

The light is mine; its rays consume
 Me: I have made a secret door
Into the House of Ra and Tum,
 Of Khephra and of Ahathoor.
I am thy Theban, O Mentu,
 The prophet Ankh-af-na-khonsu![34]

## Practical Considerations

Having established the theoretical basis for doing Resh, let's walk through the text with an eye toward practical considerations. The text begins:

 0. These are the adorations to be performed by aspirants to the A∴A∴.

As we saw, Liber Resh is not just for aspirants to the A∴A∴ but for all Thelemites. The next line of the text reads:

 1. Let him greet the Sun at dawn, facing East, giving the sign of his grade.

The next three sections begin similarly, with modifications made for the time of the day:

 2. Also at Noon, let him greet the Sun, facing South, giving the sign of his grade.

 3. Also, at Sunset, let him greet the Sun, facing West, giving the sign of his grade.

---

34 AL III.38

4. Lastly, at Midnight, let him greet the Sun, facing North, giving the sign of his grade

There are at least three senses dawn can have. It can mean astronomical dawn. This begins when the Sun is 18 degrees below the horizon. It can mean nautical dawn, when there is enough illumination for sailors to distinguish the horizon at sea. This begins when the Sun is 12 degrees below the horizon. And there is civil dawn, which is when there is enough light for most objects to be distinguishable. This occurs when the Sun is 6 degrees below the horizon.

One thing "dawn" does not mean is sunrise. The dawn Resh is meant to be performed before the Sun has risen.

Noon can mean either 12:00 in the daytime, or it can mean solar noon, i.e., the time when the Sun appears to contact the local celestial meridian or when it is at its highest point in the sky.

Sunset is more straightforward. It is when the upper limb of the Sun disappears below the horizon.

Midnight is either the moment when the date changes in your location, or it is solar midnight which is the time opposite to solar noon, i.e., when the Sun is at its nadir.

You can easily determine the times of these occurrences using an astronomical website such as https://www.timeanddate.com/. Brother Scott Wilde has also created an app to determine these for you based on your location. It sounds a gong when it is time to do one of the Resh adorations. https://keepsilence.org/clock/

Most practitioners of Resh are not strict about the times. It is common for people who have missed an adoration to do it when convenient. For example, it is common to do the midnight adoration upon waking.

My suggestion is that, if you have not done so, you try to do the adorations exactly at the appointed times for a period of at least a week to see what it is like. It is unrealistic to expect most people will stick indefinitely to a strict schedule, but it is valuable to try it so as to have the experience to compare with other experiences. Keep track of what happens in your magical diary.

The phrase "the sign of his grade" refers to the signs of the grades of A∴A∴. This direction is for aspirants to the A∴A∴ who are doing Resh. Crowley noted in his own personal copy of *The Equinox* 1:6 the signs that should be given by someone who is not an A∴A∴ aspirant:

Where the aspirant has no grade, let him give [...] The L.V.X. signs at dawn, 4°=7□ at noon, 2°=9□ at sunset, 3°=8□ at midnight.[35]

These signs are illustrated in Liber O, which is in the second volume of The Equinox. The L.V.X. signs are Osiris Slain (the cross), Isis Mourning (the Swastika), Typhon (the Trident), and Osiris Risen (the Pentagram). The 4°=7□ sign, given at noon, is the sign of fire and the goddess Thoum-aesh-neith. The 2°=9□ sign, given at sunset, is the sign of air or the god Shu supporting the sky. The 3°=8□ or water sign is the goddess Auramoth. You can either remain in the sign throughout the entire invocation, or you can give the sign, drop your hands to your sides, and then give the invocation.

If one is an initiate of O.T.O., they can give the sign of recognition of whatever degree they happen to be. Once one is a III°, they can give the I° sign at dawn, the II° sign at noon, the III° sign at sunset, and the o° sign at midnight.

After giving the sign, the instructions say that the practitioner is to say in a loud voice:

Hail unto Thee who art Ra in Thy rising, even unto Thee who art Ra in Thy strength, who travellest over the Heavens in Thy bark at the Uprising of the Sun.

Tahuti standeth in His splendour at the prow, and Ra-Hoor abideth at the helm.

Hail unto Thee from the Abodes of Night!

The invocation describes the solar barque, a vessel utilized by the sun god Ra throughout the course of the Sun's journey across the sky. Ra was said to use a vessel called the *Mandjet* or the Boat of Millions of Years during the day, and at night he used what was called the *Mesektet*.

The other three invocations are similar, except the gods, their stations, their qualities, their points in the journey, and their hailing abodes are different.

---

35 Aleister Crowley, Mary Desti, and Leila Waddell, *Magick Liber ABA Book Four Parts I-IV*, Second Revised Edition (Boston: Weiser Books, 2002), 655.

| Name | Ra | Ahathoor | Tum | Khephra |
|---|---|---|---|---|
| **Station** | Rising | Triumphing | Setting | Hiding |
| **Quality** | Strength | Beauty | Joy | Silence |
| **Point in Journey** | Uprising | Midcourse | Down-going | Midnight Hour |
| **Hailing Abode** | Night | Morning | Day | Evening |

The particular gods chosen are those mentioned on the Stele of Revealing, a paraphrase of which Crowley was directed by Aiwass to insert into verse 38 of chapter 3 of *The Book of the Law*. I quoted it earlier:

The light is mine; its rays consume
Me: I have made a secret door
Into the House of Ra and Tum,
Of Khephra and of Ahathoor.

Ra was considered by the Egyptians to be the king of the deities and father of all creation. He was the patron of the sun, heaven, kingship, power, and light. Ahathoor or Hathor was the goddess of love, beauty, music, dancing, fertility, and pleasure. She was depicted either with a cow's head or as a woman wearing cow's horns. Tum or Atum is the primordial god in Egyptian mythology from whom all else arose. He created both himself and is the father of Shu and Tefnut, the ancestors of all the other Egyptian gods. Khephra or Khepri is a scarab-faced god in ancient Egyptian religion who represents the rising or morning sun. He represents creation and the renewal of life.

There is evidence Crowley practiced Resh at times with different gods attributed to the quarters than those mentioned in *Equinox 6*. As Hymenaeus Beta has described in the Weiser Second Edition of Magick, Crowley gives the phrase "Harmachis in thy beauty" following "Ra in Thy Strength" in his copy of *Magick in Theory and Practice*, with a line indicating an apparent insertion or replacement. In another manuscript note to his copy of *Magick in Theory and Practice*, "Mau the Lion very lordly" is written in the margin opposite paragraph 2 of section 2 but without an insertion point in the text.[36] Crowley remarks in Letter A of *Magick Without Tears*:

---

36 Ibid, 786-87.

There is another version of these Adorations, slightly fuller; but those in the text ⟦i.e., in Equinox 6⟧ are quite alright. The important thing is not to forget.[37]

All of this suggests a certain degree of flexibility on Crowley's part over the years with regard to the specific deities utilized in this ritual.

We are always hailing the god from an abode that is passing away. For example, we greet the rising Sun from the abodes of night, the noon Sun from the abodes of morning, the setting Sun from the abodes of day, and the midnight Sun from the abodes of evening. The Sun is in our future and represents both a physical and a spiritual state we are in the process of entering.

Line 5 says:

> And after each of these invocations thou shalt give the sign of silence, and afterward thou shalt perform the adoration that is taught thee by thy Superior. And then do thou compose Thyself to holy meditation.

The Sign of Silence is given by pressing one's index finger to one's lips and symbolizes Harpocrates or Hoor-paar-kraat, who Crowley took to be the god of silence and another form of Hadit or the Silent Self. Commenting on AL II.21, he says:

> Hadith calls himself the Star, the Star being the Unit of the Macrocosm; and the Snake, the Snake being the symbol of Going or Love, and the Chariot of Life. He is Harpocrates, the Dwarf-Soul, the Spermatozoon of all Life, as one may phrase it. The Sun, etc., are the external manifestations or Vestures of this Soul, as a Man is the Garment of an actual Spermatozoon, the Tree sprung of that Seed, with power to multiply and to perpetuate that particular Nature, though without necessary consciousness of what is happening.[38]

We face and address the physical Sun—Lord Visible and Sensible, Our Lord in the Universe— and then we immediately follow this with the Sign of Silence, the sign of the Lord Within Ourselves, the Secret Lord of which the Sun is merely the outward manifestation.

The phrase the "adoration that is taught thee by thy Superior" refers to

---

37 *Magick Without Tears*, Letter A
38 New Comment on AL II.21

one's superior in A∴A∴. If one is not in A∴A∴, it is typical to recite the adoration from AL III.37-38:

Unity uttermost showed!
I adore the might of Thy breath,
Supreme and terrible God,
Who makest the gods and death
To tremble before Thee—
I, I adore thee!
Appear on the throne of Ra!
Open the ways of the Khu!
Lighten the ways of the Ka!
The ways of the Khabs run through
To stir me or still me!
Aum! let it kill me!

The light is mine; its rays consume
Me: I have made a secret door
Into the House of Ra and Tum,
Of Khephra and of Ahathoor.
I am thy Theban, O Mentu,
The prophet Ankh-af-na-khonsu!
By Bes-na-Maut my breast I beat;
By wise Ta-Nech I weave my spell.
Show thy star-splendour, O Nuit!
Bid me within thine House to dwell,
O wingèd snake of light, Hadit!
Abide with me, Ra-Hoor-Khuit!

The meditation is of one's choosing. I will lead you through one possible meditation right now. Press your index finger to your lips and close your eyes. As best you can, listen for the sound of cargo being loaded on ships at the dock on Harbor Island. Harbor Island is about nine miles from where we are right now. Given the distance, it is physically impossible for us to hear anything happening on Harbor Island right now, but try anyway. As you are listening for the sound of cargo being loaded on boats at Harbor Island, you're liable to hear other things. You may hear a car passing on the street. You may hear neighbors talking. Whatever you hear, note that you have heard it, but then renew your attempt to reach out further and hear the sound of boats being loaded on Harbor Island. A feeling of openness in the center of your chest is a sign that you are doing the exercise properly. Take a deep breath, let it out, and open your eyes.

When we hear an actual occurrence—for example someone talking or a car passing on the street—that is the natural soul making contact with matter. But when we try to hear something we cannot possibly hear, the natural soul is reaching out beyond things and into Nuit Herself. We are not just hearing at that point; we are listening. When we notice ourselves just hearing, we drop that and switch back to listening.

The feeling of openness in the chest is the sign that your feet are on the path of the open heart. That is the path which, if you follow it to its ends, leads to Our Lady Babalon and her Grail. The Thelemic spiritual path is a way of the heart. It is a way of compassion. Compassion is not sentimentality but rather acceptance and affirmation of the intrinsic goodness of existence.

Line 6 of the text reads:

Also it is better if in these adorations thou assume the God-form of Whom thou adorest, as if thou didst unite with Him in the adoration of That which is beyond Him.

The assumption of God-forms is a practice taught in A∴A∴ and is described in Liber O.

The Magical Images of the Gods of Egypt should be made thoroughly familiar. This can be done by studying them in any public museum, or in such books as may be accessible to the student. They should then be carefully painted by him, both from the model and from memory.

The student, seated in the "God" position or in the characteristic attitude of the God desired, should then imagine His image as coinciding with his own body, or as enveloping it. This must be practised until mastery of the image is attained, and an identity with it and with the God experienced. It is a matter for very great regret that no simple and certain test of success in this practice exists.

So for the dawn Resh, one would call to mind as vividly as possible the image of Ra, and they would then imagine that image of Ra coinciding with and enveloping their own body while performing the invocation. The same would be done with Ahathoor at noon, with Tum at sunset, and with Khephra at midnight.

Who is "That which is beyond Him"? I interpret this to mean the Voice of the Silence, emanating from the center and secret of the Sun. It is this which I am listening for during the meditation portion of the practice.

Finally line 7 reads:

Thus shalt thou ever be mindful of the Great Work which thou hast undertaken to perform, and thus shalt thou be strengthened to pursue it unto the attainment of the Stone of the Wise, the Summum Bonum, True Wisdom and Perfect Happiness.

## Conclusion

Liber Resh is a staple of Thelemic spiritual practice. In this lecture I have endeavored to bring it to life by connecting it with the ultimate purpose of Thelema (the Great Work) as well as our ultimate purpose as human beings.

All postmodern nonsense aside, in the deepest part of ourselves, we hunger for actual contact with reality. Reality is not something you can grasp through an adequate description of it. Contact with reality in the fullest sense is explosive of self. To have contact, we must turn ourselves inside-out. We must empty ourselves in the Cup of Our Lady Babalon. We must become pure conduits for the Holy Fire of the Interior Sun on its journey outward into the Womb of Nuit. Liber Resh is a way of participating ritualistically in this truth and physically, mentally, and emotionally enacting it four times a day.

# 6

# Light of the Shadow:
# A Meditation on Beauty &
# Eternal Truth

There is a mystery at the heart of beauty. It is the mystery of appearances and illusions. It is the mystery of shadows. When we talk about appearances, we talk about them in opposition with reality. Between these two concepts—appearance and reality—we naturally assign a hierarchy. Appearance is the lesser, and reality is the greater. We spend much of our lives attempting to get past mere appearances and to somehow arrive at the truth. We struggle every day with illusions in the world and the deceptive behaviors of other individuals. We even struggle with illusions and shadows within ourselves in our quest to understand who we truly are. So pervasive is the problem of illusion that human beings have devised a set of practices—the natural scientific method—to set limits to the basic human tendency to make things up literally all the time. Our lives are a struggle against illusion and darkness in our attempts to reach the light. And yet in the case of beauty—whether we're speaking of natural beauty, such as in the case of the beauty of a mountain or forest, or whether we are speaking about artistic beauty, as in the case of painting, sculpture, film, or a piece of music—we are concerned exclusively with appearances. We don't mind that the fruit in the painting cannot be eaten. We don't mind that the actors in the play or film are merely pretending to grapple with tragedy. When we're experiencing beauty, all the interest lies right at the surface of things. And yet despite the apparent shallowness of beauty, such experiences carry a depth and profundity of meaning that has the power to change the course of a life—sometimes forever. These experiences are purely subjective in nature. They provoke feelings rather than concrete cognitions about the world. And yet despite the fact of being subjective and merely feeling-based, the experience of beauty is so profound that human beings have seen fit to include it alongside truth and goodness as one of our highest ideals. How is it that something seemingly so weak and shallow as a mere appearance can have such power?

Reflecting upon beauty, we are drawn naturally to the question of appearances, but reflecting upon appearances naturally brings us to a consideration of the human body and its physical senses. It is because of our senses after all that we are aware of mere appearances as opposed to reality. Our souls do not have unmediated access to reality. The content is filtered through our faculty of sensation.

From the perspective of the Path in Eternity, which is dramatized in the degree initiations of O.T.O., we acquire our bodies through a process of incarnation. Each of us is essentially a spiritual being. "Every man and every woman is a star." And yet we are also told by Crowley that "each such Star, or Soul, must eat of the Fruit of the Tree of Knowledge of Good and Evil, by accepting labour and pain as its portion, and death as its doom."[1] In other words each of us takes a body. We incarnate. As a result we become subject to conditions. This process is dramatized in the Minerval and First degrees of Man of Earth. Each of us has traded the fullness of being for a world of absence. We have traded permanence for instability. We traded our self-sufficiency and freedom from conditions to exist in a world where nothing can truly be said to be I, me, or mine. We became subject to birth, aging, sickness, tragedy, death: a life of pain and suffering punctuated by the malevolence of other beings.

*What would make a god want to do this?*

We relinquish our apprehension of the light, only to spend our whole lives searching everywhere to get it back. Do gods hide their own car keys on themselves, too? What is the purpose of this? Why would anyone—let alone an omniscient and omnipotent god—want to come *here* of all places?

And yet perhaps this is not what happened at all. Perhaps we never did turn away from the light. Perhaps we looked intently into the light, and therein, in that world of stillness, eternity, and silence, we found this world of time, motion, and shadows. Perhaps we were drawn into that world of shadows precisely when we were drawn into the light. And were we able to properly perceive this world of shadows and suffering that we dwell in, we would find hidden therein that other world of light, stillness, and peace that we seek. And if we could perceive one in the other—time in eternity and eternity in time, motion within stillness and stillness within motion, silence within speech and speech within silence—then the distinction be-

---

1 New Comment on AL I.29

tween those two worlds would drop away, and our minds would leap into the heart of the mystery lying beyond any of them.

If this story is true—in other words if 0 is only to be found in 2, if 2 is only to be found in 0, if they truly are identical with one another—then we must reconsider the role of the body in our spirituality. We must reconsider the role the senses play. Because if this alternate story is true, then the senses are *not* barriers between our divine souls and reality. On the contrary the senses are divine. The problem is not that we have senses. *The problem is that we do not yet know how to use our senses properly—with the result that our senses end up using us instead.* What we therefore require is what the great German poet Friedrich Schiller referred to as an *aesthetic education*—after the Greek word for sensation, aísthēsis.

> Even as on the resounding wind-swept heights of Mitylene some god-like woman casts aside the lyre, and with her locks aflame as an aureole, plunges into the wet heart of the creation, so I, O Lord my God! There is a beauty unspeakable in this heart of corruption, where the flowers are aflame.[2]

When each of us cast aside the lyre and plunged into the wet heart of creation, we took with us into this world something from that other world. Each of us brought a seed. Crowley refers to this seed by many names: Secret Self, Aleph, "secret of secrets that art hidden in the being of all that lives," Harpocrates, Hoor-paar-kraat, the Virgin Self. This seed contains within itself a memory of the light, a memory of eternity, and a memory of what was apparently lost. It is by virtue of this seed that each of us knows of the existence of the light even though we live in a world of apparent and total darkness. When the seed came into this world, it landed in the black soil of Malkuth, and there it remained concealed within the heart of each individual. Most of us don't even know that we carry it except for the occurrence every now and again of some inchoate yearning for something else—usually something ridiculous which all the evidence of our senses tells us doesn't even exist. Yet should we turn our attention toward these seemingly ridiculous yearnings, something miraculous happens. All on its own, the seed germinates, and it begins to grow. As if by magic, it instinctively pushes through the dark soil and heads toward the light. Should we supply this new growth with its proper share of food, air, water, and sunlight, then it will grow. By

---

2  Liber LXV, IV.2-3

seed and root and stem and bud and leaf and flower it will unfold and artic-
ulate itself into the light. In the Chaldean Oracles, this flower is called the
*flower of mind*. The Theravada Buddhist tradition has a word for the fruit
this flower creates. It is called *magga phala* or fruit of the path. It is the direct
comprehension of the deathless which occurs through unbinding or *nibbana*.
In our tradition it is called *gnosis*. It is the full expression of the knowledge
of the light which was merely implicit in the Silent Seed. In time that fruit
will fall from the branch, and it will break open on the ground. The seeds
contained therein will go into the black earth once again, thereby completing
one full cycle of the cosmological process, the upward arc of which Crowley
refers to as *initiation*.

In chapter 20 of *Magick in Theory and Practice*, Crowley draws a parallel
between initiation and alchemy. In the case of alchemy, we are once again
dealing with a secret seed, this time a spiritual potential concealed within
matter. Peter Kingsley has traced this idea of a hidden spiritual essence within matter—particularly a solar essence—back to the writings of Empedocles,
a Greek-speaking philosopher, mystic, and magician of the 5th century BCE,
from whom we get our words for the four elements.[3] Empedocles claimed
there were great fires burning at the center of the earth. This subterranean
fire is in fact the origin of the sun. The sun—that very symbol of light, divinity, and oneness, the banisher of shadows, the symbol of reality—itself has
its home and origin in the darkest of dark places: hidden in the heart of the
shadows in the earth. We find a latter-day echo of this ancient idea in the 6th
collect of our own Gnostic Mass.

> Mother of fertility on whose breast lieth water, whose cheek is caressed
> by air, and in whose heart is the sun's fire...[4]

Crowley goes on to draw parallels between initiation and alchemy on the
one hand and art production, in particular painting, on the other. We are
dealing once again with a potential hidden within the heart of matter, a light
hidden in the heart of darkness, and a process which brings forth that divine
light.[5] This is precisely what happens in the transformation of mere matter
into artistic medium. Matter itself becomes the bearer or vehicle of human

---

3   Peter Kingsley, *Ancient Philosophy, Mystery and Magic: Empedocles and Pythagorean Tradition* (Oxford: Clarendon Press, 1995), ch 1-5.
4   *Liber XV*, sec 5
5   See chapter 8.

significance and meaning-making, right here on the surface of the earth. Normally we think of matter as being at odds with human meaning-making. Matter must be forced into shape to become useful in the attainment of human ends, and yet in the case of the production of a work of art, it is as though there were an intention hidden within matter itself, and rather than being at odds with human intention, matter enters into collaboration with it to produce a work of beauty which is capable of bearing and expressing human significance in ways we hitherto could not even imagine. Every work of art is the product of at least two creators: the artist and nature. In the case of the production of a work of art, it is as though the world were made by a mind like ours, for a mind like ours. Thus Crowley says that what is held in common between initiation, alchemy, and art is nothing less than the transformation of dead matter into a living being.

Nature appears alive. The shadows begin to glow with light. Our senses come alive when we enjoy works of art. Matter glows with hidden potential. Our senses themselves begin to play. As Nietzsche said, we play with the seriousness of a child—and it all happens spontaneously without us even having to try.

When we were children, each of us was completely spontaneous and totally innocent. We were like stars in their original state. We were at one not only with the world around us and with our caregivers but also with ourselves. But as a human being matures, it sheds that sense of oneness to become a separate individual. It releases or trades some of its spontaneity and its innocence for knowledge and skills and for the ability to take aim in life. As we make the passage into adulthood, we specialize. We learn skills to become more useful to others and to ourselves. The ordeal of midlife—as Nietzsche alludes—is to reclaim that sense of spontaneity we relinquished when we went through the narrow passageway from childhood into adulthood. Thus we become wise. The only difference between the wise person and the fool is that the wise person is not naïve. They understand how the world works—and they nevertheless rejoice.

Under ideal circumstances this shedding of spontaneity and of innocence is gradual and organic. Yet under conditions of trauma, rather than being gradually shed, innocence is shattered. Under such circumstances the human psyche mobilizes its divine, miraculous powers. It protects the imperishable spirit from the unthinkable. This happens entirely spontaneously, and it is indeed a divine miracle. Yet when these defenses are carried forward into adulthood, they show up as the inability to adapt or to mature emotionally.

They express themselves as a failure to find meaning in life or to move toward wholeness. We remain partial, impoverished beings, unnourished by
the power of life in a walled off world that feels increasingly dead and filled
with demonic powers. At that point the only thing that can destroy what
the human psyche created in desperation is the power of darkness.[6] We must
venture directly into the shadows and trace our wounds back to their origins,
and with the power of a magician we must heal ourselves. Very few have the
knowledge or the willingness to accept full responsibility for the darkness in
their own lives, and even fewer have the courage to march courageously into
the underworld and to stand face-to-face with the Queen of Death Herself.
Few of us can carry our fear all the way. So there we remain, locked in our
own prisons, dimly aware of the existence of something else.

Yet in experiences of beauty, something strange happens. The shadows
themselves begin to glow. A thin beam of light makes its way through a
crack in the wall. As the German poet Novalis said, chaos begins to shimmer
through the veil of order. Something calls to us. Something dormant in our
hearts begins to stir. This stirring oftentimes shows up as a crisis. You've just
finished a great novel. You're leaving the theater having just seen a play or
a film. Something inside of you stirs. Maybe the thought occurs to you: *My
God, something has to change! My life must change!*

But how?

You don't know. A work of art doesn't tell you what to do with your life.
That's not its job. Beauty is not the same thing as goodness. You don't see
a painting or hear a song and then get a download of a plan of what to do
with your life. Aesthetic experience does not generate a concept. First and
foremost, it creates a *feeling*. You are thrown back upon your own resources
to figure out what you are going to do. The aesthetic experience affirms our
radical freedom. The choice we're presented with is nothing less than that
between life and death. And yet—you do not literally fear for your life. This
is not like getting a cancer diagnosis or seeing a car barreling toward you in
the crosswalk. You're not in peril of dying. *You're in peril of dying without ever
having lived in the first place.*

There is something inside of you which is yet unrealized. It is the Silent
Seed. It is that memory of the light hidden within the darkness of your own
being. It is a precious, one-of-a-kind gift which you have neglected. And yet
that neglect has in no way harmed or deformed it. It is as bright as it ever
was. It is immortal light. It speaks to you, not in life-plans or even concepts

---

6  Frater Acher, *The Everyday Path to Your Holy Guardian Angel* (Frater Acher, 2011), 8.

or words. Like beauty itself, it makes no demand of you. The god within you is so divine that it leaves you free to turn away from it and return to your ordinary life. But should you turn toward it, it will germinate and grow. It will look out upon the world through your physical eyes, and it will behold a divine world all around it: precious, unique, engulfed in beauty. Together you will know the light all over again but as if for the very first time.

# 7

# God is an Artist: Thelema & Hermeticism

Historically there has been a close relationship between Thelema and art. Thelema has attracted many artists and musicians over the last century, and Thelemic ideas have been transmitted primarily by means of artists and musicians—far more than by occult orders. Why exactly is that? This lecture seeks to answer that question and to draw practical implications from it.

The way I propose to do that is by showing the deep inner connection between Thelema and art. We'll look at Thelema as an artistic form of spirituality and as a spiritual art. Creativity plays an important role in Thelemic theology. That will require a deep, heady dive into Thelemic theory. Then I want to look at the relationship between art and some areas of magick, particularly alchemy and initiation. And finally, I want to think about ways we can use the power of beauty to transform our lives and to make our magick more effective, both in the narrow sense of ritual but also in the broader sense of what we might term *the art of living*.

## Spiritual Art and Artistic Spirituality

The founder of Thelema, Edward Alexander Crowley, was himself an artist. Art was a huge part of Crowley's life. Crowley became a painter relatively late in life, around the age of 40. But prior to that he was also a prolific poet. Artistic expression was an enormous part of Crowley's personality. Whether he was painting or writing, he turned out art like a machine.

It's not an accident that Thelema was founded by a prolific, even compulsive artist. Creativity is imprinted upon the core of Thelema itself. This fact explains why so many artists were drawn to Thelema. During Crowley's lifetime, Austin Osman Spare and Frieda Harris were attracted to Thelema.

Later there was Marjorie Cameron, Harry Smith, and Xul Solar.

The influence of Thelema has not been limited to painters. Harry Smith also made films, and Crowley of course had a huge influence on Kenneth Anger. Horror movies since the late 60s have been important for popularizing occult themes, if not Thelema in particular. More than anything else, rock bands—The Beatles, Ozzy Osbourne, Led Zeppelin, King Crimson, Throbbing Gristle, Blue Oyster Cult, Psychic TV, and Current 93 to name a few—have popularized Thelema and Crowley. If you or any of your friends know about Crowley, odds are far more likely that you were introduced to Crowley through one of these bands, through an artist, or through a horror film than through an occult order.

When Crowley formed his magical order, the A∴A∴, he was very interested in the idea of spiritual practices and experiences to generate what he called genius. In 1912 Crowley published part one of his magnum opus, *Book Four*, the subtitle of which was *The Way of Attainment of Genius or Godhead considered as a Development of the Human Brain*. In the summary section at the end, we find this mock dialogue about genius:

Q. What is genius, and how is it produced?

A. Let us take several specimens of the species, and try to find some one thing common to all which is not found in other species.

Q. Is there any such thing?

A. Yes: all geniuses have the habit of concentration of thought, and usually need long periods of solitude to acquire this habit. In particular the greatest religious geniuses have all retired from the world at one time or another in their lives, and begun to preach immediately on their return.

In a footnote earlier in the book he says, "We have dealt in this preliminary sketch only with examples of religious genius. Other kinds are subject to the same remarks, but the limits of our space forbid discussion of these."

Genius was at the heart of Crowley's spiritual concerns. Religious genius is the focus of his study, but it's clear from the footnote that he was interested in genius more generally as well. What all forms of genius have in common is that they are discovered within oneself—not invented—once we remove the obstacles to them.

Speaking at a panel discussion in 2016, William Breeze said of Crowley:

In the introduction to his own early diaries, [Crowley] has a note which says, at later stages, when one gets truly advanced with this ... it becomes all about vision. At the Adeptus Minor/Holy Guardian Angel level, the work involves changes in your vision. You see that with these artists who have attained. Their color sense is different ... Their way of seeing changed permanently.[1]

Crowley saw a necessary relationship between creative vision and spiritual attainment. The painter Breeze was referring to here was Xul Solar, an Argentinian painter of intense occult themes. Whether Solar would have painted the way he did had he not gone through Crowley's system of spiritual attainment is a question we cannot answer. What's undeniable is that visionary capability was essential to Crowley's own sense of spirituality, and that spirituality has been influential for artists.

Another one of Crowley's students, J.F.C. Fuller, was also a painter of occult themes. Fuller is not known to the world as a genius of paint. He is known, along with Basil Henry Liddell Hart, as an innovator of *Blitzkrieg*. It is important to note that Crowley's usage of the term "genius" is general. It does not just apply to artistic creativity, and it is beyond good and evil.

When working with an artistic medium, one will often progress through the stages of experimentation, personal expression, and—in actual cases of genius—creations of works of universal significance. Particularly within the context of modern art, this last stage is associated with works that do not simply appeal to an existing audience but which *create a new audience*. This is generally what is meant by the term *avant-garde*.

We can observe a minor version of this progression when we learn to play a new musical instrument. For example, let's say that you're learning how to play guitar. You pick up the guitar, and you press your fingers on some frets, and you hit some strings. It probably sounds horrible, but you pick up a book or download a tutorial, and soon you learn to play some open chords. You learn strumming and picking, and pretty soon it starts to sound not as bad.

If you continue to develop your skill at it, you will probably reach the

---

1　Susan L. Aberth,, Jesse Bransford, William Breeze, "Panel on 'Language of the Birds: Occult and Art' at 80WSE Gallery, New York," https://www.artforum.com/video/panel-on-language-of-the-birds-occult-and-art-at-80wse-gallery-new-york-58280 stage of being able to express yourself with the instrument. Perhaps you come up with a tune in your head, and you are able to figure out how to play it on the guitar or accompany the melody with chords. This middle stage has personal significance for you. Your friends might enjoy what you're doing, not because they think it's great music, but because they think you're great, and they want to support you.

Some people achieve the third stage, though. Then they are creating music which is not only important to them and their friends; it becomes of interest to a broader audience. If the audience is broad enough, then you might create something which is part of the history of music. There's something about hitting this third stage which can't be taught. We're in awe when people hit that stage. It's a bit of a mystery because it's not just simply a level of skill.

One finds an analogous progression in visionary magick, e.g., when scrying. The magician opens their temple, they do the invocation, and then they sit there with their eyes closed. They may begin to see random images of a religious nature: a pyramid, an angel, a lion, etc. It can often be difficult at this first stage to tell whether you're having visions or just daydreaming.

But if you keep at it, sometimes you arrive at a stage where the visions are more intense and form something like a complex narrative structure. You may even begin to learn some things from these visions, as they inform your life outside the temple. This is like the second stage, because what you are seeing has personal significance to you. A large part of the value of magick is that it helps inform us about our lives. We find it useful or at least interesting.

Now once in a while, you might end up in the third stage of universal significance. At this stage, the magician is having visions that aren't so much about them personally. The visions have a transpersonal quality to them. The visions may be more intense. They may appear more like vivid dreams and have deep archetypal significance.

*The Vision and the Voice* is just full of visions like this. Jung's *Red Book* also falls into this third category. If you practice visionary magick for a long time, you may occasionally have spikes that take you into this third stage. Most of your visions may fall into the second or even first stages, but every once in awhile you have something that seems to tip the scales and go beyond mere personal expression and begin to express some kind of more general or abstract force having to do with humanity or the meaning of life.

So creativity—particularly artistic creativity—is an important part of Thelema. Genius—in particular producing genius—was a concern of Crowley's. It was arguably his primary concern, at least when he was in a certain mood. As a matter of historical fact, art and music have been natural vehicles for Thelemic and occult ideas since the middle of the 20th century. None of us first encountered Thelema through O.T.O. or *The Equinox*. We found Crowley through Ozzy.

Now I want to turn to offering an explanation for why this is, and that will lead me into the rarefied air of theology, because I think the reason there is such a tight connection between Thelema and artistic creativity has to do with the theology underlying Thelema, a theology I would describe as broadly *hermetic*.

## Hermeticism: The Theology of Thelema

Hermeticism was a Renaissance movement that grew out of interest in the writings of a figure called *Hermes Trismegistus*. These writings came into Italy after the fall of Constantinople, and not long after, the Jews were kicked out of Spain and brought Kabbalah with them to Italy as well. A lot of this is documented in Frances Yates's book on Giordano Bruno.

As Wouter Hanegraaf has pointed out, Hermeticism was not necessarily or even primarily magical in nature, though owing to historical circumstances, its adherents also tended to be interested in Kabbalah, alchemy, perennialism, prisca philosophia, Lullism, Paracelsianism, Rosicrucianism, Eckhartian mysticism, "correspondences," vitalism, and occult "sympathies".

My main concern is to analyze what we might term the Hermetic theology, which I'm going to define as constituting a middle position between Judeo-Christian theology on the one hand and pantheism on the other.

According to Judeo-Christian theology, God is a self-caused, necessarily existing, disembodied personality who created the universe by fiat. All of which raises the question: *Why?* Why exactly did God choose to create the universe, the Earth, and human beings? If God is truly self-sufficient, he did not create from any lack. One possibility is that God created from an over-abundance of love. The problem with such an answer is that it seems irrational. We don't actually get any insight into the problem with such an answer and it seems to render the entirety of creation irrational. God felt a certain way, so that's why we're here. How does that help? And if you allow this line of questioning to linger, you remain with this deep mystery of why there is anything rather than nothing.

Pantheistic theology answers this question rather differently. In pantheistic theology, God is still self-caused and necessarily existing and therefore eternal, but God is now identical with the universe as a whole. The most famous modern exponent of this view was Baruch Spinoza. In his 17th century work, *The Ethics*, he argued, quite sensibly, that if there is any substance at all, it must be an infinite substance, and you can only have one infinite substance, so everything must be part of the same infinite substance. Ergo, nature is God. (His argument is a little more complex than that, but those are the broad strokes.)

This way of answering the question gets rid of the problem of why there is anything rather than nothing. Substances exist necessarily. They are self-caused. There can never have been a time when God did not exist. But nature is God. So nature has always existed, and necessarily so. But in collapsing nature and God into one another, nature got some of the properties of God, but God also got some of the properties of nature. For instance, God no longer has a personality or freedom of choice. (In fact, neither do we.) In making the universe identical with God, we've divinized nature a bit, but there's the unavoidable sense that we've also ended up killing God and destroying any possibility of spiritual transcendence.

Now as I said, the Hermetic theology is a middle way between these two pictures. In the Judeo-Christian theology, God radically transcends the universe, so much so that we cannot figure out why the universe exists. In the pantheistic theology, God is so closely identified with the universe that we completely lose the meaning of the term God. The Hermetic move is to say that God both transcends the world and is part of the world. For the Hermeticist, the universe is the body of God (just like in pantheism), but God is not just his body. In the same way, your left hand is part of you, but if you lose your left hand, you will probably go on living. God does not reduce to a part of Himself. He is the universe, but He is also more than the universe.

In Hermeticism, God is distinct from the world, but he *needs to create the world* in order to complete Himself. Creation is now both necessary and rational. And because creation is necessary and rational, we can make sense of why we exist and what follows from that. No more throwing things back on some mysterious divine love or feeling.

A lot of these Hermetic ideas are assumed by the Kabbalah, which is a form of Jewish mysticism. The transcendent aspect of God is called *Ain*, which just means *nothing*. Imagine no universe, no matter, no space, no time, no thought, no consciousness, no nothing. That is the most mysterious and transcendent dimension of divinity. But nothingness cancels or "nothings" itself, and in canceling itself, it creates being. But beingness as such is shaky or unstable, and so it is immediately productive of duality. That is the transition from Kether to Chokmah. But then Chokmah is also incomplete or unsatisfactory, and so the subsequent spheres of Binah, Chesed, Geburah, Tiphareth and the like are also produced, until you get down to Malkuth, which is nature or the manifest universe. We live in Malkuth. "You are here."

Malkuth is important in Jewish Kabbalah, because it represents the "I" or the self-consciousness of God. God does not achieve fulfillment in nothingness. He does not achieve it in Kether, either. He achieves it all the way at the bottom, in Malkuth. This is an illustration of the Hermetic theology. You have both the transcendent and immanent aspects of God, and a dynamic process connecting them. Creation is not merely an accident but proceeds *necessarily* from the very idea of God Himself.

Here are a few quotes from the Corpus Hermeticum to illustrate some of these notions.

> If you force me to say something still more daring, it is his essence to be pregnant with all things and to make them. As it is impossible for anything to be produced without a maker, so also is it impossible for this maker [not] to exist always unless he is always making everything in heaven, in the air, on earth, in the deep, in every part of the cosmos, in every part of the universe, in what is and in what is not. For there was nothing in all the cosmos that he is not. He is himself the things that are and those that are not. Those that are he has made visible; those that are not he holds within him.[2]

The identity of God is tied up with the act of creation. It is easy to get a sense of what this is like if you are an artist or if you are close with an artist. Creation is a compulsion for an artist. Artists do not simply choose to create. Creation is part of their identity. When an artist is not creating, when the creative juices are not flowing, it can feel as though the vitality has been sucked out of life. It feels like life is not even worth living. And when an artist is creating, there's nothing unusual about it. It just feels normal. For an artist, artistic creation is as natural as breathing is for other people. That is

---

2  "A discourse of Hermes to Tat, his son: That god is invisible and entirely visible." Brian P. Copenhaver, *Hermetica: The Greek Corpus Hermeticum and the Latin Asclepius in a new English translation with notes and introduction* (Cambridge: Cambridge University Press, 1992),20.

a microcosmic version of what the Hermetic God is like. The Hermetic God is a compulsive creator.

> God's activity is will, and his essence is to will all things to be.[3]

The very essence or identity of God is acting. God is not just hanging out, dreaming of the day he'll become "A Creative". Insofar as God is, God is creating.

> For the two are all there is, what comes to be and what makes it, and it is impossible to separate one from the other. No maker can exist without something that comes to be. Each of the two is just what it is; therefore, one is not to be parted from the other [nor] from itself.[4]

The universe exists, because God exists, and because it is in the nature of God to make. When the highest principle in the universe is a God who is a creative artist, then God requires the universe to exist as much as the universe requires God to exist.

This implies a special role for us human beings:

> For God does not ignore mankind; on the contrary, he recognizes him fully and wishes to be recognized. For mankind, this is the only deliverance, the knowledge of god. It is ascent to Olympus.[5]

Wanting to know God is not particular to Hermeticism. Lots of spiritual traditions include that idea. But in Hermeticism, God always wants to be recognized by us. In particular, he wants us to know Him through His creations.

> Who is more visible than God? This is why he made all things: so that through them all you might look on him.[6]

Again, it helps to compare with actual artists. Part of the reason an artist creates is out of the compulsion to create, but plenty of artists also want their words to be appreciated. It's a bit paradoxical, because they do not necessari-

---

3   "[Discourse] of Hermes Trismegistus: The key" in Ibid, 30.
4   "From Hermes Trismegistus to Asclepius, health of mind" in Ibid, 56.
5   "[Discourse] of Hermes Trismegistus: The key" in Ibid, 33.
6   "Mind to Hermes" in Ibid, 42.

ly create in order to please an audience, but pleasing an audience is part of the reason they create. Similarly, we knowing God through His creations fulfills God. It completes Him.

So in the Hermetic theology, the individual is capable of knowing God. That part is not unique to Hermeticism. But the individual's knowledge of God is necessary for God's self-completion. That part is uniquely Hermetic. By creating the universe, God gains the individual's recognition. The individual desires to know God, but God also desires to be known. S/he wishes to recognize Him/Herself in His/Her creation. The cosmos is created so that God can know Him/Herself.

I'm twisting myself into pretzels with the personal pronouns, because in this theology, you cannot get away with calling God "it". This isn't New Age or Spiritual-But-Not-Religious spirituality where we talk generally about the universe or energy or whatnot. That's too abstract. God is a personality in this theology, because God wants personal recognition for what S/he has created. The universe is a work of art God has delivered from out of His/Her subjectivity for the appreciation by other subjectivities. You cannot get away with just reducing God to abstract ideas or forces.

By now you may be thinking, "What is all this talk about God? I thought there is no god but man."

From one perspective, "There is no god but man," is or at least seems like a statement of atheism. The focus of Thelema tends to be on finding one's true will, which Crowley identifies with the will of God.

We also find out in *The Book of the Law* that "Every man and every woman is a star." I will respect the right of each person to interpret *The Book of the Law* as they will; however, let's consider what Crowley thought the passage meant. Writing in the "Introduction" to *The Book of the Law*, he said:

"Every man and every woman is a star," that is, an aggregate of ⟦...⟧ experiences, constantly changing with each fresh event, which affects him or her either consciously or subconsciously.

At this moment, you're an individual sitting in a chair in a temple, listening to a talk, and you're surrounded by these things in the room. You have a comfortable, everyday sense of who you are. But according to Crowley, that does not reflect your essence. Your essence is that you are an aggregate of experiences. An aggregate is formed by a bunch of things lumped together into one thing. How many things? Well, how many things do you want to include?

If we're including in our aggregate your whole lifetime of experiences, then you include everything that happened in the past, at least since your birth and perhaps since before then. We must also include everything that will happen to you in the future. We must also consider all the experiences you undergo which are perhaps dimly aware of or not conscious of at all. All of these changes that occur to you do not take place in a vacuum. They are caused by things ostensibly outside of you.

So the star is the totality of your being across time, spread across your entire natural life, but it makes sense to widen it to include anything that causes those changes to happen, which means we could include the entire observable universe in it. Other than that, there is no precise limit to where the star ends. So in this concept of a star, we have the idea of the self (in other words the point of view these experiences are focused on), the universe (the causal whole giving rise to those experiences), and in the case of the concept of true will we also have the concept of God.

Crowley's notion of the star is not unlike Carl Jung's idea of the Self. The Self is either identical with God, or it's at least a closely related concept.

Now here's the puzzle: If we are really stars, why doesn't it look that way? I don't feel like the whole universe. I don't feel like God. I feel like a single person in a room having particular experiences. Why do I have this restricted view of myself if I'm so much larger?

Similarly, if existence is pure joy, why doesn't it feel joyful all the time? Why does it so often seem to be the opposite?

Crowley offers an explanation for this fact. In his commentary on *The Book of the Law*, he says:

> To know itself, each such Star, or Soul, must eat of the Fruit of the Tree of Knowledge of Good and Evil, by accepting labour and pain as its portion, and death as its doom. That is, it must reveal its nature to itself by formulating that nature as duality.[7]

Your true self is the totality of all things, but on its own, it does not have any awareness of itself. If the star is going to know itself, it does not have many options at its disposal. It cannot look at itself in a mirror. It cannot look at anything outside of itself, because it is everything. It has no outside. That means that all it can do is look inside itself. It can reflect. But then that means

---

7   New Comment on AL I.29

it must create an artificial sense of separation in itself. It has to create subject and object from itself. It has to divide itself.

It has to divide itself, but it also has to simplify itself. There has to be a reduction of myself to a few pieces of data at a time. I have to be able to say, "I begin here and end there" as a means of dealing with the complexity of experience.

As soon as the star introduces self-consciousness and duality into itself, a whole host of problems arise almost without delay. Life is full of all sorts of unpleasant experiences such as pain, disappointment, and frustration. But even more challenging than the unpleasant experiences themselves is the knowledge that they are happening *to me*. Not only do I come down with a cold, for instance. I know that I am the person who has come down with a cold, and that's just not fair. The second-order reflection introduces narrative. There's a story about a little character called "me" that is moving around in the world. And because all these bad things can happen to that character, that introduces the problem of suffering and shame.

When Adam and Eve eat the fruit of the Tree of Knowledge of Good and Evil, what's the first thing that happens? It's literally the next line after they eat the fruit. It says they discover their nakedness, and they feel ashamed. They cover themselves up. Immediately on the heels of self-consciousness comes shame.

But that's not even the worst part. With self-consciousness, I can look at myself. I know I can die. I know I can get sick. I know something bad could happen to me. And if I look at you, and if I infer you're like me and can undergo the same sorts of experiences as me, I can reasonably infer you're vulnerable like me. Sure, I can empathize with you. I can also plan your misery. Animals may tear each other to bits, but they do not plot one another's torture or destruction. So in addition to recognizing the world is a really hard place to live in, with self-consciousness comes a sizable minority of people who are evil.

So the star has to divide itself to know itself. It has to become self-conscious. But in becoming self-conscious, a world of suffering is created.

This should remind you of what we saw earlier when we considered the Hermetic God. The Hermetic God also wanted to know itself. And in order to do that, it had to involve itself in creating a world. But since the star can't create anything outside of itself, all it can do is separate off part of itself and say, "that's the world." But upon creating that world, it doesn't find divinity. It doesn't find being, consciousness, and bliss. Instead, it finds impermanence, not-self, and suffering. It finds the opposite.

Most of the world's religions since the Iron Age more or less define themselves by how they solve this problem of suffering. Crowley of course has his own response. I'm not giving away a state secret if I tell you it has to do with doing your true will. But here's another way he expresses the solution. This is from the same passage in the commentaries:

> [The star] must express itself by a series of symbolic gestures ostensibly external to it, just as a painter reveals one facet of his Delight-Diamond by covering a canvas with colours in such a way that the picture seems at first sight to represent something outside himself. It must, in fact, repeat for itself the original Magick of Nuith and Hadith which created it.[8]

With self-consciousness comes the appearance of a universe opposed to me. On bad days, existence feels like a curse. But the path to liberation involves seeing the world differently: not as something imposed upon us but rather as a medium of expression. It involves seeing the world the way an artist sees an artistic medium. And this process has something to do with love.

Crowley expresses a similar idea in somewhat different terms in a passage from Liber Samekh.

> All experiences contribute to make us complete in ourselves. We feel ourselves subject to them so long as we fail to recognise this; when we do, we perceive that they are subject to us. And whenever we strive to evade an experience, whatever it may be, we thereby do wrong to ourselves. We thwart our own tendencies. To live is to change; and to oppose change is to revolt against the law which we have enacted to govern our lives. To resent destiny is thus to abdicate our sovereignty, and to invoke death. Indeed, we have decreed the doom of death for every breach of the law of Life. And every failure to incorporate any impression starves that particular faculty which stood in need of it.

There are different ways we could conceivably deal with the problems arising from self-consciousness. We could choose to reject self-consciousness. We could use drugs and alcohol to obliterate it. We can sleep excessively. We can work too many hours or throw ourselves into distracting relationships or other pursuits.

---

8   Ibid.

But in Thelema, the medicine is also the poison. Instead of pulling back from the cause of pain, we move more deeply into it. Rather than restricting what we can experience so as to keep ourselves safe, we expand the scope of our experiences. We take in more. We affirm the consequences of our will. We begin to treat the universe as though we chose this for ourselves and are therefore responsible for everything in it.

Crolwey says that the first duty to yourself is "Find yourself to be the centre of your own Universe."[9] This does not mean staring in the mirror and saying "me me me me me." It means taking radical responsibility. It means rejecting the view that things merely happen to you. If you reject that, then bitterness can never arise.

This idea is captured in the figure of Pan, who appears on Atu XV, The Devil. Writing of this card, Crowley says:

The formula of this card is then the complete appreciation of all existing things. He rejoices in the rugged and the barren no less than in the smooth and the fertile. All things equally exalt him. He represents the finding of ecstasy in every phenomenon, however naturally repugnant; he transcends all limitations; he is Pan; he is All.[10]

This is one path toward salvation. It's the extraverted path, the path of Ayin. There is also an introverted mystical path, the path of Nun. But the extraverted path is all about enjoying all things of sense and rapture. It is learning to look at existence with the eyes of an artist.

So far we have seen that Thelema assumes a theology of the star which is very similar to the theology of Hermeticism. The Hermetic God relates to the universe as an artist relates to a work of art. This introduces an ineluctable sensuousness into the Hermetic gnosis, since God is to be found in and through nature which is His creation. This is different from ancient Gnosticism where the universe is a cage created by the Demiurge to imprison us, and then you have to be like the Count of Monte Cristo and escape your prison and kill God. That's not what Hermeticism is about.

We see something analogous in Thelema, except now we're talking about the God each and every one of us truly is, the God which Crowley calls the star. If we look at Thelema through this quasi-Hermetic lens, its soteriology

---

9 Crowley, "Duty: A note on the chief rules of practical conduct to be observed by those who accept the Law of Thelema"
10 *The Book of Thoth*, "The Devil"

makes more sense. Success on the path means learning to see the world as an artist-god would.

Now I want to consider what role aesthetics and art in particular play in spiritual realization. It's one thing to say that we should take a disinterested aesthetic attitude toward everything. But what about actual art itself? We're going to get more specific and instead of thinking about theology we're going to think about the magick particular to art itself.

## The Magick of Art

Crowley comments on the relationship between magick and art in chapter 20 of *Magick in Theory and Practice*. Commenting on what he sees as the essence underlying the diversity of ideas in alchemy, he says:

> Yet beneath this diversity, we may perceive an obscure identity. They all begin with a substance in nature which is described as existing almost everywhere, and as universally esteemed of no value. The alchemist is in all cases to take this substance, and subject it to a series of operations. By so doing, he obtains his product. This product, however named or described, is always a substance which represents the truth or perfection of the original "First Matter"; and its qualities are invariably such as pertain to a living being, not to an inanimate mass. In a word, the alchemist is to take a dead thing, impure, valueless, and powerless, and transform it into a live thing, active, invaluable and thaumaturgic.

The alchemical process begins with a substance deemed without value. This is similar to how the world initially appears in the light of self-consciousness. It's the world of duality and suffering.

The reader of this book will surely find in this a most striking analogy with what we have already said of the processes of Magick. What, by our definition, is initiation? The First Matter is a man, that is to say, a perishable parasite, bred of the earth's crust, crawling irritably upon it for a span, and at last returning to the dirt whence he sprang. The process of initiation consists in removing his impurities, and finding in his true self an immortal intelligence to whom matter is no more than the means of manifestation. The initiate is eternally individual; he is ineffable, incorruptible, immune from everything. He possesses infinite wisdom and infinite power in himself.

This equation is identical with that of a talisman. The Magician takes an idea, purifies it, intensifies it by invoking into it the inspiration of his soul. It is no longer a scrawl scratched on a sheep-skin, but a word of Truth, imperishable, mighty to prevail throughout the sphere of its purport. The evocation of a spirit is precisely similar in essence. The exorcist takes dead material substances of a nature sympathetic to the being whom he intends to invoke. He banishes all impurities therefrom, prevents all interference therewith, and proceeds to give life to the subtle substance thus prepared by instilling his soul.'

Once again, there is nothing in this exclusively "magical". Rembrandt van Ryn used to take a number of ores and other crude objects. From these he banished the impurities, and consecrated them to his work, by the preparation of canvasses, brushes, and colours. This done, he compelled them to take the stamp of his soul; from those dull, valueless creatures of earth he created a vital and powerful being of truth and beauty. It would indeed be surprising to anybody who has come to a clear comprehension of nature if there were any difference in the essence of these various formulas. The laws of nature apply equally in every possible circumstance.

We are now in a position to understand what alchemy is. We might even go further and say that even if we had never heard of it, we know what it must be.

Let us emphasize the fact that the final product is in all cases a living thing.[11]

Alchemy, talismanic magic, initiation, and art production share a similar form. That form has to do with creating a living being from dead matter. In the artistic process in particular, we are taking meaningless matter and creating something with the power to bear the weight of human significance—so much so that when other people look at it, they experience a similar sense of meaning enlivening their own lives.

The great painting, film, or piece of music is like a talisman. When it passes into somebody's "hands," the power passes to them. Art has that kind of magical power. It transmits meaning and significance into the spectator. It "saves" them in a quasi-religious sense. *Salvation* here does not mean pro-

---

11 *Magick in Theory and Practice*, ch 20

tecting the soul from an eternity in hell. It means living a life of meaning and purpose. It means feeling like no matter what is happening, no matter what suffering there may be, living is worthwhile.

The circle is a symbol of the self. It is a symbol of consciousness, perhaps because when standing on top of a mountain, we look all around us, and the horizon seems to form an encompassing circle. The circle can be thought to represent the star in its original, unconscious state. When it divides itself, it alienates part of itself, and it feels alienated as a result. As Crowley says, we crawl irritably upon the surface of the Earth before returning to it. The question we considered earlier was: How do we return to a consciousness of our own divinity?

One option would be to return to undifferentiated union with ourselves. That is essentially what happens at death. But what about in this life? Is there a way to have both self-consciousness and the experience of being divine? That would be symbolized by moving back to the center of the circle. It would be the natural consciousness—your consciousness as a finite being—taking its place in the center of the circle, thereby forming the symbol of the cross in the circle, lingam and yoni conjoined, the accomplishment of the Great Work, and the symbol of the Sun. On the Tree of Life, the House of the Sun is Tiphareth, which is the Hebrew word for *beauty*.

I mention this only to point out that these questions of beauty we're exploring are not "merely" subjective questions about what kind of art we like. These issues lie in close proximity to what might be deemed more "seriously" questions of mysticism and accomplishing the Great Work.

In his book *The Mirror of Magic or Magic, Supernaturalism and Religion*, the 20th century occultist and painter Kurt Seligmann said:

> In every man there is a child that yearns to play, and the most attractive game is occultation, mystery.[12]

Echoing a similar sentiment, Friedrich Nietzsche said:

> Mature manhood: that means to have rediscovered the seriousness one had as a child at play.[13]

---

12 Kurt Seligmann, *The Mirror of Magic or Magic, Supernaturalism and Religion* (New York: Grosset and Dunlap, 1968), 447.
13 Friedrich Nietzsche, *Beyond Good and Evil* (London: Penguin Books, 1990), 94.

We enter this world with a dispersed sense of self. We are at one with all things. We are at one with our caregivers. This is why when a little child is upset, they scream like the earth itself is shattering. It's because it is. There is hardly any self-consciousness, hardly any internal division. And so they are also completely spontaneous and able to experience joy in a way that is really remarkable and enviable. This is a little bit what the star is like before it divides itself.

But as time goes on, one goes through the normal developmental process-es. Life teaches them where their limits are. The difference between self and world emerges. If this process is traumatic, a small child may be thrown back upon their own resources in a way they're not yet ready for. They will not have the resources within themselves to cope in the normal fashion, and so the psyche mobilizes miraculous processes. It utilizes psychological defense mechanisms to protect the spirit from being destroyed. Unfortunately what starts out in childhood as a form of self-protection can be carried forward into adulthood where it shows up as dysfunction and the inability or unwill-ingness to adapt. That's how we end up in psychotherapy.

What Crowley calls "duality" can also be viewed as an overly rigid sense of myself. This is a painful sense of self that refuses to cope. It refuses initia-tion, as Crowley says. The constant flux of change is fought against. We end up feeling dead and unnourished by life. We're not able to trust other people enough to create the openings to let the vitalizing flow of life energy in. We do not allow ourselves enough spontaneity.

Art can be a safe way for us to experience that energy coming back in. When you see a particularly vibrant painting, listen to intense music at a rock concert, when you're impinged upon by these sensations, the energy of life is allowed to break through and chemically break down those walls. This is why art has the power to give us back the feeling of existence. We are exposed to something vital, and so it brings vitality back into us.

Both the wise person and the fool are "childish". The difference is that the wise person's eyes are open to the true nature of things. They approach life with the consciousness of its danger. Aesthetic experience is a way to reap-proach the playfulness of childhood but from the perspective of the adult. It gives us a sense of what wisdom and the adult reclamation of childhood can be like.

The romantic poet and philosopher Friedrich von Hardenberg (aka Nova-lis) said:

[I]n each poetic statement, chaos must shimmer through the veil of regular order.[14]

Poetry—we might say art more generally—is a window on to a life beyond the walls we have constructed against it in desperation.

Similarly the poet and philosopher Friedrich von Schiller said:

Truth lives on in the illusion of Art, and it is from this copy, or after-image, that the original image will once again be restored.[15]

Truth is connection with reality. It is love. For truth to live on in art means that it has been captured as an after-image or an ideal. It is a representation of what we have lost—and what we can start to reclaim.

To get a sense of how this can be, think of the last time you finished a great novel or powerful film. You may have had the feeling immediately after that some kind of emergency was imminent. You may have thought, "My God! Something has to change! My life has to change somehow!" But it wasn't clear what had to change. Art does not tell you exactly what needs to change. It doesn't tell you what kind of relationship you need to have or what sort of job to get. It doesn't tell you what your true will is. But it can create that sense of urgency, a feeling like you're about to die. This is not an existential threat. This is not the perception of an asteroid about to hit the earth. It's not a warning to stock up on canned goods. Death isn't what's at issue. The problem is that you haven't lived as you should have. You haven't been properly living out the mystery, the gift within yourself. You have squandered it. You have wasted it.

And so it's like something is calling to you. There is a crack in the walls you have built around yourself. You were not even aware the wall was there, and now some message is being secreted to you through a crack in it. It is calling you toward it. What are you being called toward? You are being called toward a life of meaning and purpose. You are being called to your own true will.

This is why in beauty is eternal truth revealed.

A part of the star is shining toward you. It is shining from outside of yourself.

---

14 Novalis, *Heinrich von Ofterdingen*
15 Friedrich Schiller, *On the Aesthetic Education of Man in a Series of Letters* (Oxford: Oxford University Press, 1982), 57.

In the book of Genesis, the rainbow appears as the symbol of God's promise after the flood that destroys the world. Why is the rainbow the symbol of promise? In all likelihood because it is beautiful. Beauty is the image of a better, hoped-for future. It represents, not exactly what you should be doing, but that you could be doing something better. You could reclaim the sense of being at home in the world. You can reclaim your sense of spontaneity. You can reclaim your childhood. You can reclaim your starhood.

Thelema has a strong relationship with art because of the theological significance of the sensuous world. Nature expresses the soul of God the same way a work of art expresses the soul of the artist. The Thelemite is the Hermetic artist-god of their own universe. But the world does not immediately appear to be my work of art. It appears as something alien to me. It appears as something set against me and my will. The process of coming to see the world as my artistic creation is magick and initiation.

Initiation is isomorphic with alchemy, talismanic magick, and art production. It involves the transformation of dead matter into a living being. In the experience of what is beautiful, I am experiencing the call of my true self, my star. It is calling me to live a life full of meaning and purpose. It is calling me to reclaim my true nature, my original spontaneity which I lost in the transition into adulthood. This is the spiritual significance of beauty.

Beauty is not the accomplishment of the will. All your work is still ahead of you. But it is the calling to do your will. Beauty presents you with the image of truth. It is the image of the task. It generates the urgency to accomplish the task.

Let's turn now to the implications of all of this. How can we utilize the power of beauty to enchant and change our lives?

## The Power of Beauty

Beauty has power because it excites us to actualize ourselves, to do our true wills. It is the image of what is possible if we were integrated with our lost spontaneity. This means that we can use beauty to motivate ourselves.

When I say "beauty," I don't simply mean what is harmonious. I am using "beauty" as a catch-all for what we appreciate aesthetically. It can also be dissonant. It can also be upsetting and jarring. It's about finding what excites you on an aesthetic level.

A simple way to begin this process is simply to surround yourself with art, especially where you live. Surrounding yourself with art is a way of impressing your own soul upon the space in which you live. It's a way of turning your own home into a talisman. The art does not have to be expensive. It does not have to reflect refined taste. It just has to inspire and reflect your own aesthetic sense.

In the tarot, the Magician card is associated with the Hebrew letter *Beth* which means *house*. Magick is primordially about creating a domicile. It is about the transformation of space into home. Magick means dwelling, and we start doing magick where we dwell, when we impress ourselves upon our space and turn it into our home. We begin by creating a sacred place of dwelling, and from there we move outward into the world. We use our magick to transform the rest of the world from that center of sacred order and beauty. We carry that power outward with us.

Ritual and magical ceremony offer opportunities to bring beauty into your life in a sacred context. When creating a ritual, include as many of the correspondences from 777 as possible. Bring a lot of attention to aesthetic detail. Choose from the four color scales of the path. Bring in the appropriate incense. Bring in plants and flowers. Bring in colored lights. Create an immersive, sensual experience. Don't simply go through the motions. Don't be minimalistic! Make the entire temple embody your intention and become a dwelling place for the god or spirit.

Be playful! Let the rituals be rightly performed, with joy and beauty! Magick should be a playful, joyous form of spirituality.

There are plenty of forms of spirituality where you don't have to bother with any of this shit at all. You can just sit on your knees and pray or meditate. There is no need to worry about correspondences. That's not the case in magick. Magick offers you the opportunity to go hog-wild and play. So play. Have fun.

Beauty is important and powerful when utilized in our personal lives and in our personal magick. It is also powerful when we bring it into our magical and Thelemic communities. Thelema is an artistic religion. It is a religion of artists. Saying that is nowhere near as powerful as showing it by making our group rituals and our group space as aesthetically powerful as possible. Thelema offers a unique perspective on the universe. Showing that through our aesthetic sense is more powerful than simply saying it.

## Conclusion

The connection between Thelema and art is strong. Thelema was created by an artist. Many artists have been and are drawn to Thelema. Art—particularly music—has been more important for bringing Thelema into mainstream consciousness than occult orders. I have tried to explain this by unearthing what I see as the Hermetic theology underlying Thelema. This is a theology according to which God is an expressive artist. It is in the nature of God to create. This means that the sensuous universe is not a cage for the soul but rather a mirror of God's true nature in the same way a work of art is a mirror of an artist's soul.

Crowley taught that each person is a star or a unique Hermetic creator god in their own right. The universe appears to stand over and against each of us, but the way to salvation is to see every event as an expression of our own true nature. The universe is our soul's means of expressing and knowing itself. To see the universe as an artist would see their own work is synonymous with doing one's true will.

While all experiences are expressions of will and are potentially joyous, the aesthetic experience in particular has unique spiritual significance. This is because the experience of beauty is a perception of balance between order and chaos or between the mind and the world. In beauty, our true selves call us forth into a life of meaning and purpose. This is the motivational and spiritual power of beauty.

For this reason we ought to surround ourselves with beauty where we live. We should do beautiful rituals to create a center of sacred beauty in our lives from which we can expand outward. We should create order, harmony, and stability where we live so that we may greet the chaos of the world from the place of our own true wills.

If you are part of a magical community, make your public rites as aesthetically compelling as you can. Maintain a group space which is beautiful. Communicate your iconoclastic beliefs and values with art. Don't just say what you can also show.

We must put the principle of creativity at the center of everything we do. When we rightly perform the rituals with joy and beauty, when we present ourselves as an artistic religion by utilizing religious artistry, we are able to attract individuals who share our values, and we are able to have a positive impact on the culture around us.

# 8

# Shimmering Chaos:
# The Magical Power of Art

One of the most important statements Crowley made on the subject of art production is in Chapter 20 of *Magick in Theory and Practice*, titled, "Of the Eucharist and of the Art of Alchemy." Nearly as an aside to a broader discussion of alchemy and various forms of magick, Crowley states:

> Once again, there is nothing in this exclusively "magical". Rembrandt van Ryn used to take a number of ores and other crude objects. From these he banished the impurities, and consecrated them to his work, by the preparation of canvasses, brushes, and colours. This done, he compelled them to take the stamp of his soul; from those dull, valueless creatures of earth he created a vital and powerful being of truth and beauty. It would indeed be surprising to anybody who has come to a clear comprehension of nature if there were any difference in the essence of these various formulas. The laws of nature apply equally in every possible circumstance.[1]

From a purely naturalistic perspective, paint is merely some pigmented liquid, liquefiable, or solid mastic composition which, after application with a stick, a brush, fingers, etc., converts to a solid film on a surface. And yet though they are dealing with such humble, "crude" materials, the artist is able to create something from them which expresses vitality, power, truth, and beauty.

While Crowley's statement focuses solely on the medium of paint, the same claim could be made of other forms of art such as sculpture, film, photography, poetry, or prose. While we tend to think of nature as being opposed to

---

1   *Magick in Theory and Practice* (MITAP), ch 20

consciousness or subjectivity—as something which frustrates the soul—the artist takes pieces of nature and "compels" them to "take the stamp of his soul," thereby transforming them into something of human significance.

To fully appreciate Crowley's statement on painting in particular and art generally, it helps to situate it within the context of the larger argument he is making in the chapter.

Chapter 20 of *Magick in Theory and Practice* is on the face of it quite odd. After a discussion of the fundamentals of eucharistic magick, Crowley veers off into an at-times sprawling discussion of alchemy and how it relates to topics as diverse as initiation, talismanic magick, conjuration, and the production of the Elixir of Life, before returning at the end to the subject of different kinds of eucharist.

But what makes this chapter so important, not just for the question of how Crowley viewed art but also for his views on spirituality in general, is that Crowley believed all these diverse fields shared an underlying structure as human activities. The key to understanding this chapter is to understand what that underlying structure is. That underlying structure will illuminate the essence of art from Crowley's perspective, but because this structure underlies and even defines so many disparate phenomena—all of them essential to the practice of Thelemic magick—elucidating this structure will also allow insight into the essence of the Thelemic spiritual path.

## The Unity of Chapter 20 of *Magick in Theory and Practice*

After surveying several disparate ideas from the alchemical tradition, Crowley offers us this summary:

> Yet beneath this diversity, we may perceive an obscure identity. They all begin with a substance in nature which is described as existing almost everywhere, and as universally esteemed of no value. The alchemist is in all cases to take this substance, and subject it to a series of operations. By so doing, he obtains his product. This product, however named or described, is always a substance which represents the truth or perfection of the original "First Matter"; and its qualities are invariably such as pertain to a living being, not to an inanimate mass. In a word, the alchemist is to take a dead thing, impure, valueless, and powerless, and transform it into a live thing, active, invaluable and thaumaturgic.[2]

---

2  Ibid.

According to Crowley, the essence underlying this apparent diversity of al-chemical techniques is the taking of some "first matter," which is an ordi-nary, "inanimate" object, and running it through some process, after which is revealed some "truth" or "perfection" which was immanent or implicit within the first matter. In other words the outward appearance of the first matter—what it originally presented as evidence to the senses—belied what the first matter truly was. While the first matter at first appears "dead ... im-pure, valueless, and powerless," it contains implicit within it a dimension of vitality and activity which is revealed and liberated by means of the activity of the alchemical process.

But what does Crowley have in mind here when he talks about the differ-ence between something dead and something alive? One of the peculiarities of living beings is that we feel constrained to think of them as integral wholes rather than aggregates or mere collections of parts. If I take a rock and split it in half, I end up with two rocks. If I do that with a cat, I don't end up with two cats. Living beings demand we respect their wholeness, their integrity, if we are to continue to regard them as alive.

Of course fields like biology and medicine are premised upon our ability to understand living beings mechanistically. We understand them by break-ing them down into pieces, understanding how those pieces operate inde-pendently, and then understanding how those pieces operate in relation to one another. This is the essence of the atomistic or mechanistic perspective. But from a first-person, subjective point of view, when we encounter a living being, we feel compelled *not* to treat it as a mere heap of parts but rather to regard it as a *unity*. And we regard the wholeness or unity of the being as somehow being prior to its parts in terms of importance. We think of the parts as expressing the unity of the being.

Remarking on how differently our attitudes often seem toward a stone versus a fly, the philosopher Ludwig Wittgenstein remarks:

Look at a stone and imagine it having sensations.—One says to oneself: How could one so much as get the idea of ascribing a sensation to a thing? One might as well ascribe it to a number!—And now look at a wriggling fly and at once these difficulties vanish and pain seems able to get a foot-hold here, where before everything was, so to speak, too smooth for it.

And so, too, a corpse seems to us quite inaccessible to pain.—Our attitude to what is alive and to what is dead, is not the same. All our reactions are different.—If anyone says: "That cannot simply come from the fact that a living thing moves about in such-and-such a way and a dead one not", then I want to intimate to him that this is a case of the transition 'from quantity to quality'.[3]

Realizing something is alive rather than dead provides an entire orientation for how to think about that being and how to relate to it. The experience of something being alive provides a "foothold" for the application of other concepts. This is precisely what we expect from a conceptual orientation or a conceptual framework: it is a way of looking that, in turn, determines further ways of looking at something. We feel that there is a fundamental difference between the concept of "aliveness" and other concepts. It would be odd to say, "Jeff is 6' tall, has brown hair, lives in Missouri, is alive, and works as an engineer." Being alive is not just another property alongside other properties but rather determines how we're going to assign other properties to Jeff. If I told you Jeff fell out a 10 story window and landed in the street below, the story would have a much different impact if I told you he had already been dead for two days. Whether something is alive or dead tends to determine our entire attitude toward it. But as we will see shortly, this distinction and transformation between the living and the dead is at the heart of all of these related forms of magick, including art production.

Crowley goes on to compare alchemy with initiation, finding the structure of the former in the latter:

> The reader of this book will surely find in this a most striking analogy with what we have already said of the processes of Magick. What, by our definition, is initiation? The First Matter is a man, that is to say, a perishable parasite, bred of the earth's crust, crawling irritably upon it for a span, and at last returning to the dirt whence he sprang. The process of initiation consists in removing his impurities, *and finding in his true self an immortal intelligence to whom matter is no more than the means of manifestation.* The initiate is eternally individual; he is ineffable, incorruptible, immune from everything. He possesses infinite wisdom and infinite power in himself.[4]

In the case of alchemy, the first matter was presumably some inert clod of earth or one of the base metals. By means of the alchemical process, some

---

3  Ludwig Wittgenstein, *Philosophical Investigations* (Oxford: Blackwell Publishing, 1999), 98
4  MITAP, ch 20, emphasis mine

vital, presumably "solar," quality was revealed to lie hidden at the heart of it. In the case of an initiate, the first matter is a human being in their natural state, which Crowley describes as "a perishable parasite ... crawling irritably for a span" upon the surface of the Earth. We might with some justification also describe such a person as subject to "the Darkness of Matter, and the strife of contending forces" as described in *Liber Librae sub figura XXX*. Crowley contrasts this natural condition with the condition of the initiate who has found his "true self" and for whom "matter is no more than the means of manifestation."

Notice the contrast between an atomistic and a holistic perspective in this passage. For the initiate, "matter is no more than the means of manifestation" of their "immortal intelligence". The unity of the whole takes precedence over the parts. The individual is not a mere aggregate of parts or modules. They are in a sense greater than the sum of their parts. The parts function as vehicles to express the immortal, spiritual principle, and therefore that spiritual principle has metaphysical priority. This notion of an individual's unity preceding the parts—which Crowley refers to as true will—is central to Thelema, and realizing and living in accordance with this principle is central to walking Thelema as a spiritual path. As Crowley summarizes the issue in Liber Samekh:

> The Adept must accept every "spirit", every "spell", every "scourge", as part of his environment, and make them all "subject to" himself; that is, consider them as contributory causes of himself. They have made him what he is. They correspond exactly to his own faculties. They are all— ultimately—of equal importance. The fact that he is what he is proves that each item is equilibrated. The impact of each new impression affects the entire system in due measure. He must therefore realize that every event is subject to him. It occurs because he had need of it. Iron rusts because the molecules demand oxygen for the satisfaction of their tendencies. They do not crave hydrogen; therefore combination with that gas is an event which does not happen. All experiences contribute to make us complete in ourselves. We feel ourselves subject to them so long as we fail to recognise this; when we do, we perceive that they are subject to us.[5]

We saw in the case of alchemy that, in order for a being to be alive, it had to maintain unity in the face of physical or biological change. The "aliveness"

---

5   Liber Samekh, point 2, section B

of a living being had less to do with the parts composing it and more how those parts related to one another in service to that higher unity. True will is the subjective correlate of this. It is the *feeling* of being alive which complements the objective *fact* of being alive. This feeling arises when we learn to view the events of our lives, not as circumstances impinging upon us and determining us, but rather as expressing the higher unity defining our true selves. To live life in accordance with true will, therefore, is not one decision among others but rather consists in the application of a framework which tells us how to interpret all our other decisions. In this way it is analogous to the shift in perspective we saw earlier when we transitioned from viewing something as dead to viewing it as alive.

Crowley's analyses of talismanic magick and evocation are almost identical with what he has said so far about alchemy and initiation, with one small exception:

> This equation is identical with that of a talisman. The Magician takes an idea, purifies it, intensifies it by *invoking into it the inspiration of his soul*. It is no longer a scrawl scratched on a sheep-skin, but a word of Truth, imperishable, mighty to prevail throughout the sphere of its purport. The evocation of a spirit is precisely similar in essence. The exorcist takes dead material substances of a nature sympathetic to the being whom he intends to invoke. He banishes all impurities therefrom, prevents all interference therewith, and proceeds to give life to the subtle substance thus prepared *by instilling his soul.*[6]

When we were examining alchemy and initiation, we saw that they should be understood as isolating and liberating a vital potential implicit within the first matter itself. In other words, the alchemist/initiator was not getting anything out of the first matter/candidate which wasn't already there.

> There is an obvious condition which limits our proposed operations. This is that, as the formula of any Work effects the extraction and visualization of the Truth from any "First Matter", the "Stone" or "Elixir" which results from our labours will be the pure and perfect Individual *originally inherent in the substance chosen*, and nothing else. The most skilful gardener cannot produce lilies from the wild rose; his roses will always be roses,

---

6  MITAP, ch 20, emphasis mine

however he have perfected the properties of this stock.[7]

Alchemy and initiation are about the "extraction and visualization" of a latent potency within the first matter. It is a making-visible of the invisible in ordinary matter. In the cases of talismans and evocations, however, we see a slightly different structure. Now the operator is invoking or instilling "the inspiration of his soul" *into* the material substratum. Indeed, we saw Crowley make a similar remark earlier with regard to painting, where the materials "take the stamp of [the artist's] soul".

We can deal with such a contradiction in one of two ways. We can regard it either as a mistake on the part of the author (the result of sloppy thinking), or we can view the contradiction as symptomatic of a tension within the subject-matter itself. The first is an analytical method, the second a dialectical method of treating contradiction. I will choose to treat this contradiction using the latter method, though my account will come later when I turn to the issue of authorship.

As far as eucharistic magick goes, Crowley regards it as a subset of alchemy.

> [T]he Eucharist, with which this chapter is properly preoccupied, must be conceived as one case—as the critical case—of the Art of the Alchemist.[8]

As such its structure is identical with that of alchemy. By means of the magical operation, the divine essence "originally inherent in the substance chosen, and nothing else" will be brought forth. For this reason, the final result of the eucharistic operation will depend upon the substance or substances started with.

> According to the nature of the Sacrament, so will its results be. In some one may receive a mystic grace, culminating in Samadhi; in others a simpler and more material benefit may be obtained. [9]

As near as possible, one ought to "Take a substance symbolic of the whole course of nature, make it God, and consume it."[10]

---

7  Ibid, emphasis mine
8  Ibid.
9  Ibid.
10 Ibid.

For example in the Gnostic Mass, each element of the eucharist—bread and wine—represents a complete, complementary cycle of the natural process. Bread sustains the exercise of labor, and labor in turn produces bread. Wine inspires labor, and labor in turn finds solace in intoxication with wine.

The closer this substance is to representing the whole course of nature, the more universal will be the sense of God drawn forth from it. For this reason the ideal eucharist is what Crowley refers to as the eucharist of one element.

> The highest form of the Eucharist is that in which the Element consecrated is One.

> It is one substance and not two, not living and not dead, neither liquid nor solid, neither hot nor cold, neither male nor female.

> This sacrament is secret in every respect.[11]

> The highest sacrament, that of One element, is universal in its operation; according to the declared purpose of the work so will the result be. It is a universal Key of all Magick.[12]

As the substance started with already presents a unity of opposites, so too will the divinity purified and brought forth from it—presumably the Holy Guardian Angel—have a universal character. This helps make sense of Crowley's claim in this chapter that, "To a Magician thus renewed [by eucharistic magick] the attainment of the Knowledge and Conversation of the Holy Guardian Angel becomes an inevitable task."[13]

In the same chapter, Crowley speaks of the "Medicine of Metals" or the "Elixir of Life" in similar terms.

> The Universal Medicine will be a menstruum of such subtlety as to be able to penetrate all matter and transmute it in the sense of its own tendency, while of such impartial purity as to accept perfectly the impression of the Will of the Alchemist. This substance, properly prepared, and properly charged, is able to perform all things soever that are physically possible,

---

11 Ibid.
12 Ibid.
13 Ibid.

within the limits of the proportions of its momentum to the inertia of the object to which it is applied.[14]

The production of the Medicine of Metals is the supreme secret kept within the Sanctuary of the Gnosis of O.T.O. It is a universal substance which can be molded by the magician into any state of affairs whatsoever.

> [O.T.O.] possesses the secret of the Stone of the Wise, of the Elixir of Immortality, and of the Universal Medicine.[15]

But the universality of this magical force owes to the universality of the first matter from which the operation starts, same as in any other alchemical operation.

So far we have seen that art production, alchemy, initiation, talisman-ic magick, and evocation all share the same basic underlying structure and operate according to the same principles. All of them have to do with the creation of a living thing from a dead thing. And in each case, the operator is not able to bring forth any "truth" from the first matter which was not already implicit within it. In other words, the nature of the first matter is only brought forth and made visible by the operator, not created in it.

Furthermore, we have also seen that this very same structure is implicated in the main work of both A∴A∴ and O.T.O. Initiation is the main concern of the work of A∴A∴, and the production of the Universal Medicine or Eucharist of One Element is the main concern of O.T.O. So not only is this structure essential to virtually all forms of Thelemic magick. It must be im-portant to an understanding of Thelemic spirituality generally for it to lie so close to the heart of both of Crowley's life-long spiritual projects.

Finally the fact that this structure is also shared by art production means that, far from being a mere peripheral matter, art production actually has an important, even essential relationship with Thelemic spirituality.

But what, precisely, is the nature of this structure? What exactly does it mean to transform a dead thing into a living thing? How is it done? And what does it mean exactly that the issue of life and death lies at the heart of Thelemic spirituality? What does that imply about the essence of the Thele-mic spiritual path?

Before turning to the dark star around which all these issues revolve, I

---

14  Ibid.
15  Liber 52, Sec 4 (Manifesto of the O.T.O.)

want to circle back on art production and draw out some of the implications lying on the table so far.

## Medium Specificity

In the cases of the first matter of alchemy, the candidate for initiation, and the substrate of eucharistic magick, the final result depends almost entirely on the implicit nature of the first matter. The alchemical process, the initiation process, and the eucharistic process only have the power to make explicit what was lying in wait as potential in the first matter. The job of the operator is not to impose something divine on matter from the outside but rather to transform the first matter in such a way as to reveal what the first matter was truly all along. If we apply this same logic to art production, we get the notion of *medium specificity*.

Medium specificity is the idea that there are unique qualities inherent to each artistic medium, and the function of the artist is to reveal and bring these inherent qualities into relief in the work of art. Medium specificity is often contrasted with representationalism or the idea that the work of art is representing some state of affairs in the world. Gotthold Ephraim Lessing is considered to have invented the notion of medium specificity in the 18th century, but its most famous proponent was the 20th century art critic, Clement Greenberg.

> It quickly emerged that the unique and proper area of competence of each art coincided with all that was unique in the nature of its medium. The task of self-criticism became to eliminate from the specific effects of each art any and every effect that might conceivably be borrowed from or by the medium of any other art. Thus would each art be rendered "pure," and in its "purity" find the guarantee of its standards of quality as well as of its independence. "Purity" meant self-definition, and the enterprise of self-criticism in the arts became one of self-definition with a vengeance.[16]

If it were possible to speak of an artistic medium having "true self" or "true will," that would be its specificity as a medium. When an individual is following their true will, events do not "happen to" them. Every single interaction with anything whatsoever is seen as an expression of self or will. Similarly

---

16 Clement Greenberg, "Modernist Painting," in *Forum Lectures* (Washington, D.C.: Voice of America, 1960)

in the case of an artistic medium, it's no longer about anything external to the medium itself. The job of the artist is to allow the medium to express itself and its own potencies. Medium specificity is a way of looking at artistic medium which is conducive to abstract, non-representational art.

> To achieve autonomy, painting has had above all to divest itself of everything it might share with sculpture, and it is in its effort to do this, and not so much—I repeat—to exclude the representational or literary, that painting has made itself abstract.[17]

Aside from being a life-long poet, essayist, and prose writer, Crowley himself became a painter in his 40s and exhibited his work in Berlin in the 1930s. Crowley was by no means an abstract expressionist. His paintings have been favorably compared with German expressionists like Ernst Kirchner.[18] But while medium specificity as an account of art production is probably most at home with abstract expressionism, Greenberg identifies it as a trend that defines most modernist painting. It involves a movement away from what we might think of as an "accurate," 3-dimensional portrayal of objects in space and more toward an approach that emphasizes the flatness of the canvas. Crowley's own style of painting is part of that overall trend toward abstraction and medium specificity.

The spiritual and magical importance of medium specificity is that it is about giving intrinsic meaning—what Crowley might have called "vitality"—back to matter. Take a force of nature like gravity as an example. We don't think of there being anything numinous about the fact that objects, when released, fall to the earth. The ancients didn't view things that way at all, though. The fact that something fell to the earth when released said something important about its intrinsic nature as compared with fire or air— or for that matter as compared with the planets which they viewed as being composed of a different, more divine substance altogether. For us the fact of something falling to the earth has been demystified and demythologized. It's been rendered a "dead," merely mechanical result, expressible as an abstract equation.

But in the context of Jackson Pollock's drip paintings, gravity comes into play as an essential factor. Pollock would paint by standing over his canvas

---

17 Ibid.
18 See Frank van Lamoen's "Foreword" in Tobias Churton, *Aleister Crowley, The Beast in Berlin: Art, Sex, and Magick in the Weimar Republic* (Rochester Vermont: Inner Traditions, 2014), xi.

and letting the paint fall over it in drops and dramatic streaks. His process of painting revealed gravity, not as a mere lifeless mechanism, but also as a vehicle of human expression. This is the transformation of gravity as "first matter" into an artistic medium. Gravity became a partner with human desire, thereby allowing both the painter and the spectator to feel at home in the world. Gravity is "reenchanted" for a moment in the context of our aesthetic appreciation. The same could be said for other dimensions of paint. Sensuous qualities—shapes, lines, movements, forms, things we would normally think of as mere lifeless "data" of the senses—invigorate the imagination and show up as living, divine beings.

This has implications for the function of the artist. Medium specificity implies that there is a certain "will" on the side of the artistic medium, be it paint, sound, film, stone, plastic, language, etc. It is not simply the will of the artist which is coming out in the final work of art. Even in the case of expressionism—the type of painting Crowley did—there is a particular *meaning* which is being delivered by means of the work of art which cannot be unequivocally reduced either to objective reality or the inner state of the artist. Every work of art has dual authorship. There is the intention the artist brings to the medium—that which they seek to express through the medium—and then there is the truth implicit within the medium itself which is seeking its own expression. Even in writing this talk, language is not appearing to me as a transparent, obedient vehicle of my commands or thoughts. I have some idea, I set out to write it, and the final result is not just of me but rather expresses a partnership between some felt life within me and some life I feel myself pushing up against in the form of language. It is not my confrontation with nature I am experiencing but rather nature's confrontation with itself, resulting in words, which in some sense represent some objective state of affairs, but which also must be seen in their magical aspect, as incantations meant to evoke images and thoughts in your mind, the way a magical operator, standing in a circle, evokes a spirit into a triangle.

This is why the ambiguity Crowley leaves between imprinting one's soul on an object (as in talismanic magick or painting) versus realizing some truth implicit in the first matter is not a mistake. It's exactly correct. It is the line between the will inherent in ourselves and the will inherent in nature which is effaced through magical creation. The greater the work of art, the more impossible it is for the artist to sign it. Every great artist is NEMO.

Having explored art production and art medium in light of the principle Crowley identifies at the root of alchemy, I would now like to return to that principle and consider it more abstractly. As I mentioned before, the fact that this structural principle underlies most forms of Thelemic magick—as well as the central mysteries of A∴A∴ and O.T.O.—makes it worthy of special consideration.

## IAO: Of the Living and the Dead

In all the cases we have looked at thus far, we are subjecting some first matter to a process whereby its implicit truth is made explicit. The first matter is invariably some natural object, something we find ready-made in nature. But it does not exist according to its "truth". Its "truth" is buried or concealed within it. And so whether it appears that way or not, the natural object is really "dead" according to Crowley. It is possible for this "dead" object to become vivified—to experience its own vitality, which really means existing in accordance with its own nature or its own principle—but this requires it to first undergo a process. This process is invariably destructive of the original, outward form of the first matter. In the case of alchemy, it requires the first matter to undergo the *nigredo* or blackening stage. In the case of initiation, it requires one to pass through the Dark Night of the Soul and experience the destruction of separateness in *samadhi*. In the case of the work of art, matter must be transformed into artistic medium.

This three-part structure we have been looking at in which an object in its natural state undergoes a destructive process only to be reborn in a perfected state is symbolized by the magical formula IAO.

Describing this formula in Chapter V of Magick in Theory and Practice, Crowley says:

This formula is the principal and most characteristic formula of Osiris, of the Redemption of Mankind. 'I' is Isis, Nature, ruined by 'A', Apophis the Destroyer, and restored to life by the Redeemer Osiris. The same idea is expressed by the Rosicrucian formula of the Trinity:

Ex Deo nascimur. [We are born from God.]
In Jesu Morimur [We die in Jesus.]
Per Spiritum Sanctum reviviscimus. [We are reborn through The Holy Spirit.]

[...]

> The doctrine of resurrection as vulgarly understood is false and absurd. It is not even 'Scriptural'. St. Paul does not identify the glorified body which rises with the mortal body which dies. On the contrary, he repeatedly insists on the distinction.

> The same is true of a magical ceremony. The magician who is destroyed by absorption in the Godhead is really destroyed. The miserable mortal automaton remains in the Circle. It is of no more consequence to Him than the dust of the floor. But before entering into the details of 'I.A.O.' as a magick formula it should be remarked that it is essentially the formula of Yoga or meditation; in fact, of elementary mysticism in all its branches.[19]

IAO was an important formula in the context of the Golden Dawn Adeptus Minor initiation where it symbolized resurrection or a second birth through self-sacrifice. In that context Apophis (also known as Apep), the Great Serpent and enemy of the sun-god Ra, "ruins nature". But this ruination is redeemed through the suffering of Osiris, who is seen as isomorphic with Jesus Christ. By sharing in the suffering of Osiris/Jesus Christ, we too can be redeemed and participate in deification.

The parallel between this tripartite formula of destruction and resurrection and the process of alchemy was noted by Crowley himself in an adjacent passage.

> The Alchemists themselves taught this same truth. The first matter of the work was base and primitive, though "natural". After passing through various stages the "black dragon" appeared; but from this arose the pure and perfect gold.[20]

However, it must also be noted that Crowley regards this formula of redemption through suffering as abrogate. As we saw above, he regards the doctrine of resurrection itself as absurd. And while he considers the notion of mystical attainment described by IAO as valid so long as it is divorced from the glorification of suffering, it is no longer the "supreme attainment".

While the similarity between IAO and the alchemical-artistic processes we've been looking at so far is clear, it is also worth noting a key difference. In the IAO formula of the Golden Dawn, Apophis is the destroyer of nature

---

19 MITAP, ch 5
20 Ibid.

and the enemy of Ra whose havoc must be redeemed vicariously by means of Osiris. But in the sorts of activities we have been looking at, it is the destructive or transformative process itself which valorizes the first matter by releasing its truth or perfection from captivity within the blind forces of matter. The alchemist blackens the first matter in order to release gold from it. The candidate brings themselves through the ordeal of initiation in order to reorient themselves toward the immortal part of themselves. The magician-conjurer arranges matter so that it can bear the spiritual. The artist transforms mere matter into artistic medium so it can bear and communicate human significance. In all of these cases, the artist-magician has taken up the place of Apophis in the operation, not Osiris, and their action does not ruin nature in anything other than a superficial sense.

This has bearing on another doctrine which has importance both to the Golden Dawn and to Thelema, the doctrine of the pentagrammaton. The pentagrammaton, or יהשוה, represents the descent of spirit, represented by the Hebrew letter Shin, down into the midst of the four elements, represented by Yod-Heh-Vau-Heh. By descending into their midst, spirit "redeems" the four elements from their fallen, blind state. This doctrine of pentagrammaton is connected in Golden Dawn spirituality with the aforementioned doctrine of redemption of "ruined" existence through suffering and self-sacrifice. The five letters together are pronounced "Yeheshua," a reconstructed form of the name "Jesus".

Not only was this doctrine rejected by Crowley, but again, it is quite different in kind from the formulae we've been examining so far. In all of these cases, matter is in no way being "redeemed" by something spiritual injected from outside of it. On the contrary what we keep seeing over and over again is that there is already a spiritual reality implicit within matter itself in its natural state. What makes the first matter "untrue" isn't that it is "mere" matter in some spiritually dejected sense. It's that it either lacks unity or lacks orientation toward the principle of its own unity. That situation is remedied, not by bringing in something extra from the outside, but rather— if anything—by taking something away, by destroying something in the first matter. This destructive process itself liberates and makes visible the "truth" implied in the first matter.

In the fifth chapter of *Magick in Theory and Practice*, Crowley offers a reconstruction of IAO that is a better fit to the processes we have been looking at so far. He refers to that formula as **VIAOV**.

THE MASTER THERION, in the Seventeenth year of the Aeon, has reconstructed the Word I A O to satisfy the new conditions of Magick imposed by progress. The Word of the Law being Thelema, whose number is 93, this number should be the canon of a corresponding Mass. Accordingly, he has expanded I A O by treating the O as an Ayin, and then adding Vau as prefix and affix. The full word is then:

ו י א ע ו

whose number is 93. We may analyse this new Word in detail and demonstrate that it is a proper hieroglyph of the Ritual of Self-Initiation in this Aeon of Horus.[21]

Rather than a formula of redemption of destruction through self-sacrifice, the formula of VIAOV describes a process of initiation through reduction and reorientation.

According to Crowley the "first process" of this formula of initiation "is to find the I in the V—initiation, purification, finding the Secret Root of oneself, the epicene Virgin who is 10 (Malkuth) but spelt in full 20 (Jupiter)."[22]

This is almost exactly the same way Crowley described initiation in Chapter 20 when he compared initiation with alchemy:

> The process of initiation consists in removing his impurities, and finding in his true self an immortal intelligence to whom matter is no more than the means of manifestation.[23]

The "epicene Virgin" is a reference to Heh-final of Tetragrammaton, which is also Malkuth.

> This Yod in the "Virgin" expands to the Babe in the Egg by formulating the Secret Wisdom of Truth of Hermes in the Silence of the Fool.[24]

We went from V to I—this was the initial process of initiation and purification—and now we have just transitioned to A. However, A is no longer the

---

21 Ibid.
22 Ibid.
23 MITAP, ch 20
24 MITAP, ch 5

ruiner of nature. A no longer represents some condition we need to redeem ourselves from. Rather, A represents the "Babe in the Egg," a symbol Crowley equates with the Egyptian god of silence, Harpocrates.

> Now consider the traditional form of Harpocrates. He is a babe, that is to say, innocent, and not yet arrived at puberty; a simpler form of Parsifal, he is represented as rose pink in colour [...] This *babe is in an egg of blue,* which is evidently the symbol of the Mother. This child has, in a way, not been born; the blue is the blue of space; the egg is sitting upon a lotus, and this lotus grows on the Nile. Now, the lotus is another symbol of the Mother, and the Nile is also a symbol of the Father, fertilizing Egypt, the Yoni."[25]

Harpocrates is an important symbol in Thelema, representing, among other things, the Secret Self or Holy Guardian Angel of each individual.

> Harpocrates is also the Dwarf-Soul, the Secret Self of every man, the Serpent with the Lion's Head.[26]

> But the 'Small Person' of Hindu mysticism, the Dwarf insane yet crafty in many legends in many lands, is also this same 'Holy Ghost,' or Silent Self of a man, or his Holy Guardian Angel.[27]

Notice that the connection with the symbol of the serpent has been retained. We saw earlier that Apophis, the destroyer of nature, was the Great Serpent Apep. Crowley has retained this connection in the A-phase of the IAO formula, but now rather than representing a condition which humanity must free itself from through self-sacrifice, the Serpent represents the saving power itself. Indeed, the candidate calls upon the serpent, Apep, as such in Liber Pyramidos.

> Hail! Asi! hail, Hoor-Apep! Let
> The Silence speech beget! Two strokes on Bell.
> Banishing Spiral Dance.
> The Words against the Sons of Night

---

25 *Book of Thoth,* "The Fool," emphasis mine
26 New Comment on AL II.8
27 New Comment on AL I.7

Tahuti speaketh in the Light.
Knowledge & Power, twin warriors, shake
The Invisible; they roll asunder
The Darkness; matter shines, a snake.
Sebek is smitten by the thunder
The Light breaks forth from Under.[28]

Harpocrates does not only represent the Holy Guardian Angel of each individual. They also represent the preeminent divine reality from which Crowley received *The Book of the Law* and with it the spiritual path of Thelema.

Aiwass is called the minister of Hoor-paar-kraat, the God of Silence; for his word is the Speech of the Silence.[29]

Behold! it is revealed by Aiwass the minister of Hoor-paar-kraat.[30]

Aiwass is the representative of the God of Silence. His speech, *The Book of the Law*, can therefore be thought of as the Speech of Silence. Liber Tav tells us what the function of the speech of silence is. It is the path of Peh, the Mouth of the Beast. It is Destruction.

This inversion of the symbol of the serpent—its transformation from a symbol of evil into a symbol of liberation—is one of the core, distinctive features of Thelemic spirituality. But this deification of the serpent does not transform it into a force for "good". It does not make it a friend. The characteristic mode of behavior of the serpent Apep is still to destroy, to poison.

Then was there silence. Speech had done with us awhile. There is a light so strenuous that it is not perceived as light. Wolf's bane is not so sharp as steel; yet it pierceth the body more subtly. Even as evil kisses corrupt the blood, so do my words devour the spirit of man. I breathe, and there is infinite dis-ease in the spirit. As an acid eats into steel, as a cancer that utterly corrupts the body; so am I unto the spirit of man. I shall not rest until I have dissolved it all.[31]

---

28 Crowley, Liber Pyramidos
29 Old Comment on AL I.7
30 AL I.7
31 Liber LXV, I.12-17

To turn toward Thelema and to reorient oneself toward the preeminent spiritual reality it represents means a turn toward darkness, toward what one without any exaggeration might call the *demonic*.

This turn toward the demonic is born out in the next step of the VIAOV process, which takes us from A or Harpocrates to O or Baphomet.

> The second main point is the completion of the A, babe Bacchus, by the O, Pan [...] He acquires the Eye-Wand, beholding the acting and being adored. The Inverted Pentagram—Baphomet—the Hermaphrodite fully grown—begets himself on himself as V again.[32]

Baphomet is of course the famous idol allegedly worshiped by the Templars. He is the Goat of Mendes, the Devil.

> We have therefore no scruple in restoring the "devil-worship" of such ideas as those which the laws of sound, and the phenomena of speech and hearing, compel us to connect with the group of "Gods" whose names are based upon Sht, or D, vocalized by the free breath A. For these Names imply the qualities of courage, frankness, energy, pride, power and triumph; they are the words which express the creative and paternal will.

> Thus "the Devil" is Capricornus, the Goat who leaps upon the loftiest mountains, the Godhead which, if it become manifest in man, makes him Aegipan, the All.[33]

This treatment of Harpocrates as the silent, menacing prelude to a violent, even demonic explosion of energy occurs elsewhere in Crowley's writings, where he links it with the explosion of true will represented by Ra-Hoor-Khuit or Horus.

> But on His appearing, He assumes the active form twin to Harpocrates, that of Ra-Hoor-Khuit. The Concealed Child becomes the Conquering Child, the armed Horus avenging his father Osiris. So also our own Silent Self, helpless and witless, hidden within us, will spring forth, if we have craft to loose him to the Light, spring lustily forward with his cry of Bat-

---

tle, the Word of our True Wills.[34]

For two things are done and a third thing is begun. Isis and Osiris are given over to incest and adultery. Horus leaps up thrice armed from the womb of his mother. Harpocrates his twin is hidden within him. Set is his holy covenant, that he shall display in the great day of M.A.A.T., that is being interpreted the Master of the Temple of A∴A∴, whose name is Truth.[35]

Following the climactic moment of the Gnostic Mass in which the Priest and Priestess together depress the particle of bread into the cup of wine, the Priest strikes his breast and three times cries, "O Lion and O Serpent that destroy the destroyer, be mighty among us." The Lion-Serpent he is calling upon is the very same spiritual power we have been contemplating, the very same force, Hoor-Apep, whose poison corrupts and dissolves us utterly. That very same destructive power is now called upon at a crucial moment in the central religious rite of O.T.O. for the purpose of "destroying the destroyer". But who or what exactly is the destroyer we are calling upon the Lion-Serpent to destroy? What is the spiritual function of this power of destruction? Why would someone want to submit themselves to being "poisoned"? How can one make a spiritual path out of embracing darkness? And what does this imply about the function of art and of the artist? I will address these now in the final part of my talk.

## Destroy the Destroyer

In Chapter XXI of *Magick in Theory and Practice*, Crowley declares,

The Devil does not exist. It is a false name invested by the Black Brothers to imply a Unity in their ignorance muddle of dispersions. A devil who had unity would be a God.[36]

How are we to reconcile such a statement with the rampant devilry we just witnessed in chapter V? The clue lies in his reference to unity and disunity. As we saw in our discussion of alchemy, the difference between the living and the dead is the difference between that which demands we approach it

---

34 New Comment on AL I.7
35 Liber A'ash vel Capricorni Pneumatici, 7
36 MITAP, ch 21

as a unity versus that which is a mere aggregate of parts or pieces. In the case of the initiate, it is all a matter of coming to see the events of one's life, pleasant or unpleasant, boring or difficult, as expressions of that higher unity of the true self and the true will. Being alive is the objective side of which doing one's true will is the subjective correlate. Doing one's will is what it feels like to be alive.

But unity is beyond good and evil. It is light and it is night and it is that which is beyond them. It is speech, and it is silence, and it is that which is beyond them. It is life, and it is death, and it is that which is beyond them. It is war, and it is peace, and it is that which is beyond them. It is weakness, and it is strength, and it is that which is beyond them.

This is true in a lofty metaphysical sense. Kether transcends the duality of Chokmah and Binah. Subtle experiences such as jhana or samadhi transcend the duality of subject and object. But even the concrete sense in which an organism maintains its unity is beyond good and evil. Arsenic is "evil" to us, because it decomposes the relations of our parts, one to another, until our unity is ultimately dissolved and we perish. But from the point of view of arsenic, it is merely declaring its own unity in relation with our bodies, ex-pressing its own intrinsic nature, and therefore it is doing good by killing us.

"Do what thou wilt" allows for the concept of evil, but it is a concept of evil relative to the will of each. It is relative to the unity which expresses the true nature of each organism. To be evil means to live in such a way that your own relations decompose. It means the loss of your own unity. By contrast, to be good means to live in accordance with and to express that underlying unity. But living in accordance with your own unity, your own good, gives no guarantee that, from the perspective of another being, your impact on them is not evil. In fact you can be certain that there are many perspectives from which the activities of your best, divine self are evil.

This might seem like a terrible fate—and *fate* in the sense it had for the ancients is precisely the right term for it—but the truth is that we cause even more mayhem when we do not live in unity with ourselves. The more we concern ourselves with the wills of others, the more damage we do. We become mere aggregates of impulse. Our final "decisions" are nothing of the kind. They are merely the sums of competing force vectors from within and without and around. In Crowley's language we are like countries divided against ourselves, bodies wracked with cancer. From the perspective of our higher selves, we are in a fallen, evil state. This is how Crowley describes the run-of-the-mill human condition.

But if we're not living in accordance with our own natures, if we are not organizing according to our own principle of unity, then we are not truly alive. We merely think we are. So many of our decisions are motivated by the fear of death and the desire to avoid death. In reality the worst thing imaginable has already happened to us. If we had any sense, we wouldn't fear death. We would fear never having lived in the first place.

When this realization occurs—if it ever occurs—it is accompanied by the feeling of horror: horror in the sense of revulsion and terror, but also horror like a horror film. What is a monster really other than our own repressed natures projected onto a shadow? The monster is the illusion of dead matter erupting with life. It is a false unity grotesquely imposed upon and animating a shadow—almost the exact terms Crowley used to describe the Devil. One of the first horror novels ever written, Mary Shelley's *Frankenstein*, is about exactly the issues we have been exploring this evening: life, death, and the difference. Horror continues to be about this issue. It presents an image of dark matter pregnant with a coiled serpent about to spring. It is the mere image or illusion of what we in fact are: the walking dead.

The reason we require an encounter with darkness is simple. Darkness is the only thing in heaven or hell that has the power to destroy what we have erected in desperation.

There is something here akin to the ancient idea of the Gnostics that we are spiritual beings trapped in matter that must seek their release. The Gnostic god, Chnoubis, is isomorphic with the Lion-Serpent, the Holy Guardian Angel of Thelemic tradition. But the similarity stops there.

The purpose of releasing this potential trapped at the heart of disorganized matter is not so it can escape to some remote celestial region. There is no pleroma to retreat to for perfection. What is freed in this world is freed *for* this world, because it was always *of* this world. If you want to know what heaven, the body of Nuit, looks like, look around you. When you discover and do your true will, you will do it right here, right now, in this world. And it may very well be destructive of other things in this world—in fact it almost certainly will be at least some of the time. Full consciousness, apprehension, and ownership of one's own vitality require one to accept and face this fate. One will probably encounter this fate as darkness outside of oneself, darkness which one must descend into on a solitary journey to the underworld, to the realm of the dead. If you want the keys to open your prison cell, you need to go to the only person who has them. She is the Queen of the Dead. Her name is Kore. She is also called Malkah or Heh-final of Tetragrammaton. Her destiny is Babalon, the Mother of Us All. She lies at the center of the Earth. I do not mean she is at the center of the planet. I mean she is at the heart of all matter. She is everything we have been looking at for the last hour. You can see her and feel her literally anywhere you look—so long as you know how to look. And that is a large part of the spiritual path: learning how to look, learning the proper use of the senses. It is the acquisition of an "aesthetic" education—after the Greek word for sensation, *aisthesis*.

And so we return to the function of the artist and the spiritual role of the work of art. The artist affects liberation and release of what is spiritual at the heart of matter. The transition from mere matter to artistic medium is the same as the journey of initiation. The artist is the hierophant, and matter is the candidate. If the initiation is successful, the work of art is a window allowing chaos to shimmer through the regular order of being. When we are face-to-face with great art, whatever the form, we are having a direct experience of that spiritual reality which lies all around us and in us, but which we are not usually able to see or appreciate until we have learned to see with the eyes of a mystic—or an artist.

# 9

# The Spirit in the Letter:
# Truth and the Gnostic Mass

## The Purpose of the Gnostic Mass

Our most important source for understanding the Gnostic Mass comes from what its author, Aleister Crowley, wrote about it in his autobiography, *The Confessions of Aleister Crowley.*

> During this period [1913] the full interpretation of the central mystery of freemasonry became clear in consciousness, and I expressed it in dramatic form in *The Ship.* The lyrical climax is in some respects my supreme achievement in invocation; in fact, the chorus beginning:
>
> Thou who art I beyond all I am ...
>
> seemed to me worthy to be introduced as the anthem into the Ritual of the Gnostic Catholic Church which, later in the year, I prepared for the use of the O.T.O., the central ceremony of its public and private celebration, corresponding to the Mass of the Roman Catholic Church.
>
> Human nature demands (in the case of most people) the satisfaction of the religious instinct, and, to very many, this may best be done by ceremonial means. I wished therefore to construct a ritual through which people might enter into ecstasy as they have always done under the influence of appropriate ritual. In recent years, there has been an increasing failure to attain this object, because the established cults shock their intellectual convictions and outrage their common sense. Thus their minds criticize their enthusiasm; they are unable to consummate the union of their individual

souls with the universal soul as a bridegroom would be to consummate his marriage if his love were constantly reminded that its assumptions were intellectually absurd.

I resolved that my ritual should celebrate the sublimity of the operation of universal forces without introducing disputable metaphysical theories. I would neither make nor imply any statement about nature which would not be endorsed by the most materialistic man of science. On the surface this may sound difficult; but in practice I found it perfectly simple to combine the most rigidly rational conceptions of phenomena with the most exalted and enthusiastic celebration of their sublimity.[1]

From this passage we gather that the Gnostic Mass is a religious ceremony—analogous to the Mass of the Roman Catholic Church—the purpose of which is to "consummate the union of [our] individual souls with the universal soul," an experience of which should allow us to "enter into ecstasy". By doing this, Crowley sees himself as fulfilling the traditional purpose of religion, a purpose which has been forgotten and repressed over the years by an excess of superstition. And so in writing the Gnostic Mass, Crowley wanted to avoid implying anything about nature that might be deemed supernatural.

One of the difficulties presented by this statement of purpose is that the Gnostic Mass is not an ecstatic ritual. There is no singing, dancing, or chanting in it. It is uncommon for congregants to begin writhing on the floor or speaking in tongues. If they do, the fire department usually shows up. While a celebration of *Liber XV* should be more edifying than a celebration of the Mass of the Roman Catholic Church, Crowley admits that the rituals are not different in kind.

One possibility is that Crowley was exaggerating the potential effects of the Gnostic Mass. Another possibility is that we are doing the ritual improperly. I don't think either of these is true. Instead I'm going to make the case that the Gnostic Mass is supposed to lead us to an understanding of ourselves and the world, the fruition of which is ecstasy. And if the ritual fails to lead us to ecstasy, it is because we have failed to understand and apply its truth. We have failed to heed the spirit in the letter.

Crowley speaks of the potential of religion to bring us to an encounter with truth in *Equinox III*. There he says:

---

[1]    *Confessions*, ch 73

The world needs religion.

Religion must represent Truth, and celebrate it.

This truth is of two orders: one, concerning Nature external to Man; two, concerning Nature internal to Man.

Existing religions, especially Christianity, are based on primitive ignorance of the facts, particularly of external Nature.

Celebrations must conform to the custom and nature of the people.

Christianity has destroyed the joyful celebrations, characterized by music, dancing, feasting, and making love; and has kept only the melancholy.

The Law of Thelema offers a religion which fulfils all necessary conditions[2]

The purpose of religion generally—and of a Thelemic religious rite such as the Gnostic Mass in particular—is to represent and to celebrate what Crowley calls "Truth". This Truth, he says, takes two forms: truth concerning nature external to us and truth concerning nature internal to us.

## External Truth: The Sun of the Cosmos

Crowley's criticism of the way in which Christianity has based itself on a superstitious account of external nature reflects his desire, expressed in the quote from *Confessions*, to "celebrate the sublimity of the operation of universal forces without introducing disputable metaphysical theories" and to remain committed to a "rational [conception] of phenomena". The Gnostic Mass fulfills this criteria by being a ritual of nature worship. Thus prayers are made throughout the course of the ritual extolling the life-giving virtues of the Sun, the Moon, and the Earth, as well as other natural phenomena such as birth, life, and even death.

Natural forces are described in the Gnostic Mass in such a way as to relate them back to basic human activities, in particular production and leisure or what the Gnostic Mass refers to as *labor* and *enjoyment*. The light of the Sun is adored because it makes labor and enjoyment possible. The Lord is signif-

---

2  *Equinox III*, "Editorial"

icant as the motive power of our labor and a source of abundant joy. The Moon is extolled for the ways in which she makes hunting, loving, toiling, and sailing possible. The Lady is significant for the role she plays in giving and receiving joy. The Saints are those who adore the Lord of Life and Joy. The Earth is the site of labor, the womb of all life who answers the prayers of labor. The Principles grant health, wealth, strength, and pleasure and allow each to accomplish their wills.

Labor and enjoyment—or life and joy—together constitute an important binary focus of the Gnostic Mass. What they both have in common is that they are modifications or potentials of our bodies. Building, creating, farming, imagining, love-making, relaxing, dreaming—in short, all willed human activities—are impossible without bodies. Notwithstanding the possibility of entities that have only astral and not physical bodies, without the "labor and heroism of incarnation," the will is an abstraction bordering on meaninglessness. It is only in bodies situated upon the surface of the Earth, with a sunlit or star-studded sky above them, joys and sorrows behind them, and hopes and dreams laid out in front of them, that we can realize our wills. The body is represented in the Gnostic Mass as a two-in-one phenomenon of Life and Joy.

The two-part eucharist of the Gnostic Mass is also referred to Life and Joy. The Cake of Light is the "life of man upon earth". It is both the product of labor and that which, by being consumed, sustains a new round of labor. The cup of wine is the "vehicle of the joy of Man upon earth". It both provides us relief at the end of a day of work and inspires new forms of creativity the following day. It is precisely this life and this joy which are offered up as sacrifices to the Sun, and which are later returned to the Priest as the "life of the Sun" and the "joy of the Earth". The Miracle of the Mass itself is a transubstantiation of these two fundamental modes of embodied human being in the world.

This transubstantiation or sacrifice is represented as taking place through a process of unification or love. The Priest places the particle of the Cake of Light on the end of the lance, and together, he and the Priestess depress both into the cup. Together they cry, "HRILIU," a word from *The Vision and the Voice* which represents "the shrill scream of orgasm," an exemplary form of human joy.[3]

Procreation is the creation of a new Life which is inaugurated by an act culminating in Joy or the bliss of orgasm. As simultaneous labor and enjoy-

---

3   *The Vision and the Voice*, 2nd Aethyr

ment, it is an exemplary mode of the two-in-one nature of the human qua embodied, natural being.

The act of procreation is the source of our embodiment. Each of us can trace our respective existences back to our births, and before that, to a single orgasm. As such, procreation is a source of ambivalence. On the one hand, we would be unable to do our wills without bodies. Whatever labor we engage in, be it the ordinary kind we get paid for or the exalted labor of the Great Work, none of it is possible outside the context of our embodiment. On the other hand, the body is the source of all our limitations. Because we are embodied, we are vulnerable. Our minds are susceptible to hurt feelings, wounded pride, and betrayal. Our physical bodies are susceptible to illness and infirmity. To be born is immediately to incur the penalty of death. Womb and tomb are combined in the symbol of Babalon in the Gnostic Mass. Thus all the spiritual significance and ambivalence associated with our embodiment is condensed into the symbol of procreation.

Procreation has further spiritual significance insofar as it presents us with a way in which, even as finite mortal beings, we can experience immortality. While the individual may suffer death, the human race continues through procreation. Insofar as one reproduces, cares for, and properly raises offspring, they get to participate in this higher purpose of the species. Thus both birth and continuing knowledge from generation unto generation are extolled in the Collects of the Gnostic Mass.

Following the usage of Richard Payne Knight and Hargrave Jennings, Crowley refers to the generative principle as the *Phallus*. The Phallus is not the male organ *per se*. Rather it is the procreation of the species, the collapse of labor and joy into a single act: the orgasmic union of male and female. The Phallus is represented in the Gnostic Mass by the lance, but its perfection is its union with the grail, culminating in the shrill cry of orgasm.

Summarizing this process, the Priest says, "TOUTO ESTI TO SPERMA MOU. HO PATÊR ESTIN HO HUIOS DIA TO PNEUMA HAGION" or "This is my seed. The Father is the Son through the Holy Spirit." On a naturalistic reading, the particle of the Cake of Light represents the Priest's spermatozoon. It is the Lion-Serpent that destroys the destroyer or which vanquishes death. The Priest realizes immortality: he lives in the Son. This naturalistic portrayal of immortality is what Crowley refers to as the Lesser Mystery of the sword and the disk. It pertains to one layer of meaning of the Gnostic Mass.

Crowley summarizes many of these points in the New Comment on AL

III.22.

There are to be no regular temples of Nuith and Hadit, for They are in-commensurables and absolutes. Our religion therefore, for the People, is the Cult of the Sun, who is our particular star of the Body of Nuit, from whom, in the strictest scientific sense, come this earth, a chilled spark of Him, and all our Light and Life. His vice-regent and representative in the animal kingdom is His cognate symbol the Phallus, representing Love and Liberty. Ra-Hoor-Khuit, like all true Gods, is therefore a Solar-Phallic de-ity. But we regard Him as He is in truth, eternal; the Solar-Phallic deities of the old Aeon, such as Osiris, "Christ", Hiram, Adonis, Hercules, &c., were supposed, through our ignorance of the Cosmos, to 'die' and rise again'. Thus we celebrated rites of 'crucifixion' and so on, which have now become meaningless.[4]

In the Creed of the Gnostic Mass, we say, "I believe in one ⟦...⟧ star in the company of stars ⟦...⟧ and one father of life ⟦...⟧ Chaos, the sole vice-regent of the Sun upon the Earth..." These are references to the Sun and the gen-erative principle or phallus. The Sun is the principle of Light and Life in the macrocosm; the Phallus is the principle of Love and Liberty on the Earth or in the microcosm. Together they form Ra-Hoor-Khuit, the Lord of the Aeon. So even though Ra-Hoor-Khuit is never mentioned by name in *Liber XV*, as the Solar-Phallus, He is the primary object of adoration in the ritual.

Ancient religions' notions of immortality and salvation were based upon the observation that God, the Sun, died and was reborn again daily and over the course of the equinoxes and solstices. The Copernican revolution in astronomy established that the Earth in fact moves around the Sun, not vice versa. The Sun is not dependent upon our sacrifices for its immortality. Rather, the Earth depends for its existence on the Sun, as it is "but a frozen spark" of that star. Likewise the finite individual is not the essence; the spe-cies is. We are merely vehicles for the propagation of genes. To acknowledge the priority of the species relative to the individual is akin to acknowledging the priority of the Sun relative to the Earth.

In making embodied human activity and enjoyment along with the con-ditions that make them possible a focus of a religious ceremony, Crowley has fulfilled his promise to remain committed to a rational conception of phenomena. He may be using poetic language to describe these conditions,

---

4  New Comment on AL III.22

but the picture presented in the ritual is broadly naturalistic and anchored in pragmatic human activities like labor and leisure. Even the view of immortality offered is merely figurative. As natural individuals we are not immortal. We are ineluctably finite, embodied beings. Awareness of our connection to this larger, impersonal process makes our temporary lives meaningful. All that we must sacrifice to be part of it is our illusion of separateness from it. Thus the individual is represented as connected with a higher power which sustains their life's most important activities.

In his New Comment on AL III.48-49, Crowley describes this hierarchical relationship between the individual and the cosmos.

> Each man's 'child'-consciousness is a Star in the Cosmos of the Sun, as the Sun is a Star in the Cosmos of Nuith.[5]

This interconnectedness with something larger is both represented and celebrated in the drama of the Gnostic Mass.

If we were to create an updated version of the Gnostic Mass—a ritual celebration that took into account scientific discoveries since 1913—we might add discoveries in the field of cosmology of certain facts that we know are indispensable to life. For example astronomer Martin Rees has argued that

> six numbers underlie the fundamental physical properties of the universe, and [...] each is the precise value needed to permit life to flourish [...] Why are we here? As Rees puts it, "These six numbers constitute a recipe for the universe." He adds that if any one of the numbers were different "even to the tiniest degree, there would be no stars, no complex elements, no life."[6]

In addition to celebrating sexual reproduction, we might add into our modern religious celebration acknowledgement of basic facts of chemistry that make DNA replication or the Krebs cycle possible.

But is this what we're really looking for in a religious celebration? By restricting the object of adoration to those conditions which make human activity and rest possible, Crowley has satisfied the requirement that the presuppositions of his ritual remain committed to a rational account of phenomena. No disputable metaphysical beliefs have been introduced. This satisfies

---

5  New Comment on AL III.48-49
6  Brad Lemley, "Why is There Life?" from November 2000 issue of *Discover* magazine

the instinct of reason, but does it satisfy the *religious* instinct?

The instinct of reason is to search for rational explanations of phenomena. The reason it rains is because water vapor in the air condenses. The reason there is water vapor in the air is that it evaporated from the sea. It evaporated from the sea, because photons from the sun impacted the water and transferred heat to it. The reason the sun emitted photons is because of the fusion of protons in the core of the sun. The reason protons fuse to release photons is because of conditions holding at the origin of the universe. These in turn are explained by the as yet unknown physics of the multiverse. Those conditions are explained either by further physical or perhaps supernatural conditions.

For any "why?" type question you ask, the answer given has to fall into one of three categories. (1) It has to be a brute assertion of fact that itself lacks justification, (2) it has to be a reason which itself is in need of further justification, or (3) it is an answer that assumes what it hopes to ground. So if everything was set in motion by God snapping his fingers for no other reason than because He felt like it, that is a brute assertion of fact without justification, in which case existence is senseless. If He snapped His fingers for some antecedent reason, then we can ask after the reason for that reason and so on and so forth. We end up with an infinite regress. If He snapped His fingers because He snapped His fingers, then we are reasoning in a circle.

For this reason Crowley says that the image we form of the universe by means of reason—what he calls the *Ruach*—is ultimately painful and unsatisfying. But that is one use of reason: its theoretical use. There is also a practical use of reason.

Practical reason is at play in the symbolism of the Gnostic Mass. The Gnostic Mass does not portray the universe through the lens of "why?" questions. It portrays nature as a system of conditions that enable labor and enjoyment. We don't know why anything rather than nothing exists. All we know is that nature exists, and it supports our willed activities. That alone justifies the worship of nature as a higher power.

It is common today for many Thelemites to understand Thelema by means of this kind of pragmatic, means-ends framing. According to this view, there is no univocal meaning to life. Each person has their own end, and that end is ineluctably subjective, individual, and private. We cannot say what is ultimately good in life. All we can say is whether certain means successfully attain certain ends. Morality and ultimately spirituality are reduced to technical problems.

The problem with this framing is that it is an interpretation of Thelema purely from the perspective of practical reasoning. It may not be the perspective of the universe through theoretical reasoning, but it is still a view of the world framed exclusively in terms of our powers of direct and indirect control, which is still a component of the Ruach. This is not bound to satisfy the religious instinct, either, because religious or mystical experiences are ones in which we lose control. These are not experiences in which all that exists is relativized to the intellect or the personal will. They are experiences in which the opposite occurs. We are decentered. Our normal conceptions of self and world are radically disrupted. This is accompanied by awe, wonder, and sometimes even terror. These are not experiences in which we assimilate the world to our needs. Rather the opposite occurs. We attain an insight which demands we accommodate ourselves to it.

We have the closely related problem of trying to make sense of Crowley's claim that a religious ceremony in general, and the Gnostic Mass in particular, ought to "consummate the union of ⟦our⟧ individual souls with the universal soul" and enable us to "enter into ecstasy". In order to have a rational understanding of something, I must stand apart from it and from myself. I have to stand apart from it to observe and measure it, and I have to stand apart from myself to ensure my biases don't get in the way of my reasoning. We are similarly detached and calculating when we take a pragmatic stance toward nature as a mere means of fulfilling our individual ends. And yet the religious instinct is not for detachment but for deep mutual participation and involvement in nature.

Religion must represent and celebrate the truth of nature external to the individual. Part of that requires us to represent nature in a way which avoids superstition. In this case *truth* can be understood as a property of our thoughts or statements about the world. The quality of *being true* is then to be understood as the opposite of *being false*. We can tell if a proposition about the world is false by comparing it with the actual state of affairs in the world. But Crowley observed a problem with this notion of truth in the aptly named *Little Essays Toward Truth*.

What is Truth? It is absurd to attempt to define it, for when we say that S is P, rather than S is Q or S is R, we assume that we already know the meaning of Truth. This is really why all the discussions as to whether Truth depends on external correspondence, internal coherence, or what not, neither produce conviction, nor withstand analysis.[7]

What Crowley describes as definitions of the type S is P is what we are calling *propositions*. Propositional knowing is the ability to make statements of fact or to make valid inferences from those facts to other conclusions. For example we may infer from what we hear outside that it is raining. Our statement that it is raining is true if it is in fact raining.

Crowley's point here is that what makes a statement like "It is raining" true is not self-evident. Let's assume truth is the correspondence of some proposition P with some state of affairs in the world S. But such an assumption is itself a proposition. We can put it in quotes—"truth is the correspondence of some proposition P with some state of affairs in the world S"—and now it is a proposition. What is the state of affairs in the world that it has to correspond to? It has to correspond to what truth really is. We've gone in a circle. That's what Crowley calls the correspondence theory of truth.

The internal coherence theory says that truth has nothing to do with states of affairs. Rather truth is the proper logical relations between propositions. One could raise multiple problems with this. For example it applies well enough to a statement such as "John is a bachelor and is unmarried," where the truth of the statement depends exclusively on the definitions of the terms. But what about a statement about the age of the earth or even whether it is really raining outside? Such a conception of truth does not seem able to account for how we ever *learn* anything. How are our minds ever challenged on this view to accommodate something outside of them?

This is why Crowley says that our attempts to understand truth at the level of propositions do not produce conviction or withstand analysis. He doesn't mean there is no such thing as truth; nor does he mean that it makes no difference what we say or think about things. As Crowley says in the New Comment on AL II.28:

> We must not suppose for an instant that *The Book of the Law* is opposed to reason. [...] It makes reason the autocrat of the mind. [...The mind] should be a perfect machine, an apparatus for representing the universe accurately and impartially to its master.[8]

Statements can be true or false. Truth and falsity are properties belonging to

----

7   *Little Essays Toward Truth*, "Truth"
8   New Comment on AL II.28

them. But truth does not *originate* with them. The source of truth is something non-propositional. The source of truth is in what he calls *Neschamah*.

> Briefly, Truth is an idea of a supra-rational order, pertaining to Neschamah, not to Ruach. That all rational conceptions imply that we know Truth, and that Truth is in their propositions, only shows that these so-called rational ideas are not really rational at all.[9]

The terms *Neschamah* and *Ruach* are terms from Hebrew Kabbalah. They refer to parts of the soul. What Crowley calls *Ruach* is what we are calling propositional knowing. He contrasts Ruach with *Neschamah*, which he equates with the *Self* of the individual.

> Now the same Truth, which is Light, which is implicit in each spark of the Intelligible; what is it but the Self of Everyman? It is this that informs his every motion, this that lies closest to his heart and soul, being indeed their mainspring and their dial, the principle of section and of measure.[10]

By *Self* Crowley does not mean the personality of the individual. Personality, memory, desire, and power of choice all belong to what Crowley calls the *Ruach*. By contrast the *Self* or the *Neschamah* is the true self of the individual that transcends what we normally take to be ourselves. It is addressed in the Gnostic Mass's Anthem as "Thou who art I beyond all I am, who hast no nature and no name". It is only encountered through the process Crowley calls *initiation*.

> Now Initiation is, by etymology, the journeying inwards; it is the Voyage of Discovery (oh Wonder-World!) of one's own Soul. And this is Truth that stands upon the prow, eternally alert; this is Truth that sits with one strong hand gripping the helm!

> Truth is our Path, and Truth is our Goal; ay! there shall came to all a moment of great Light when the Path is seen to be itself the Goal; and in that hour every one of us shall exclaim:

---

9 *Little Essays Toward Truth*, "Truth"
10 Ibid.

"I am the Way, the Truth, and the Life!"[11]

Thus the truth of external nature—propositional truth about external states of affairs which we may contrast with superstition or falsehood—finds its basis in *inner truth*. The claim is not that external truth is relative to our feelings or wants. If you walk off a cliff, you will immediately fall and probably die, regardless if you look down. Thelema isn't Looney Tunes. You're not Wile-E-Coyote.

The claim is that our ability to make true and false statements about the world rests upon a condition external to reason. Therefore we cannot introspect upon it, and we cannot control or manipulate it, since all acts of introspection or manipulation assume it.

Crowley calls this condition *Self*, *Soul*, or *Neschamah*. In the New Comment on AL II.9, he refers to it as the *Silent Self* and the *Sun of the Soul*, the internal counterpart of the Sun in the cosmos.

> He will choose the object of his passion at the nod of his Silent Self. He will not allow the prejudice, either of sense, emotion, or rational judgement, to obscure the Sun of his Soul.[12]

Our inquiry into the essence of religious truth generally and of the Gnostic Mass in particular has led us to one of the foundational ideas of Thelema, the idea that every man and every woman is a *star*.

## Internal Truth: The Sun of the Soul

Crowley explains the concept of the star and its relationship to the Thelemic view of the universe in his 1938 "Introduction" to *The Book of the Law*.

> This Book explains the Universe.

> The elements are Nuit—Space—that is, the total of possibilities of every kind—and Hadit, any point which has experience of these possibilities. (This idea is for literary convenience symbolized by the Egyptian Goddess Nuit, a woman bending over like the Arch of the Night Sky. Hadit is symbolized as a Winged Globe at the heart of Nuit.)

---

11 Ibid.
12 New Comment on AL II.9

Every event is a uniting of some one monad with one of the experiences possible to it.

"Every man and every woman is a star," that is, an aggregate of such experiences, constantly changing with each fresh event, which affects him or her either consciously or subconsciously.[13]

The world described by *The Book of the Law* is composed of two elements. There is space and the matter occupying it—what we have been calling external nature or what Crowley refers to as the sum total of all possibilities—and any "point" that has experience of nature by realizing one of the possibilities in it. These two principles are symbolized in the book by two deities that appear on the funerary stele of Ankh-f-n-khonsu, a priest of the Egyptian god Mentu who lived in Thebes around 725 BCE. The first is symbolized by the Egyptian sky goddess, *Nuit*, and the second by the winged solar disk, *Hadit*.

The star is defined as the union of Nuit and Hadit.

Hadit is the 'core of every star,' [...] He is thus the Impersonal Identity within the Individuality of 'every man and every woman.' [...] Hadit seems to be the principle of Motion which is everywhere, yet is not extended in any dimension except as it chances to combine with the "Matter" which is Nuit. There can evidently be no manifestation apart from this conjunction. A *Khabs* or Star is apparently any nucleus where this conjunction has taken place.[14]

Furthermore Hadit represents the immortal essence of each individual and is distinct from the personality or who we normally take ourselves to be.

It follows that, as Hadit can never be known, there is no death. The death of the individual is his awakening to the impersonal immortality of Hadit. This applies less to physical death than to the Crossing of the Abyss; [...] One may attain to be aware that one is but a particular 'child' of the Play of Hadit and Nuit; one's personality is then perceived as being a disguise.[15]

---

13  "Introduction" to *The Book of the Law*
14  New Comment on AL II.2
15  New Comment on AL II.6

Again we see the idea that the core or the essence of the self transcends the personality. Here we are also introduced to the idea of the personality being an outward display or disguise—essentially a tool of expression—of Hadit which is otherwise distinct from everything we take ourselves to be. Again we come to know all of this by means of initiation, what Crowley is here referring to as Crossing the Abyss.

Every event—that is, every change from one state to the next—is the result of Hadit uniting with Nuit. As Crowley puts it in the New Comment on AL I.1:

> The theogony of our Law is entirely scientific, Nuit is Matter, Hadit is Motion, in their full physical sense.[16]

This is a continual, ongoing process. A star is the course taken by a particular Hadit on His path through Nuit. The aggregate or sum-total of all these experiences—across innumerable incarnations—makes up the essence of an individual.

Crowley's term for the unification of Hadit with Nuit that occurs moment-to-moment is *love*.

> In order to have Motion one must have Change. In fact, one must have this in order to have anything at all. Now this Change is what we call Love, thus "love under will" is the Law of Motion.[17]

> We may say briefly that Hadit is Motion, that is, Change or 'Love.' The symbol of Godhead in Egypt was the Ankh, which is a sandal-strap, implying the Power to Go; and it suggests the Rosy Cross, the Fulfilment of Love, by its shape. [18]

The ground of propositional truth was found to be inner truth. Inner truth is itself grounded in the essence of the individual, which is the Soul, the Self, the Neschamah, or the star. But the star is nothing other than the continual, ongoing coition between Hadit, the impersonal drive of the individual to become, and nature or Nuit. Therefore the ground and essence of truth is *love*.

---

16 New Comment on AL I.1
17 New Comment on AL I.19
18 New Comment on II.7

## Truth as Love

There is an ongoing, continual, dynamic coupling taking place all the time between the impersonal depths of ourselves and nature or the environment we find ourselves to be in. We are constantly being pushed out beyond ourselves into the world. Even when we are as still as we can be, one moment passes to the next and to the next—the sign of the constant coitus between Hadit within us and Nuit without.

Hadit is the impersonal core of the individual. His union with Nuit is taking place below the level of conscious awareness. We cannot introspect upon this process, because every act of introspection is also being driven or pushed by this process. As Crowley says in the New Comment on AL II.4:

> Hadit is hidden in Nuit, and knows Her, She being an object of knowledge; but He is not knowable, for He is merely that part of Her which She formulates in order that She may be known.[19]

Anything known is Nuit, not Hadit. This applies to knowledge of mental events with the same force it applies to knowledge of external physical events. Any experience whatsoever—be it of nature or of mental events—is the end result of the union of Hadit with Nuit.

The world of objects, people, events, morals, political and social customs, etc., that we find ourselves in is the result of the ongoing dynamic coupling of the unknowable interior of ourselves with nature. Because that world is there for us, we can develop a theoretical understanding of it. We can make true and false claims about it. We can also learn how to cope with it. We can learn practical skills like reading, writing, talking, bike riding, flute playing, meditating, etc. But because theoretical and practical reasoning assume the existence of a changing world resulting from the union of Hadit and Nuit, we can never come to either a theoretical understanding or develop practical control over that preconscious process of coupling. We are always going to be one step behind it, only ever in a position to appreciate the downstream effects of it. As Crowley says:

> Truth is an idea of a supra-rational order, pertaining to Neschamah, not to Ruach.[20]

---

19 New Comment on AL II.4
20 *Little Essays Toward Truth*, "Truth"

The deepest part of yourself—Thou who art I beyond all I am, who hast no nature and no name—strives to have contact with the deepest part of reality. We can infer this truth from many experiences in life such as being in the zone, skill-acquisition, experiences of natural beauty, creation of art, and most especialy falling in love.

If the essence of truth is love, and if religion must represent and celebrate truth, doesn't it make sense that a proper religious celebration should portray a *love story?*

The Gnostic Mass depicts the relationship between an individual and what is most real as a love relationship. It is a story of mutual, accelerating opening and disclosure.

The Priestess pulls down the veil over the tomb. She reveals the Priest to the congregation and the temple, an act which simultaneously dramatically expands the Priest's own world. His contact with her is not a detached, purely theoretical or purely practical affair. He does not come away from the encounter with a few more facts about the world or a few more skills to add to his resume. He is a changed man. The encounter transforms him from a mere "man among men" into an Adept.

Shortly thereafter he does the same for her. Parting the veil, he discloses her, this time in a more exalted, more vulnerable manner. At the climax of the ritual, he opens himself so radically to her that he symbolically turns himself inside-out. The fullest experience of truth is one of total participation, surrender, and reciprocal disclosure with what is real, so that nothing is held back. This is the total loss of the knower in the known. The experience transforms him into a God.

The Gnostic Mass represents truth as a drama in which one falls in love with what is real. The congregants observe this, but they themselves are also participating in it insofar as they are saying or singing their parts and taking communion at the end of the ritual. Eating is a primal and direct form of participation.

When the ritual is over, they go back to their lives, and if they understand what the ritual was trying to represent, they may begin to notice the ways in which their own relationship with reality takes the form of mutual disclosure. They may notice the subtle ways in which their self shifts and changes shape to fit reality, and the ways in which reality responds by opening up and showing its secrets.

Next week, when they attend the ritual again, they may notice more subtle details in the drama. They may pick up on nuances of the symbolism and dialogue they had not noticed before. They now see deeper into the ritual.

As a result, when they go back out into the world, they take those insights with them. They notice even more subtle ways in which the sense of self changes in relation to how reality discloses itself. The insight they acquired into the ritual carries over and enhances their insight into and participation with reality. When they return to see the ritual again, their insight into the ritual and hence their sense of self once again opens on to new depths.

This is how the Gnostic Mass succeeds in consummating the union of our individual souls with the universal soul. It can lead to a series of cascading insights, an upward spiral the culmination of which can be religious ecstasy.

Not all religious insights occur during meditation or in the middle of spiritual practices. They can occur at quite ordinary times. My own religious experience happened when I was standing in my kitchen, opening a beer. You never know when the light of Neschamah will shine on you. You never know when the voice of the Silent Self will speak to you. We don't have control over these sorts of events; we can only make them more likely to happen.

To say that the Gnostic Mass represents and celebrates truth is not to say that it gives us all the correct ideas about the world. It's not a newspaper article or a study on the effects of trans fats. It is not even to say that it represents a fully accurate account of what we know about nature. It would be impossible for a ritual written in 2000 to do that, let alone one written in 1913. That is not the value of the Gnostic Mass, and that is not the most important truth embodied in it.

Nor does the value of the Gnostic Mass consist in some supernatural effect attendant upon saying all the words and doing all the actions in the correct order, exactly as written, according to custom in 1913, now, or any other time. The Gnostic Mass is not a tool to achieve an end, whether that end be to attract members, to fulfill our lodge's quota, or to achieve our individual heart's desire. Its value cannot be reduced to a simple technique.

To say that the Gnostic Mass represents and celebrates truth means that it is a means of insight into the nature of truth itself. That truth is not a set of facts—natural or supernatural—but rather a dynamic process of reciprocal disclosure between the depths of ourselves and the depths of nature that has the qualities of a love relationship. We see a relationship with what is real portrayed through the ritual's drama, and that affords us the ability to see real patterns in the world outside the ritual. That in turn allows us to see more deeply into the ritual, which affords more insight yet into reality.

We do not have the ability to reflect upon the depths of ourselves. Hadit is not available for reflection. And we have no way to work magically with Hadit, as every act of magick is itself the result of the going of Hadit.

Nor do we have the ability to comprehend the infinite vastness of nature. The world is a "marvel beyond imagination ... before whom time is ashamed, the mind bewildered, and the understanding dark". That being said, we are able to engage with the attunement between the depths of nature and with our own beings indirectly, when we engage with it through the image of love.

## Conclusion

Tonight we considered the purpose of the Gnostic Mass. We saw that it is a religious ceremony—analogous to the Mass of the Roman Catholic Church—the purpose of which is to satisfy the religious instinct. Crowley defined this as consummating the union of the soul of the individual with the universal soul, thereby bringing about ecstasy.

We saw that the purpose of a religious rite in general, and of the Gnostic Mass in particular, must be to represent and celebrate external and internal truth. External truth is symbolized by the Sun, and internal truth is symbolized by the star or the Sun of the Soul. We came to understand these truths by means of analogies.

As the Earth is to the Sun, so are we to nature in general and our species in particular. We are part of a larger, interconnected web of life, without which we would be unable to accomplish our wills. This is because we are dependent upon our physical bodies, which are represented in the Gnostic Mass as the two-in-one phenomenon of labor and enjoyment. Labor and enjoyment become one in us in the act of procreation, through which we can participate in a kind of immortality. The continuity of the species is like a reflection on the earth of the immortality of the Sun in the heavens.

Truths of external nature are represented in the Gnostic Mass as something to be grateful for, to be celebrated. They are also represented in the ritual in order to serve as a check against superstition and absurdity. This accords with Crowley's desire to stick as closely as possible to a rational conception of phenomena.

But there's a third function of the representation of truths of external nature. Truths of external nature can lead us by analogy to truths of internal nature. As the Earth is to the Sun, so are we to our souls. The Sun is the center of the solar system, not the Earth. Likewise the personality is not the center of the individual; the star or soul is. As embodied individuals, we are dependent upon the interconnected web of life to support us in our going. We must serve nature in order to serve ourselves. Likewise our individual personalities and bodies are mere means for our souls to experience the universe, themselves, and other individuals. In both instances we are invited to step into larger contexts and understand ourselves and find meaning in relationship to them.

Just as the union of male and female in the act of procreation allows us to participate in the immortality of the species, so does the union of male and female in us—or the union of opposites more generally—lead the way toward understanding God within each of us. This is because the immortal God within us is the constant, ecstatic union of opposites. So in addition to representing biological reproduction, the Gnostic Mass also represents the internal truth of each individual.

External truth is dependent upon internal truth. The normal, hierarchical way we tend to think about things has to be reversed. We can understand the inner on analogy with the outer, and in fact we have to. We cannot reflect directly on the inner processes that allow perception and reflection to take place; we can only symbolize them, and as we'll see next time, that is the main function of a living religious tradition as opposed to a dead ceremony.

But upon reaching inner truth—by means of initiation—we discover that the inner has primacy, and the outer is merely a reflection. In other words we see our bodies, our sexuality, and nature more generally as the expression of an inner living spirit, the nature of which is love—and annihiliation.

> O Lion and O Serpent that destroy the destroyer, be mighty among us!
> O Lion and O Serpent that destroy the destroyer, be mighty among us!
> O Lion and O Serpent that destroy the destroyer, be mighty among us!

We have just scratched the surface of this ritual. But understanding what the ritual has to accomplish and why is key to understanding the rest of its symbolism. An interpretive framework beginning from the truth of the Gnostic Mass helps orient the rest of our interpretation, and it helps orient ritual celebrants toward the ritual in such a way as to ensure continual and tight contact or fittedness between its inner depth and its external manifestation, thereby vivifying the external letter with the living spirit of truth.

# 10

# The Living and the Dead:
# Truth Embodied in *Liber XV*

## The Khabs and the Khu

To continue and build upon our discussion of truth in the Gnostic Mass, we need to continue and build upon the Thelemic account of the individual. Last time we considered the Khabs of the individual as the source of inner truth and indirectly as the source of outer truth. We saw that the Khabs is the secret "true self" of the individual, the Sun of the Soul around which the other aspects of the personality (including the ego or the sense of self and the freedom of choice) orbit, analogous to the way in which planets orbit around a star. Tonight we're going to talk more about that which is symbolized by the planets in this analogy and the way in which light and life are conducted from the center of ourselves to reach these outer parts.

If the secret center of ourselves is called the Khabs, Crowley's word for the elements of the personality revolving around the Khabs is the *Khu*. This term comes from the eighth and ninth verses of the first chapter of *The Book of the Law* which read:

> The Khabs is in the Khu, not the Khu in the Khabs. Worship then the Khabs, and behold my light shed over you![1]

Crowley defines the Khu as the "magical garment" of the Khabs.

> Khabs is the secret Light or L.V.X.; the Khu is the magical entity of a man.[2]

---

1   AL I.8-9
2   Old Comment on AL I.8

[The Khabs] or 'Inmost Light' is the original, individual, eternal essence. The Khu is the magical garment which it weaves for itself, a 'form' for its Being Beyond Form, by use of which it can gain experience through self-consciousness[3]

[The] Khabs needs a Khu or Magical Image, in order to play its part in the Great Drama. This Khu, again, needs the proper costume, a suitable 'body of flesh', and this costume must be worthy of the Play.[4]

The Khabs on its own is unable to gain experience either of itself or of the universe. In order to do that, it has to create the Khu, the function of which is to enable the Khabs to "gain experience through self-consciousness."

The Khabs itself, we are told, is "beyond form". In other words, it is unmanifest. It doesn't appear or look like anything. As we saw last time, the interior depth of each individual is inaccessible to reflection. But we are told that the Khu is the "form" that the Khabs "weaves for itself". In other words the Khu is the means by which the Khabs manifests itself to itself and to the rest of the world.

As we saw last time, Hadit is the principle of going, change, or love. It is anonymous and impersonal. But we are not anonymous beings, and we do not find ourselves going aimlessly. We find ourselves in a particular situation, having a particular kind of experience. We have come from some origin in the past, and we find ourselves going toward some particular destination in the future.

Crowley adds that "This Khu, again, needs the proper costume, a suitable 'body of flesh'".[5] In order for experience and self-awareness to be possible, we need bodies. This is ultimately why the Khabs incarnates. It needs a mind and a body in order to participate in the "Great Drama" of life. But this decision to incarnate and thereby become dependent upon a mind and a body comes with a price.

## The Human Condition

With the decision to incarnate comes the illusion of duality.

---

3   New Comment on AL I.8
4   New Comment on AL II.70
5   Ibid.

To know itself, each such Star, or Soul, must eat of the Fruit of the Tree of Knowledge of Good and Evil, by accepting labour and pain as its portion, and death as its doom. That is, it must reveal its nature to itself by formulating that nature as duality.[6]

By "duality" Crowley primarily means the difference we make in our minds between subject and object. I am a particular individual consciousness occupying a particular portion of space. From my perspective, part of the universe, over there, is made manifest to my consciousness over here. While we saw that the Khabs in itself is the ecstatic union of Hadit with Nuit, of the unfathomable depths of ourselves with the depths of nature, in fact the depths of ourselves are not in immediate contact with external nature. The mind and the body—the Ruach and the Nephesh—*mediate* or *come between* the divine depths of ourselves and the divine depths of nature. The mind and the body make nature manifest and available to our divine depths; however, in doing so, they create the illusion of separation between the interior of ourselves and the depths of nature. There is the appearance of a separation between myself and my mind and the world it perceives and acts upon. Crowley identifies this fact of human experience as the source of our suffering. Writing in *Liber CL*, he says:

> Understand now that in yourselves is a certain discontent. Analyse well its nature: at the end is in every case one conclusion. The ill springs from the belief in two things, the Self and the Not-Self, and the conflict between them. This also is a restriction of the Will. He who is sick is in conflict with his own body: he who is poor is at odds with society: and so for the rest. Ultimately, therefore, the problem is how to destroy this perception of duality, to attain to the apprehension of unity.[7]

In order to have experience of itself and the universe, the Khabs must "weave" for itself the Khu. It must manifest itself and the universe by means of a mind and a body. But the mind and the body can only represent the universe by means of the artifice of duality: a sense of the separation of subject and object. Yet by introducing a distinction between subject and object, the world becomes a painful place. The star experiences something akin to a fall from grace, as indicated by the metaphor of consuming the fruit of the Tree

---

6   New Comment on AL I.29
7   *Liber CL: De Lege Libellum*

of Knowledge of Good and Evil. The result is that the individual is typically

> ...bewildered by the irrational character of the universe, which he takes to be real; and he cannot but regard it as aimless and absurd. The adventures of his body and mind, with their desires for material and moral well-being, are obviously as foredoomed to disaster as Don Quixote's. He must be a fool if he struggles on (against inexorable fate) to obtain results which he knows can only end in catastrophe, a climax the more bitter as he clings the more closely to his impossible ideals.[8]

The human being in their natural state is therefore

> ...a perishable parasite, bred of the earth's crust, crawling irritably upon it for a span, and at last returning to the dirt whence he sprang.[9]

Crowley's term for this near-hopeless state of most people is the *Man of Earth*, a term that comes from AL I.40:

> Who calls us Thelemites will do no wrong, if he look but close into the word. For there are therein Three Grades, the Hermit, and the Lover, and the man of Earth. Do what thou wilt shall be the whole of the Law.[10]

Crowley symbolizes the Man of Earth by "the Inverted Pentagram, matter dominating spirit. The Hanged Man and the Fool, the condition of those who are not adepts."[11]

*Spirit* in this case symbolizes the star, the true essence of the individual. It is "dominated" by matter, meaning, the individual has confused themselves with thoughts and matter as revealed by the mind and the body. Until such a person has remedied this confusion—by becoming the upright pentagram in which spirit rules over matter—they must remain "bewildered by the irrational character of the universe".[12]

The human condition—at least in its default, uninitiated state—is an unhappy one. Several lines in our Holy Books reflect this state of affairs. For example, AL II.17-18 read:

---

8   New Comment on AL I.29
9   *Magick in Theory and Practice*, ch 20
10  AL I.40
11  Appendix 21 to the New Comment
12  New Comment on AL I.29

> Hear me, ye people of sighing! The sorrows of pain and regret Are left to the dead and the dying, The folk that not know me as yet. These are dead, these fellows; they feel not. We are not for the poor and sad: the lords of the earth are our kinsfolk.[13]

Commenting on these verses, Crowley says:

> But 'the poor and the outcast' are the petty thoughts and the Qliphotic thoughts and the sad thoughts. These must be rooted out, or the ecstasy of Hadit is not in us. They are the weeds in the Garden that starve the Flower.[14]

By *Qliphotic* Crowley does not mean *demonic*, as many occultists understand the term. What he means is *disordered*. As *Liber XXX: The Book of the Balance* reads:

> Know then, that as man is born into this world amidst the Darkness of Matter, and the strife of contending forces; so must his first endeavour be to seek the Light through their reconciliation.[15]

Because we have not found the true center of ourselves, the inner truth represented by the Khabs, we take external truth to be the only kind of truth there is. As Crowley says:

> [To fall in love with the Khu] is to forget our Truth. If we adore Form, it becomes opaque to Being, and may soon prove false to itself.[16]

We become subject to the capriciousness of our thoughts and feelings about unstable and unreliable external states of affairs. *The Book of the Law* likens these individuals to the dead and the dying. Crowley goes on to say:

> The dead and the dying, who know not Hadit, are in the Illusion of Sorrow. Not being Hadit, they are shadows, puppets, and what happens to them does not matter. [17]

---

13 AL II.17-18
14 Old Comment on AL II.17
15 *Liber XXX*, 1
16 New Comment on AL I.9
17 New Comment on AL II.17

Those who sorrow are not real people at all, not 'stars'—for the time being.[18]

The default condition of most people, Crowley says, is a kind of living death. We have not realized our true natures. It has not yet been fully incarnated in us. The deepest part of ourselves desires to have contact with the deepest part of nature, and yet it remains frustrated by the confusion inherent in the very instrument it has contrived to make that very nature manifest. In attempting to bring Nuit closer to Him, Hadit has seemingly only pushed Her further away.

We fear biological death, but what we should really fear is that we will never have actually lived. We will never really have been born. This state of being alive in one sense but dead in another is described in *Liber VII* as a "grey land":

Farther and farther we float; yet we are still. It is the chain of systems that is falling away from us. First falls the silly world; the world of the old grey land. Falls it unthinkably far, with its sorrowful bearded face presiding over it; it fades to silence and woe.[19]

Far from being a place of evil, the Qliphoth is a "grey" place. It is neither white nor black, neither fully alive nor fully dead, neither this, nor that, nor anything really. It is a poorly defined middle place, a "silly" place of sorrows.

## Liberation

So what does it mean to liberate ourselves from the condition of the Man of Earth, to extract ourselves from the "old grey land" of the Qliphoth? There are many different ways Crowley symbolically represents the path of liberation. Let's stick with the symbolism we've been working with so far, that of the Khabs and the Khu or the unknown soul of the individual and its magical garment. If suffering arises because the attempt of Hadit within to unite with Nuit without is frustrated, then the overcoming of that frustration and the reunion of Hadit with Nuit will bring at least a temporary end to that suffering. Crowley says of the liberated individual that:

he has freed Hadit, in the core of his Star, from the illusion-veils of the

---

18　New Comment on AL II.18
19　*Liber VII*, V:36-38

Khu, so that the two Infinities become one, and none...[20]

But since the Khu is necessary for the Khabs to have any experience at all, this liberation cannot consist in getting rid of the Khu altogether. Instead, it must consist in a modification of the Khu.

> Our minds and bodies are veils of the Light within. The uninitiate is a "Dark Star", and the Great Work for him is to make his veils transparent by 'purifying' them. This 'purification' is really 'simplification'; it is not that the veil is dirty, but that the complexity of its folds makes it opaque. The Great Work therefore consists principally in the solution of complexes. Everything in itself is perfect, but when things are muddled, they become 'evil'.[21]

The Khabs is a light shining within us which is metaphorically obscured by "folds" in the "magical garment". We're confused about the nature of what we're perceiving. We're falling in love with form, with manifestation, taking that to be the ultimate reality. We become identified with our thoughts and our feelings about things. This perpetuates the sense of division between us and what we're looking for in life. The solution to this is to transform the Khu so that it does its job properly, which is to conduct the "light" within us outward into manifest existence, so as to alleviate the sense of separation from reality.

Crowley contrasts this idea with that of the Gnostic idea of the pleroma.

> Why are we told that the Khabs is in the Khu, not the Khu in the Khabs? Did we then suppose the converse? I think that we are warned against the idea of a Pleroma, a flame of which we are Sparks, and to which we return when we 'attain'. That would indeed be to make the whole curse of separate existence ridiculous, a senseless and inexcusable folly. It would throw us back on the dilemma of Manichaeism. The idea of incarnations "perfecting" a thing originally perfect by definition is imbecile. The only sane solution is as given previously, to suppose that the Perfect enjoys experience of (apparent) Imperfection.[22]

---

20 New Comment on AL I.14
21 New Comment on AL I.8
22 Ibid.

*Pleroma* is a Greek word (πλήρωμα) which literally means *fullness*. It is a technical term in the texts of Gnostic Christianity where it refers to the totality of divine powers. Crowley tended to think of it as an "impersonal unity" analogous to Brahma or Ain Soph. For instance, in his 1902 essay, "Berashith," he remarks:

> [In the Advaist idea], personality, bereft of all its qualities, disappears and is lost, while in its place arises the impersonal Unity, The Pleroma, Parabrahma, or the Allah of the Unity-adoring followers of Mohammed.[23]

Crowley tended to view the pleroma as an impersonal unity in which individuality is lost.

According to Gnostic cosmogony, the world we find ourselves in is outside of the pleroma; however, each individual carries a bit of the pleroma within themselves. If you find this pleroma within yourself, you can save yourself from a state of "deficiency" characteristic of the material world and restore yourself to an otherwise inaccessible sense of divine "fullness". An example of this doctrine may be found in the 2nd century Valentinian Gnostic writing, *The Gospel of Truth*:

> Thus fullness [pleroma], which has no deficiency but fills up deficiency, is provided to fill a person's need, so that the person may receive grace. While deficient, the person had no grace, and because of this a diminishing took place where there was no grace. When the diminished part was restored, the person in need was revealed as fullness.[24]

Gnosticism entails that the material world is in and of itself deficient. Its creation was an unfortunate tragedy. And by virtue of being embodied souls, we ourselves have fallen into a state of deficiency. To be born is a tragedy. This state of deficiency can only be overcome by withdrawing from embodiment and returning to a more original, undifferentiated identification with the pleroma, which functions like a divine over-being.

Thelema bears a superficial resemblance to this. We're in something like a fallen state which can only be corrected by overcoming our sense of separateness. And *Liber XV* is called *The Gnostic Mass*. That may lead one to

---

23 "Berashith: An Essay in Ontology"
24 "The Gospel of Truth" in *The Nag Hammadi Scriptures*. Edited by Marvin Meyer. (San Francisco: HarperOne, 2009).

believe that the Mass dramatizes Valentinian Gnostic doctrine of the type I just quoted. But there are key differences.

First of all, while incarnation does give rise to suffering, it does not give rise to it directly but only indirectly. According to *The Book of the Law*, incarnation entails suffering or "hurt", not because matter is evil, not because the universe was created outside the Pleroma, and not because the universe or we are in some way deficient in divinity. On the contrary, we are told in *The Book of the Law* that space and the matter filling it are a goddess and that existence itself is pure joy.

Second, this implies that the source of suffering is not to be found in the deficiency or evil of matter or anything else that exists. Rather, the source of the suffering is to be found in us. Suffering arises from the dualistic mode of *representing* the universe.

Third, this has implications for what liberation consists in. If you think that matter is evil or even just deficient in divinity—because of its distance from the One, because it was created by a delusional Demiurge, or just because of its impermanence and instability—then incarnation can only be viewed as a loss. The soul taking a body can only be viewed as a tragedy, the natural remedy of which would be the abandonment of this world. That might mean transcending the planetary spheres as in Gnosticism or Hermetism. It might mean extinction as in the version of Buddhism Crowley would have been familiar with. But the only viable paths would be ascetic, renunciate paths.

We would also expect such a path to either be suspicious of magic or be hostile to it. In Gnostic cosmogony in particular, angels tend to function as agents of the Demiurge. Any angel or spirit you contact by means of magic would be just as likely to attempt to delude you and keep you imprisoned in this world. For this reason, Gnosticism tends to be a path of mysticism rather than magic.

But Thelema differs from Gnosticism in all these respects. It's a non-renunciate path. The goal is not to escape existence but rather to realize and incarnate the pure joy of existence—right here in this universe, in this life. This is accomplished by means of meditative techniques, but it is also accomplished through ritualistically working with the divine energies of manifest existence. In other words it includes both yoga and magic. This is not a superficial difference. The reasons for these differences are deep and are entailed by what *The Book of the Law* says the universe is and what the human being is.

Liberation in Thelema does not consist in escaping manifest existence. The solution is not to dissolve ourselves in some kind of over-mind. The solution to suffering is to be found in and through existence. And yet it is the very duality of manifest existence that gives rise to suffering. So now we appear to be in a double-bind. The Thelemic solution to suffering is to overcome duality, and yet duality is unavoidable.

We could frame the problem another way and say that *relationality*—the quality of being in relation to some reality outside my control—is an unavoidable fact of life. No matter how much control I exert over myself or my environment, I can still be impinged upon in ways that are potentially upsetting or even destructive to me. My vulnerability is an essential facet of my existence. My being is *porous* all the way down. This follows from the fact that there is no way for the Khabs to know itself or the universe without opening itself to that universe. So then the question becomes: *How do we relate to vulnerability and openness in such a way that we become free?*

This is the opposite of vulgar Thelema. Vulgar Thelema says that you assert your autonomous individuality over and against the universe and everyone around you. You use magic and an unhealthy dose of fantasy to become super-autonomous and self-possessed. As we'll see in a moment, Crowley calls this a masturbatory fantasy.

The actual path of Thelemic liberation—which is *a path of erotic liberation*—is working with duality until it expresses individuality. In other words, the living symbol of individuality is going to be *dividual*. As Crowley says:

> The Great Work is the uniting of opposites. It may mean the uniting of the soul with God, of the microcosm with the macrocosm, of the female with the male, of the ego with the non-ego—or what not.[25]

This is why so many of the symbols of the liberated individual or what Crowley refers to as the God-Man are 2-in-1 or at least express the unity of opposites: Beast and Babalon conjoined, Baphomet, the Adept and the Holy Guardian Angel, the Sphinx—and of course in the Gnostic Mass, lance and grail, Priest and Priestess, male and female united in the symbol of the Sun. These are all ways of manifesting unmanifest inner truth, of presenting in dualistic form that which transcends duality.

Let's now take a look at how Crowley symbolizes the process of working with the divine energies of manifestation to embody truth.

---

25 *Magick Without Tears*, Letter C

## Symbols of the Way to Liberation

Crowley taught different magical and mystical techniques for ritualistically working with these energies of the Khu. These are the tasks of the grades of the outer order of his magical order, A∴A∴. Crowley utilizes more than one metaphor to describe that process of transformation whereby the Khu becomes transparent to the light of the Khabs. In fact the language of Khabs and Khu is itself a symbol set which he utilizes to represent processes which are in fact invisible matters of internal truth.

In a moment, I'm going to present you with an interpretation of the first part of the Gnostic Mass, the section called The Ceremony of the Introit. But before doing so, I want to introduce you to two additional symbol sets. They are ways of symbolizing the process of disciplining the Khu we have seen so far, but they utilize symbols which help tie these principles closer to the drama of *Liber XV*. The first is referred to as the *sacrament of penance*. The second is one we've considered already, the *phallus*.

### The Sacrament of Penance

Crowley describes the sacrament of penance in chapter 4 of part 2 of *Magick*. The sacrament of penance is the work of the scourge, the dagger, and the chain. These "represent the three alchemical principles of Sulphur, Mercury, and Salt."

> Sulphur represents the energy of things, Mercury their fluidity, Salt their fixity. They are analogous to Fire, Air and Water [...] An almost exact analogy is given by the three Gunas of the Hindus; Sattvas, Rajas, and Tamas. Sattvas is Mercury, equable, calm, clear; Rajas is Sulphur, active, excitable, even fierce; Tamas is Salt, thick, sluggish, heavy, dark

> [...]

> The Scourge is Sulphur: its application excites our sluggish natures; and it may further be used as an instrument of correction, to castigate rebellious volitions. It is applied to the Nephesh, the Animal Soul, the natural desires.

> The Dagger is Mercury: it is used to calm too great heat, by the letting of blood; and it is this weapon which is plunged into the side or heart of the

Magician to fill the Holy Cup. Those faculties which come between the appetites and the reason are thus dealt with.

The Chain is Salt: it serves to bind the wandering thoughts; and for this reason is placed about the neck of the Magician, where Daath is situated.

〚...〛

The Scourge keeps the aspiration keen: the Dagger expresses the determination to sacrifice all; and the Chain restricts any wandering.[26]

The sacrament of penance is carried out as preparation for a magical working. Striking oneself with the scourge fights off torpor and stimulates aspiration. It excites that fervor and ardency necessary to pursue our spiritual ends. Cutting oneself with the dagger represents severing the connection between the appetite and reason, between the lower parts of the self and the will to unite with the divine. It represents the act of discrimination. And finally the chain binds wandering thoughts. It fixes the mind to the object of the magical working.

In the context of meditation, close analogies would be the mental qualities of ardor, alertness, and mindfulness. When these three qualities cooperate and mutually support one another, concentration naturally arises. Concentration or union between the mind and its object is not something we simply will. It is the natural outcome of the energies of the mind balancing and supporting one another. This quality is represented in *Magick* by the Holy Oil, which is described in the next chapter.

The Holy Oil is the Aspiration of the Magician; it is that which consecrates him to the performance of the Great Work 〚...〛 this aspiration is not ambition; it is a quality bestowed from above 〚...〛 It is not the Will of the Magician, the desire of the lower to reach the higher; but it is that spark of the higher in the Magician which wishes to unite the lower with itself.[27]

Once the energies of the mind and body are properly balanced and directed toward the proper end, the "spark of the higher in the Magician"—what we have been calling the Khabs—unites itself with the lower parts of the soul.

---

26 *Magick*, part 2, chapter 4
27 Ibid, chapter 5

We do not *will* contact with the Khabs; instead we turn ourselves into the medium through which that light can flow. This is consonant with the idea that the Khu is a veil, the folds of which must be resolved to allow the light to penetrate.

## The Phallus

Crowley represents a similar dynamic between lower and higher parts of the self in chapter 15 of *The Book of Lies*, this time utilizing the symbols of the pyramid and the phallus.

### THE GUN-BARREL

> Mighty and erect is this Will of mine, this Pyramid
> of fire whose summit is lost in Heaven. Upon it
> have I burned the corpse of my desires.
> Mighty and erect is this φαλλός
> > of my Will.  The
> seed thereof is That which I have borne within me
> from Eternity; and it is lost within the Body of
> Our Lady of the Stars.
> I am not I; I am but an hollow tube to bring down
> Fire from Heaven.
> Mighty and marvellous is this Weakness, this
> Heaven which draweth me into Her Womb, this
> Dome which hideth, which absorbeth, Me.
> This is The Night wherein I am lost, the Love
> through which I am no longer I.[28]

The chapter—which has the same number as *Liber XV*—opens by introducing two symbols—the pyramid and the phallus—both of which are equated with the personal will. Both of these words in Greek—*puramis* and *phallos*—add up to 831 by isopsephy. Both are described as being mighty and erect. Upon the pyramid in particular, the corpse of my desires has been burned.

The phallus in particular is described as bearing within it a seed. It is described as having been carried within me from eternity. This is reminiscent of

---

28 *The Book of Lies*, ch 15

the symbolism of the Sun of the Soul or the Khabs, the secret seed or core of which is Hadit. It should also bring to mind the final stanza of our church's creed: "I confess my life one, individual, and eternal that was, and is, and is to come."

But now a shift in the symbolism occurs. "I am not I". The letter "I" here has a dual significance. On the one hand, it is the personal pronoun. It refers to the subject of experience, both in the sense of the person who accomplishes mundane tasks such as going to the grocery store or going to work, but also in the sense of the person who accomplishes far more exalted tasks such as erecting the pyramid or attempting to accomplish the Great Work.

At the beginning of this chapter, both the erect pyramid and the erect phallus are described as *mine* and as expressive of *my* will. They *belong* to me. I take credit for them. I *own* them. They are the result of *my* self-discipline. But now a shift takes place, and this sense of ownership over the work is effaced.

This shift mirrors the one we considered a moment ago between the sacrament of penance and the application of the Holy Oil. The Holy Oil is applied after the sacrament of penance, but unlike the sacrament of penance, which is a sacrament of self-discipline, the Holy Oil does not represent one's personal ambition. It represents "a quality bestowed from above" and by "grace". "[I]t is that spark of the higher in the Magician which wishes to unite the lower with itself."

"I am not I; I am but an hollow tube to bring down Fire from Heaven." This mirrors a line from the Anthem of the Gnostic Mass in which the Priest addresses the Secret Self as "the true fire within the reed".

The penis as an organ of penetration. It ejaculates seed. It projects its essence or its power onto and into another. Similarly the self subjects the world to itself. It judges the world. It investigates it.

*I* get at the truth. *I* pursue spiritual truth. *I* impose self-discipline. *I* act. *I* do my will.

But at its culmination, at its point of maximum self-assertion, the will turns into its opposite. It becomes passive. The phallus is no longer an organ of penetration; instead it is penetrated. It becomes vaginal and receptive. The phallus becomes a hollow tube to bring down Fire from Heaven. The first stanza of the Creed of *Liber XV* says:

I believe [...] in one Star in the Company of Stars of whose fire we are created, and to which we shall return[29]

The fire of the Sun enters the erect phallus. The building up of the pyramid or the phallus—the direction of the will toward the ultimate spiritual goal—puts one's ordinary sense of self into relation with the Khabs or the Sun of the Soul. But once that relationship is established, one's being is filled with the fire or the light of the Khabs. The polarity switches. The Khabs now has agency, not me.

The relationship to inner truth is not like our relationship to external truth. We pursue external truth. We investigate, and we "get to the truth". We possess it. We finally know it. Internal truth is not at all like that. It's not possessed. You enter into relation with it and are transformed by it. The discipline of getting at external truth is the discipline of careful observation and not letting our biases get in the way of our investigation. The discipline required of inner truth is the discipline to remain in relation and therefore to *hold oneself open*. Crowley's word for this capacity is *chastity*. Paradoxically the discipline of chastity is what defines the whore, Babalon.

The inescapable fact that I am in relation to and dependent upon a reality outside of myself is at the root of my capacity to suffer. My body is permeable. It can be invaded by pathogens. The genes expressing proteins in my cells can become corrupted by radiation. I can be pierced by steel or bullets. And because I'm a social being, because I'm psychologically dependent upon other people for a sense of belonging and fulfillment, I can be hurt by other people's words or actions that express or imply rejection. I am not a self-enclosed, autonomous unit. My life from beginning to end is marked by openness, relation, vulnerability, and therefore the prospects of injury, humiliation, abandonment, betrayal, death, and all the other perennial problems of life.

Writing in his essay, "Compensation," Ralph Waldo Emerson remarked:

Achilles is not quite invulnerable; the sacred waters did not wash the heel by which Thetis held him. Siegfried, in the Nibelungen, is not quite immortal, for a leaf fell on his back whilst he was bathing in the dragon's blood, and that spot which it covered is mortal. And so it must be. There is a crack in every thing God has made.[30]

---

29 *Liber XV*, creed, article 1
30 Ralph Waldo Emerson, "Compensation," https://archive.vcu.edu/english/engweb/transcendentalism/authors/emerson/essays/compensation.html

We are creations or extensions of the gods at the centers of our beings. We're cracked, broken, and imperfect instruments.

The answer to the problem of suffering, according to Crowley, is unity. But unity is not the same thing as the self-assertion of one's autonomy from the rest of the world and the people in it. Such an attitude is described by Crowley in chapter 60 of *The Book of Lies*, which is titled, "The Wound of Amfortas," so-called because, "Amfortas was wounded by his own spear, the spear that had made him king."

> The Self-mastery of Percivale became the Self-
>    masturbatery of the Bourgeois.
> Vir-tus has become "virtue".[31]

Commenting on this passage, Crowley says:

> In paragraph 1 the real chastity of Percivale or Parsifal, a chastity which did not prevent his dipping the point of the sacred lance into the Holy Grail, is distinguished from its misinterpretation by modern crapulence.[32]

As a representation of what we can build ourselves up into, the phallus is not completely self-enclosed. It is permeable. Its attempt at self-completion must always be deferred. Nor is it self-fulfilled; it is hollow. "I am not I". I (phallus in the shape of "I") can never fulfill myself; any attempt to do so undoes itself.

Yet rather than being a mere limitation to its fulfillment, the failure of its self-enclosure provides the opening through which may flow the divine essence. Ironically, were there no opening—were we to fulfill for ourselves what we imagine it must be like to be gods—the experience of God would become impossible.

There is a crack in everything, but, as Leonard Cohen added, "that's how the light gets in."

The Great Work of uniting ourselves with God requires us to take up our vulnerability, our failure of closure, and to hold ourselves open Godward with unflinching discipline. It means rejecting every temptation to recoil out of fear and to close the heart to the pain the universe will inevitably conduct our way.

---

31  *The Book of Lies*, ch 60
32  Ibid.

## Raising the Dead

Having established this framework, let's now use it to begin interpreting the Gnostic Mass, starting with the Ceremony of the Introit.

The Ceremony of the Introit is part III of *Liber XV*, though it is the first part of the dramatic performance of the ritual. It starts with the Deacon admitting the congregation. It ends when the Priestess strokes the lance 11 times, says "Be the LORD present among us!", and the congregants give the hailing sign and say "So mote it be."

The Ceremony of the Introit represents in dramatic form the abstract principles we've been considering. It represents the condition of the Man of Earth or the individual in their natural state. It represents how the relationship between that individual and their star or soul has the potential to bring them out of that state. And it shows how the relationship between the individual and their soul is mediated by the Khu or the magical garment so as to begin to create the 2-in-1 relationship that drives the Gnostic Mass to its climax.

This part of the ritual is also important because it establishes the identity, the role, and the trajectory of the Priest for the rest of the ritual. What is done on the west side of the temple at the tomb is in a certain sense undone later on the east side of the temple. Crowley was motivated by the idea of balance through action and reaction. Understanding the ritual's setup in part III puts us in a better position later on to understand its culmination.

We're going to skip the Creed for now. The Creed is a profession of the theology of Thelema. The theology of Thelema is dramatized over the course of the entire ritual. Tonight I want to focus on just one part of the ritual and just one part of the theology.

When the Priestess enters the temple, she is described in the rubric as the *Virgin*. Writing in Appendix 47 to his commentaries, Crowley describes the High Priestess:

> She is his Silent Self, virgin beyond all veils, made free to teach him, by virtue of this third ordeal wherein, passing through the abyss, he has stripped from him every rag of falsehood, his last complexes, even his phantasy that he called 'I'.[33]

In the New Comment on AL III.22, he says:

---

33  Appendix 47 of the New Comment

The Kingdom of *Malkuth*, the Virgin Bride, and the Child is the Dwarf-Self, the Phallic consciousness, which is the true life of Man, beyond his 'veils' of incarnation.[34]

We encountered this idea of the Silent Self in the last lecture. It is synony-mous with the Sun of the Soul or the Khabs.

He will choose the object of his passion at the nod of his Silent Self. He will not allow the prejudice, either of sense, emotion, or rational judge-ment, to obscure the Sun of his Soul.[35]

At the outset the Priestess represents the Priest's star or Khabs. His union with her by means of the union of the lance and the grail represents the ful-fillment of his true individuality as the 2-in-1 male-female, the byproduct of which is the 2-in-1 eucharist.

She takes a serpentine path to the tomb, "involving 3 and a half circles of the Temple." Writing in his commentary on the Gnostic Mass, Frater Saba-zius and Tau Helena say:

The Kundalinî, prior to rising up the spine, is said to be coiled 3 1/2 times around the Svayambhu Linga located in the Mulâdhâra Chakra at the base of the spine.[36]

Crowley associates the Mulâdhâra Chakra with either Yesod or Malkuth on the Tree of Life. In AL II.22 we read:

I am the Snake that giveth Knowledge & Delight and bright glory, and stir the hearts of men with drunkenness.[37]

Commenting on this passage, Crowley says:

Hadit now identifies himself with the Kundalini, the central magical force in man.[38]

---

34 New Comment on AL III.22
35 New Comment on AL I.52
36 Sabazius X° and Tau Helena, *Mystery of Mystery: A Primer of Thelemic Ecclesiastical Gnosticism* (Berkeley, CA: Conjoined Creation, 2015), 39
37 AL II.22
38 Old Comment on AL II.22

Whether we're talking about the Khabs, the Sun of the Soul, the Silent Self, the Virgin Self, or the Kundalini, we're referring to the same underlying spiritual principle: the divine force within us which wants to live and which wants to take its fill of reality. This impulse within us gives rise to the sense of time passing and events happening. The Gnostic Mass is a means of dramatizing—as a love story and a story of resurrection—what it means for this god-like power within us to live to its fullest potential in the course of a human life.

Approaching the tomb in the west, the Priestess draws her sword. She tears down the veil enclosing the Priest in the tomb. She says:

> By the power of ✠ Iron, I say unto thee, Arise. In the name of our Lord the ✠ Sun, and of our Lord ✠..., that thou mayst administer the virtues to the Brethren.[39]

The Priestess has just described the role of the Priest in this ritual: to "administer the virtues to the Brethren."

Any interpretation of the Gnostic Mass has to explain how the different parts of the ritual serve to fulfill this task which has been appointed to the Priest. To answer this question fully would require an interpretation of the latter parts of the Mass, which we're not going to get to tonight. Suffice to say the "virtues" mentioned refer to the sacrament administered at the end of the ritual. It is a sacrament that is consecrated "by the virtue of the rod". The "brethren" in question are the congregants.

The Priest issues forth from the tomb. He gives what are called the three regular steps and the three penal signs. These are the steps and the signs of the first three initiatory degrees of O.T.O. as they existed when the ritual was written in 1913. Those rituals symbolize birth, life, and death, and together they make up the Man of Earth initiations.

As we saw the Man of Earth is the individual in their natural, uninitiated state. They are in the "grey land," the Qliphoth, which is not a land of demons but rather a place of confusion and bewilderment, a kind of living death. This association between death and what we ordinarily call life is emphasized by the Priest starting in a tomb. The tomb shows he is not only subject to death but is also subject to suffering resulting from the general confusion about who and what he really is.

After handing the lance over to the Priestess, the Priest kneels, and with

---

39 *Liber XV*, part 3

both hands he adores the Lance.

He says—we might imagine with a note of despair in his voice—"I am a man among men." In other words, "I am a Man of Earth, just like the congregants." And now perhaps plaintively he asks, "How should I be worthy to administer the virtues to the Brethren?"

His question implies that the actions the Priestess is about to take are capable of remedying the poor condition he finds himself in. We Men and Women of Earth ought to take careful note. We're being taught an important lesson by the Priestess on how to straighten ourselves out.

The nature of those actions is hinted at when the Priest kneels. In the rubric it says, "He then kneels and worships the Lance with both hands. Penitential music." This signals the sacrament of penance—the work of the scourge, the dagger, and the chain—or more generally the application of the three alchemical principles of sulfur, mercury, and salt.

The dagger does not appear in the Gnostic Mass, but the sword does. The Priestess uses it to cut down the veil over the tomb, thereby revealing and releasing the Priest. This is the faculty of discrimination, which separates the essence of the Priest from the inessentials of the environment he finds himself in. It is capable of cutting away the "husks" (i.e., the Qliphoth) from the wood.

No chain appears in the Gnostic Mass, but salt does. As we saw the chain represents the alchemical principle of salt. It is mixed with water which is then used to make three crosses on the Priest: one over his forehead, another over his chest, and a third over his body. This is paralleled in *Liber Pyramidos*, a ritual of self-initiation, which reads, "Scourge, dagger, and chain purge body, breast, and brain!"

Making the three crosses, the Priestess says, "Be the PRIEST pure of body and soul!"

"Purity," Crowley says, "means singleness [...] If one littlest thought intrude upon the mind of the Mystic, his concentration is absolutely destroyed; and his consciousness remains on exactly the same level as the Stockbroker's."[40]

Purifying the Priest with salt-water symbolizes the work of the chain, which is to bind the Priest's wandering thoughts.

Then she makes the same three crosses over him again, this time with the burning incense. "Be the PRIEST fervent of body and soul!" This reflects the purpose of the scourge: to stimulate aspiration.

---

40 *Magick in Theory and Practice*, ch 13

This first part of the Ceremony of the Introit dramatizes the application of three forms of discipline to the Priest in the form of the three alchemical principles. First there has to be the determination to sacrifice all. When the Priest steps out of the tomb, that action represents his conscious rejection of the grey land and the living death of the Qliphoth.

Then his wandering thoughts are restricted. He acquires the purity of mind represented by the salt water. In the context of spiritual practice, this is called mindfulness: thought directed in an engaged way at the task at hand. To be mindful means to know what you are doing as you are doing it.

Finally the work of sulfur—as represented by the incense smoke—is to stoke the fires of aspiration.

As we saw a moment ago, the sacrament of penance is followed by the application of the Holy Oil, which represents "that spark of the higher in the Magician which wishes to unite the lower with itself."

The anointing with Holy Oil does not take place at all in the Gnostic Mass. Instead the Priestess performs three entirely different actions on the Priest: she clothes him in a robe, she crowns him, and she kneels and strokes his lance 11 times.

First the Priestess dresses the Priest in a robe of scarlet and gold. She says, "Be the flame of the Sun thine ambience, O thou PRIEST of the SUN!" The Sun is our Lord and Father in the universe, the visible Sun which is responsible for all life on Earth. It is also the Khabs or the Sun of the Soul, the essence of each individual. Turning toward the inner Sun fills us with inner light, awakening us from the dead.

Gold is the king scale color of Resh, which is associated with Atu XIV, the Sun. Scarlet is the king scale color of Aries. Aries is the Agnus Dei or the Lamb of God. The Lamb of God in Christianity was Christ, the God-Man. The Priestess is gradually transforming the Priest into a 2-in-1 God-Man.

Then she places the Uraeus serpent crown on his head. She says, "Be the Serpent thy crown, O thou PRIEST of the LORD!" As we have already seen, the serpent is a symbol of Hadit.

The serpent is the symbol of divinity and royalty. It is also a symbol of Hadit, invoked upon them.[41]

The Serpent is the Uraeus, with the powers of Life and Death, wise, ecstatic, immortal; winged and hooded, that he may go as a god swiftly and

---

41 Old Comment on AL I.18

silently. It refers in this place especially to Hadit.[42]

This is also the Secret and Ineffable Lord of the Creed, the Lord Secret and Most Holy of the 2nd collect, and "Thou who art I beyond all I am" of the Anthem.

Finally she kneels, she strokes the lance 11 times, raises her arms, and cries, "Be the LORD present among us!" All give the Hailing Sign of the Magician and in unison say, "So mote it be."

Who is the "Lord" the Priestess is referring to? A clue is given in the Priest's next line. This is the first time he's spoken since asking the Priestess how he ought to be made worthy to administer the virtues to the brethren. He says, "Thee therefore whom we adore we also invoke. By the power of the lifted Lance!"

There is a Lord who is described in the Gnostic Mass as being adored. He is the Lord of Life and Joy of the 5th Collect.

Lord of Life and Joy, that art the might of man, that art the essence of every true god that is upon the surface of the Earth, continuing knowledge from generation unto generation, thou adored of us upon heaths and in woods, on mountains and in caves, openly in the marketplaces and secretly in the chambers of our houses, in temples of gold and ivory and marble as in these other temples of our bodies, we worthily commemorate them worthy that did of old adore thee and manifest thy glory unto men...[43]

The Lord of Life and Joy of the 5th Collect is adored in heaths, woods, mountains, caves, in temples, in nature, in our bodies—in short, everywhere on the surface of the Earth. He is clearly visible and sensible. So He cannot be the Secret Lord. The Secret Lord is unmanifest. The Secret Lord also cannot be adored. He is described as that "secret of secrets that art hidden in the being of all that lives, not Thee do we adore, for that which adoreth is also Thou. Thou art That, and That am I." So whoever we and the Saints are adoring, it cannot be Hadit, who is always the adorer and never the adored.

But He is not Our Lord and Father the Sun, either. The Sun is visible and sensible, but He is Our Lord in the Universe "who travelest over the heavens." While the light of the Sun may strike the Earth and make life possible, the Sun Himself is not god on the surface of the Earth like our Lord of Life

---

42 New Comment on AL I.18
43 *Liber XV*, part 5

and Joy is.

That leaves only one possibility. Consider the first stanza of the Creed:

I believe in one secret and ineffable LORD...[44]

That is the Lord Secret and Most Holy or Hadit.

...and in one Star in the Company of Stars of whose fire we are created, and to which we shall return...[45]

That is Our Lord in the Universe the Sun—or alternatively it is the Sun of the Soul.

...and in one Father of Life, Mystery of Mystery, in His name CHAOS, the sole viceregent of the Sun upon the Earth...[46]

Who is this Chaos person? Crowley describes him as the "sole viceregent of the Sun upon the Earth". That identifies Chaos with the surface of the Earth, just like our Lord of Life and Joy of the 5th Collect. But we have encountered this term "viceregent" before. We saw it in a quote I showed you in the last lecture.

Our religion therefore, for the People, is the Cult of the Sun, who is our particular star of the Body of Nuit, from whom, in the strictest scientific sense, come this earth, a chilled spark of Him, and all our Light and Life. His vice-regent and representative in the animal kingdom is His cognate symbol the Phallus, representing Love and Liberty.[47]

The Lord of Life and Joy of the 5th Collect, Chaos (the Father of Life of the Creed), and the phallus are all different ways of symbolizing the way God or divinity presents itself on Earth, in what Crowley is here calling the animal kingdom. We know from what we looked at earlier that the erect phallus is one of several ways Crowley describes the process whereby we discipline our minds and bodies to become mediums through which the fire of the Khabs can freely flow outward and make contact with the universe.

---

44 Ibid, part 3
45 Ibid.
46 Ibid.
47 New Comment on AL III.22

When the Priest addressing the Sun says, "Let thy light crystallize itself in our blood, fulfilling us of Resurrection," he is likely referring to this idea. To put ourselves into conscious relation with inner truth releases the light trapped within us. It then floods our beings, releasing us from living death. Our lives are filled with a sense of beauty and purpose. There is no obstacle between the interior depth and the exterior depth, and so there is the feeling of making love with reality that is characteristic of so much mystical experience.

The raising of the lance in the Gnostic Mass symbolizes a mystical experience of a particular kind, that which Crowley refers to as the Knowledge and Conversation of the Holy Guardian Angel.

> [T]he innocent and impotent Harpocrates Babe becomes the Horus Adult by obtaining the Wand. "Der reine Thor" seizes the Sacred Lance. Bacchus becomes Pan. The Holy Guardian Angel is the Unconscious Creature Self—the Spiritual Phallus. His knowledge and conversation contributes occult puberty.[48]

With the raising of the lance, the Priest is no longer a Man of Earth. He is a Lover or an Adept. Everything he does from that point forward in the ritual is not done under his own power as an ordinary mortal being. It is done "by the power of the lifted lance". It is done by virtue of him rendering himself open and receptive to the power of the secret and unknown god within him, who is using his physical and mental powers to accomplish the Great Work.

## Conclusion

This evening we continued our exploration of the nature of the human being, their relationship to truth, and how that relationship to truth is dramatized in *Liber XV: The Gnostic Mass.*

We saw how the Khabs or soul of each individual desires to know itself and the universe, and how the only means it has of doing this is to weave the Khu or what Crowley calls the "magical garment."

We saw that when the Khabs weaves the Khu and takes a body for itself—in other words when it is incarnated—it becomes subject to conditions of duality. This has the effect of making the world seem like a place of suffering and dissatisfaction. As a result, the natural human condition—the

---

48 *Liber Samekh*

condition of the uninitiate—is a painful one in which spirit is submerged in matter and one seems a pawn of fate. Crowley's term for this default condition of man is the Man of Earth.

We saw that liberation for Crowley consists in the reunion of the two infinities, Hadit within and Nuit without, but that this cannot entail the complete elimination of duality. The elimination of duality would mean death and a lack of experience. To experience liberation in this life, one must instead resolve the "complexes" in the Khu and make it transparent to the light within. This is also symbolized as the creation of unity from duality, represented by the various 2-in-1 symbols in Thelema.

We also saw that liberation does not entail the return of the star to undifferentiated union with some higher reality or superconsciousness but instead requires the full incarnation of the Khabs. One must become completely alive for the first time. This is why Crowley rejects the Gnostic idea of return to the Pleroma—or any ascetic, life-rejecting path—in favor of a path in which we engage magically with duality so as to create an image of unity from it.

We then looked at two other important ways Crowley represents the path of liberation. We considered the sacrament of penance, which is the work of the three alchemical principles of sulfur, mercury, and salt. We saw how the application of these principles prepares the lower part of the soul to receive the spark or the fire from the higher.

And we considered the symbol of the phallus, which when erect becomes "an hollow tube to bring down fire from heaven". Similar to the sacrament of penance, the lower self becomes the passive medium for the influx of the higher self, as symbolized by the Holy Oil.

We contrasted this use of the phallus or the will with that represented by Amfortas. While the erect phallus represents the Adept who is open to the flow of the fire of heaven, Amfortas represents self-enclosure and overweening self-mastery which Crowley likens to masturbation.

We then utilized this theoretical framework to interpret the Ceremony of the Introit, the first part of the Gnostic Mass. We saw how the tomb and the Priest in it represent the human condition and the Man of Earth. We saw how the Priestess's work with the sword, the salt-water, and the incense represents the sacrament of penance or the application of the three alchemical principles of mercury, salt, and sulfur respectively.

We saw how the influx of the higher represented by the application of the Holy Oil is represented in the Gnostic Mass by the Priestess adorned the Priest with the robe, the crown, and the stroking of the lance. We saw how the raising of the lance is analogous to the erect phallus in chapter 15 of The Book of Lies. We saw that the raising of the lance also represents the Priest's "occult puberty" or the Knowledge and Conversation of his Holy Guardian Angel. It transforms the Priest from a mere Man of Earth into a Lover or Adept. It represents the lower part of the Priest's soul rendered disciplined and open to receive the fire of the Khabs, and how everything else the Priest accomplishes in the ritual is by virtue of the power of the raised lance—in other words, his will a mere vehicle of the divine will.

The three alchemical principles by which the Priest has been disciplined are represented by the Hebrew letters Aleph (mercury), Mem (salt), and Shin (sulfur). By virtue of this discipline, the Priest is united with a three-part god represented by the robe (the Sun or Father), the crown (the Secret Lord or Holy Spirit), and the erect lance (Chaos or the Son). This god is represented by the three Hebrew letters Yod, Aleph, and Vau—IAO. The union of these two triads gives us the hexagram, AShIAVM, the Star of the Serpent-Messiah. As the hexagram, 6 (Vau), the Priest can now work with the Priestess, who is Heh or 5, to accomplish the Great Work which is 6 + 5 = 11, thereby setting the stage for the rest of the ritual.

# 11

# An Introduction to the Creed

## I Believe...

The text of the Creed occurs in the third section of *Liber XV*, The Ceremony of the Introit. Though it is the third section of *Liber XV*, it is the first part of the ritual that is performed. After the Deacon admits the congregation, he kisses *The Book of the Law* three times, opens it, and places it on the super-altar. He addresses the congregation in the name of IAO, a god whose name we will return to when considering the first article of the Creed. He then returns to his place between the black cubical altar and the font and leads the congregation in the recitation of the Creed. The full text of the Creed reads:

I believe in one secret and ineffable LORD; and in one Star in the company of Stars of whose fire we are created, and to which we shall return; and in one Father of Life, Mystery of Mystery, in His name CHAOS, the sole viceregent of the Sun upon Earth; and in one Air the nourisher of all that breaths.

And I believe in one Earth, the Mother of us all, and in one Womb wherein all men are begotten, and wherein they shall rest, Mystery of Mystery, in Her name BABALON.

And I believe in the Serpent and the Lion, Mystery of Mystery, in His name BAPHOMET.

And I believe in one Gnostic and Catholic Church of Light, Life, Love and Liberty, the Word of whose Law is THELEMA.

And I believe in the communion of Saints.

And, forasmuch as meat and drink are transmuted in us daily into spiritual substance, I believe in the Miracle of the Mass.

And I confess one Baptism of Wisdom whereby we accomplish the Miracle of Incarnation.

And I confess my life one, individual, and eternal that was, and is, and is to come.

AUMGN, AUMGN, AUMGN.[1]

The Creed is not referred to as such in the rubric of the ritual that Crowley published in *Equinox III:1* or in *Magick*. The practice of referring to it as the Creed likely derives from the fact that the Latin *credo* means, "I believe," a phrase which is repeated several times throughout this section, as well as similarities between this section of the ritual and the Nicene Creed of the eastern and western Christian churches.

## The Thelemic Background of the Gnostic Mass

One of the conspicuous features of the Creed is the absence from it of the major personages of *The Book of the Law*: Nuit, Hadit, or Ra-Hoor-Khuit. Instead we profess belief in a Secret Lord, in Chaos, in Babalon, in Baphomet, in the Saints, in the Miracle of the Mass, the Miracle of Incarnation, and the immortality of the soul. We see few mentions of them throughout the course of the ritual, the exceptions being a brief mention of Nuit and allusions to Hadit and Ra-Hoor-Khuit during part four. Instead there is a greater deal of emphasis placed on IAO, the Sun, and the Secret Lord throughout *Liber XV*.

Nevertheless *The Book of the Law* is the key to understanding the theology of the Gnostic Mass and its Creed. *The Book of the Law*, also known as *Liber AL vel Legis sub figura 220*, is the foundational document of Thelema. Crowley took *The Book of the Law* to describe the fundamental nature of the universe, the human being, and the path to spiritual liberation in this life. What follows are the broad strokes of that view.

---

1   *Liber XV*, part 3

The Universe is explained by the interaction of what Crowley calls two "elements," but which we can also think of as two fundamental principles or causes. These two principles are mutually *opposed* and mutually *exclusive*. In other words, they cannot be understood through one another. But they work together and complement one another to give rise to the universe or what Crowley also calls manifest existence.

The first principle is called *Nuit*. Crowley describes Nuit as extended substance, matter, space, all that exists, form, and the object of experience. The second principle is called *Hadit*. Hadit is the indivisible point, motion, the cause of change, concealed force, the unique individual, and the experiencer.

At the most general, most abstract level, Nuit is the cause of form or appearance. I'm using the terms *form* and *appearance* in ways that may seem unusual. A physical object has form. For example, the chair is a blue, soft, three-dimensional solid. It shares those qualities in common with other physical objects that are blue, soft, or three-dimensional. But as I'm using the term, a social convention such as *Wednesday* also has form or appearance. The form or appearance of Wednesday is that it is a day of the week. It occurs between Tuesday and Thursday. Even a thought, like my thought of the number 2, has form, because at a bare minimum, any act of thinking *takes time*, and *duration* is a quality.

Anything that is or could be something *for us*—anything we actually or theoretically could be conscious of, whether it's physical or not—*appears* a certain way, and that appearance is caused by Nuit. Another way of saying this is that Nuit is the unity of being. To be is to be a member of the body of Nuit.

Hadit is not a being; nor is He the unity of being. Hadit is the *unique individual* who stands opposed to being. He is aloof and alone. As such, He has no appearance and no form. He expresses what Crowley calls *unique individuality*. So for example, even though this chair shares features in common with other soft, blue, three-dimensional solids, it is also a unique individual. It is also *this chair here*. The uniqueness of the chair cannot be explained in terms of its appearance or form, because form is what it has in common with the other chairs.

So while Nuit is the unity of being, Hadit is the unity of the unique individual. These two causes cannot be understood through one another. Hadit cannot be understood through his form or qualities, because He has none. If He had a quality, He would have to share that quality in common with something or someone else, and therefore He would not be absolutely unique. Likewise, there is nothing absolutely unique in Nuit nor anything that stands absolutely apart. Everything in Nuit is connected to everything else.

While these two causes are opposed to and exclude one another at least in thought, in reality they cannot exist apart from one another. This is what Crowley refers to as the central truth of the Thelemic philosophy. Any conjunction between the two is called the *Khabs*, which is the Egyptian term for star. If Hadit is the idea of the unique individual, and if Nuit is the idea of form or appearance, then the *star*—as the conjunction of the two—is the idea of a manifested individual. It is a unique individual showing itself—indirectly—through its qualities.

Nuit is the totality of being, the totality of anything that can appear in the most general sense of the term. Any interaction of Hadit with Nuit brings some subset of those total possible appearances into existence. But because Hadit is a unique individual or "this here"—or as *The Book of the Law* says, a "point"—Hadit is only ever realizing some particular facet of Nuit. He does not reveal her all at once. It happens over time. No sooner does an appearance arise than it passes away and is replaced by another appearance. This is a constant, ongoing, unending process. The aggregate of appearances across time for a particular Hadit is the course of a star through Nuit.

If Nuit is the unity of manifest being, and if Hadit is the unity of the unique individual or the point, then in the star—also called *Ra-Hoor-Khuit*—we have a third kind of unity. The star is the unity of the manifest individual. It is the unity maintained by the unique individual over the course of its changes in outer appearance or form.

Here are some helpful analogies:

The gravity of Earth is a unified force that expresses itself through many objects being attracted to the center of the Earth. In this analogy, Hadit is to the attractive force of gravity as Nuit is to the objects pulled toward the center of the Earth.

A particular organism maintains its structural integrity even while its component cells are constantly dying and being replaced. In this analogy the individuality of the organism is Hadit, and the constantly changing component parts are Nuit. The totality or the organic whole is the star or Ra-Hoor-Khuit.

A company like Apple has an identity it maintains through changes in leadership and personnel.

An individual mind maintains its identity as it thinks successive thoughts.

Identity and form are different from one another, but they are interdependent. If Apple's new leadership brings the company in a direction that no longer reflects the values of its founder, then the company will lose what we call its integrity, and it will cease to be.

Likewise, certain changes to an organism will cause it to die, and its identity will cease.

These three kinds of unities—the unity of being, the unity of the unique individual, and their combination in the unity of the manifest individual—serve as keys to understanding the Gnostic Mass and its Creed.

## The First Article

The first article of the Creed reads:

> I believe in one secret and ineffable LORD; and in one Star in the Company of Stars of whose fire we are created, and to which we shall return; and in one Father of Life, Mystery of Mystery, in His name CHAOS, the sole viceregent of the Sun upon the Earth; and in one Air the nourisher of all that breathes.[2]

The Secret Lord is mentioned or alluded to several times throughout the course of the Gnostic Mass. When the Priestess raises the Priest from the tomb, she says

> By the power of ✠ Iron, I say unto thee, Arise. In the name of our Lord the ✠ Sun, and of our Lord ✠ ..., that thou mayst administer the virtues to the Brethren.[3]

The ellipses there refer to the Secret and Ineffable Lord.

The Priestess alludes to the Secret Lord when she places the serpent crown on the Priest's head: "Be the serpent thy crown, oh thou, Priest of the Lord!"

The Priest refers to Him as "O secret of secrets that art hidden in the being of all that lives" in the second veil speech.

The Deacon refers to Him as "Lord Secret and Most Holy, source of light, source of life, source of love, source of liberty" in the second collect.

---

2   Ibid.
3   Ibid.

The Priest addresses Him as "Thou who art I, beyond all I am" in the Anthem and again as "Lord most secret" when blessing the elements.

The Secret Lord is Hadit. He is the unfathomable depth of unique individuality, abstracted from any form. Because He is opposed to form, He has no properties. That's why He has no nature and no name. He is the infinitely contracted and concealed force, and therefore He is secret.

The "one Star in the Company of Stars" is the Sun. The Sun is addressed and alluded to many times throughout the course of the Gnostic Mass by all three of its officers.

As the cycles of the days and seasons pass, the Sun maintains His individuality. He is the representation in the heavens of the third kind of unity, that pertaining to the manifest individual produced by the conjunction of Hadit with Nuit. For this reason, we worship the Sun as God.

In his third veil speech, the Priest addressing the Sun says:

Thou that art One, our Lord in the Universe the Sun, our Lord in ourselves whose name is Mystery of Mystery, uttermost being whose radiance enlightening the worlds is also the breath that maketh every God even and Death to tremble before Thee...[4]

The same kind of unity that pertains to the Sun is also to be found within ourselves. There it is called "Mystery of Mystery," "Father of Life," "Chaos," or the generative principle. It is the unity maintained by the species as the individuals composing that species are born and die. Following the usage of Richard Payne Knight and Hargrave Jennings, Crowley calls this unity the *Phallus*. Following Freud and Jung, he also terms it the *libido* or the *unconscious*.

The Phallus is represented in the Gnostic Mass by the Priest's lance, particularly when it is raised. But the Phallus is not the male sex organ *per se*—because *Babalon* is also the Phallus.

The Phallus is also referred to in the Gnostic Mass as the "Lord of Life and Joy," the "might of man," and "the essence of every true god that is upon the surface of the Earth, continuing knowledge from generation unto generation".

Together the Sun and the Phallus form Ra-Hoor-Khuit, the Solar-Phallic god worshiped in the Gnostic Mass.

Ra-Hoor-Khuit or the Lord of the Aeon is one half of a pair. Concealed

---

4  Ibid, part 4

within Ra-Hoor-Khuit is His twin, Harpocrates or Hoor-paar-kraat, described in the Gnostic Mass as the Secret Lord or the "centre and secret of the Sun".

The Sun is the Father or I. Harpocrates or the Secret Lord is the Holy Spirit or A. Chaos or the Phallus is the Son or O. Together they are the three-in-one god, IAO, whose spirit presides over the Gnostic Mass.

Air is barely mentioned again after this point in *Liber XV*. The Priestess says, "Let the Fire and the Air make sweet the world!" as she puts incense in the censer, and the Deacon describes the Earth's cheek caressed by air. The ancient Greek word for breath—*pneuma*—is spoken by the Priest after he breaks off the particle of the Cake of Light. There it signifies *to pneuma hagion*, the Holy Spirit. Air is the physical correlate of Harpocrates or the Holy Spirit.

Air also signifies steam produced by the combination of fire and water. Air is a necessary ingredient in the alchemical Magnum Opus, a theme implied in the second article.

## The Second Article

The second article of the Creed reads:

> And I believe in one Earth, the Mother of us all, and in one Womb wherein all men are begotten, and wherein they shall rest, Mystery of Mystery, in Her name BABALON.[5]

The one Womb is the idea of Nuit Herself, just as the Secret Lord is the idea of Hadit Himself. As Hadit travels through Nuit, experiencing the variety of forms latent within Her, those forms arise from her Womb and pass back away into them.

Nuit is pure possibility, but she can be understood on analogy with pure, infinite space. Imagine yourself floating in space, far from any planets or stars. There is no up or down in this space. Assuming no forces are being applied to you, you cannot tell if you are in motion or at rest. We have no sense of orientation in purely abstract space.

But as soon as we introduce the Earth, there is now a source of gravity. With a source of gravity, we can differentiate between up and down. We can tell when we are in motion. The force within us has something to apply

---

5  Ibid, part 3

itself against. This gives rise to the feeling of the will. With the motions of the celestial bodies, the cardinal directions naturally emerge. The Earth gives us a sense of orientation. She allows us to do more than simply exist in the universe. We are now able to dwell.

As the Sun expresses the idea of manifest individuality in the heavens, the Earth expresses the very same idea, but now as solid matter.

In the individual human being, Earth is that part of themselves which they show to the world as a physical body, and it is that part of themselves through which they know the physical world around themselves. It is also called the Nephesch or the natural soul.

The Deacon addresses the Earth in the sixth collect. He says:

Mother of fertility on whose breast lieth water, whose cheek is caressed by air, and in whose heart is the sun's fire, womb of all life, recurring grace of seasons, answer favorably the prayer of labour, and to pastors and hus-bandmen be thou propitious.[6]

The Sun's fire is a reference to the core of the Earth. As the Earth conceals within Her heart the Sun's fire, so do all flesh and blood human individuals conceal within themselves—beyond the veils of their minds and bodies—that unity pertaining to the Sun or God. This is the spiritual or subterranean Sun, that part of themselves that is eternal and not subject to birth and death but which utilizes birth and death to express itself.

To establish contact with this internal Sun, one must make the inward journey. They must travel through the unconscious, which Crowley also terms hell. They must discipline their natural soul—what Crowley also terms the *libido*—and direct its energies toward union with God. This path of self-discipline of the Nephesh is represented in the Gnostic Mass by the Priestess cutting down the tomb veil from over the Priest and by means of the application of salt, water, fire, and air to the Priest's body and soul.

This path of self-discipline transforms the perishable substance of the Priest's body and soul. That substance is shown to have a principle of im-mortality concealed within it. That principle of immortality—the divine in-dividuality of the Priest—is represented by the robe of the Sun, the crown of the Secret Lord, and by the consecrated lance of Chaos, which together form the 3-in-1 god, IAO. The revelation of the God within the Priest is his occult puberty or the Knowledge and Conversation of his Holy Guardian Angel. It

---

6  Ibid, part 5

transforms him from a Neophyte into an Adept and is signaled by the raising of the lance.

The lowered lance which the Priest emerges with from the tomb represents his natural will. It is the same natural will we are all born with, despite our assigned sex at birth. Following the appropriate purification and consecration, the Priest raises the lance. The raised lance represents that very same natural soul or libido dedicated exclusively to union with God, a condition Crowley refers to as *chastity*.

In order for this transformation to occur, one must relinquish one's will in favor of the divine or true will. One must become an instrument or passive medium of its expression. One must become, as Crowley says in *The Book of Lies*, "an hollow tube to bring down fire from heaven".[7] The Phallus must cease to be an organ of penetration and instead become penetrated.

This process whereby the natural soul becomes passive and is ceaselessly penetrated by god within, is termed by Crowley the raising of the Daughter to the Throne of the Mother. It is the transformation of the soul into a Whore. It is the alchemical transformation of the black Earth of Malkuth, first into the gold of Tiphareth, then into the redness of Binah. It is the replacement of the natural phallus with the purified phallus, or Babalon.

The name Babalon spelled with an "a" instead of a "y" is composed of three words. *Bab* is Arabic for *gate*, *Al* means *God*, and *ON* is the ancient Egyptian name for *Heliopolis*, the *City of the Sun*. Thus to become Babalon is to become *the Gate of the God ON* or the living receptacle of the solar fire within.

## The Third Article

The third article reads:

> And I believe in the Serpent and the Lion, Mystery of Mystery, in His name BAPHOMET.[8]

Baphomet takes two forms in Thelema, one represented by Atu o, the Fool, the other represented by Atu XV, the Devil.

Baphomet in the form of The Fool is also referred to as the Holy Spirit. The Creed also refers to this form as the Secret Lord, and He is symbolized

---

7   *The Book of Lies*, ch 15
8   *Liber XV*, part 3

in the Gnostic Mass by the serpent crown and by the broken off particle of the Cake of Light. Raising the particle the Priest says, "This is my seed. The Father is the Son through the Holy Spirit."

When the natural soul is purified and becomes radically open, the fire of the Holy Spirit leaps up into the soul. This is the "true fire within the reed". It is as if the hidden solar god within—who is called ON or THERION— has ejaculated its seed into the soul as if it were a womb.

That seed on its own is hermaphroditic. It is "male-female, quintessential one". When it unites with the soul, it is represented by the Beast and Baba-lon Conjoined or the serpent coiled around the egg.

As a result of this intercourse, the soul becomes pregnant with the Babe in the Egg of Blue. This is "man-being veiled in woman form". It is represented by the particle in the cup of wine.

This gives rise to a fourth kind of unity which we have not yet seen. Nuit is the unity of possibility. Hadit is the unity of the unique individual. Ra-Hoor-Khuit is the unity of the manifest individual. We now have a fourth kind of unity, the unity of the deified flesh and blood individual: half god, half human being. This is the unity Crowley refers to those "Sons of the Lion and the Snake" or the Saints.

The Child—the Babe in the Egg of Blue—manifests Himself as Pan or the Devil of Atu XV. XV is the number of this ritual, *Liber XV*. The Devil is manifestation in its most masculine form, yet He shares certain character-istics with His mother, namely, the equal enjoyment of all things. For this reason Crowley says Babalon is the female equivalent of Pan, and Pan is the male equivalent of Babalon.

## The Fourth Article

The fourth article reads:

> And I believe in one Gnostic and Catholic Church of Light, Life, Love and Liberty, the Word of whose Law is THELÊMA.[9]

Light, Life, Love, and Liberty are the four emanations of the Secret Lord. This Secret Lord is ineffable and concealed, and yet He shows Himself indi-rectly through the Sun, who is Light and Life, and Chaos, who is Love and Liberty. In other words, the Holy Spirit lives most fully in each of us when

---

9  Ibid.

we align our natural souls—our minds and bodies, our unconscious, our libido—with the god within. Then we become living symbols of truth. We
become vehicles to radiate divine power outward. This divine will within
ourselves which we must align ourselves with and radiate is called *THELÊ-
MA*, the Greek term for *will*. To do one's will means to be oriented toward
the true will, the spiritual sun within, and to radiate His light outward into
the world.

Ecclesia Gnostica Catholica—the Gnostic Catholic Church—is the same
instrument of the Holy Spirit, but in the form of a religious institution rather
than an individual human being. The purpose of E.G.C. is to radiate Light,
Life, Love, and Liberty out into the world through its central ritual, *Liber
XV: the Canon of the Mass of the Gnostic Catholic Church.*

The Gnostic Mass is more than a tool to broadcast Thelemic belief. It also
dramatically portrays these ideas using action and symbolism. To attend the
Gnostic Mass is more than to passively listen to a message. It means directly
participating in Thelemic truths using our minds, our hearts, our voices, and
our bodies. This is done by saying certain words together such as the Creed
and the Anthem, but this participation is greatly aided by having some idea
of what Crowley intended those words to mean.

Participation is also achieved through physical movement—for example
the steps and signs—and by taking communion. When we eat the Cake of
Light and drink the glass of wine, we are taking the truths represented by
those elements into ourselves and incorporating them on a cellular level. This
is in part what is intended when we say "There is no part of me that is not
of the gods."

E.G.C. also forms a religious community which holds Thelemic values and
a Thelemic worldview in common. This means recognizing and accepting
basic truths such as "Every man and every woman is a star," that each of us
has a unique god within ourselves which we alone are answerable to, that
it is each person's responsibility to serve the will of that god into the world,
and to transform the world so that all beings express their latent divinity.
This latter duty is the establishment of the Kingdom of Ra-Hoor-Khuit on
Earth: the Greeting of Earth and Heaven.

## The Fifth Article

The fifth article reads:

And I believe in the communion of Saints.[10]

The Saints are described as those "sons of the Lion and the Snake" who adore the Lord of Life and Joy of the fifth collect.

The Sons of the Lion and the Snake are those who have given birth to themselves by becoming Babalon and allowing themselves to be impregnated by the All-Father. They have been deified, thus becoming "man-being veiled in woman-form". The process whereby an ordinary individual becomes a Saint is dramatized in every celebration of the Gnostic Mass. It is the path of love.

The Communion of Saints is also called the *interior church* or the A∴A∴. The interior church is to the exterior church as the Sun's fire is to the Earth, as the true self is to each individual, as genetic coding is to the human race, as Harpocrates is to Ra-Hoor-Khuit, or as the center and secret of the Sun is to the Sun itself.

All manifest existence is created from the mutual participation of two opposed elements: Nuit, the principle of being or form, and Hadit, the concealed force driving change in being or form. They need each other and must exist together.

The interior church has no doctrine of its own. Like Hadit, it is formless. This is why the interior church can take the form of different religions that have diametrically opposed teachings. But this is also why the interior church *needs* the exterior church. The interior church on its own would be like Hadit without Nuit. It would be like a soul without a body.

But because the interior church must always take an outer form, that means it is always possible to confuse the inner with the outer. It is also possible to freeze the outer form in place and to take that frozen outer form to be eternal truth. This is how the letter of a teaching becomes divorced from its animating spirit.

Owing to the dependence of the inner on the outer, it is necessarily the case that, over time, a church's outer form will become detached from its inner spirit. This means that religion must continually be renewed through what is termed the Baptism of Wisdom, which we shall learn about shortly.

Nor is ossified doctrine the only form this separation of the inner from the outer takes. It can also take the form of excessive attention to technique. Focusing all of our attention on doing the Gnostic Mass a certain way, while paying almost no attention at all to *understanding* what we're doing is also a

---

10 Ibid.

way of divorcing the ritual from its animating fire.

Likewise, treating the Gnostic Mass as a magical vending machine we put a dollar in to get a prize is another way of exsanguinating it.

The purpose of lectures such as these is to try to keep as tight a fit as possible between the outer form and the inner truth which makes the former a living symbol of truth.

## The Sixth Article

The sixth article is:

> And, forasmuch as meat and drink are transmuted in us daily into spiritual substance, I believe in the Miracle of the Mass.[11]

The Miracle of the Mass is that more general process by means of which mere matter is made or shown to be divine. The purification of the natural soul, which has been so significant a theme of today's talk, is an example of the Miracle of the Mass.

Read carefully, the sixth article of the creed implies that normal digestion is an *example* of the Miracle of the Mass, not its essence. While the orientation of the Gnostic Mass is naturalistic, it is not reductionistic. The actions portrayed in the Gnostic Mass are not simply thinly veiled representations of sexual intercourse and the consumption of sexual fluids for magical ends.

Crowley himself said that the orgasm is an example of the Miracle of the Mass, not the other way around. As the Earth is the outer form of the Sun's fire, as the generative principle is the outer form of God in nature, so are basic activities like eating, drinking, and procreating outer forms of inner spiritual truths.

To purify our natural souls and to become Babalon means learning to accept all occurrences as issuing from the will of God. It means to accept every change as a necessary part of reality, the totality of which is divine. This is a technique which Crowley refers to as "destroying evil".[12] It means in particular overcoming our instincts of lust and revulsion and learning to appreciate the divinity in all things. This is the transmutation of mere matter into god of which the consecration and consumption of the eucharist is merely one example.

---

11 Ibid.

12 See *Liber V vel Reguli*

# The Seventh Article

The seventh article reads:

> And I confess one Baptism of Wisdom whereby we accomplish the Miracle of Incarnation.[13]

This is the inverse of the previous article. The Miracle of the Mass is the transformation of matter into spirit; the Miracle of Incarnation is the submerging of spirit into matter. This is a process that is dramatized in the first two initiation rituals of Mysteria Mystica Maxima: Minerval and Lustration.

The Man of Earth initiation rituals teach us that our minds and bodies are mere instruments by means of which "adventuring gods" come to appreciate their divinity and the divinity of the cosmos. The first two initiation rituals in particular tell the story from the perspective of the adventuring god, and they dramatize the introduction of those conditions of incarnation which will lead to that god forgetting His or Her true nature once they are born. Subsequent initiations teach the "Magick of Baphomet" by means of which one's divinity may be rediscovered in the context of a flesh and blood existence.

One of the implications of these rituals is that incarnation is, for most of us, an incomplete process. There is the first incarnation by means of which a god is wedded to a mortal body. This results in physical birth. But most of us lead our lives subject to the blind forces of matter, unaware that our true selves are eternal.

Incarnation is completed when the adventuring god comes to fully inhabit His or Her mortal vessel. This occurs with the purification of the natural soul and its transformation into Babalon. At that point one is able to receive the influx of fire from the spiritual Sun. This is also called the "true fire within the reed," the reception of Baphomet or the Lion-Serpent into the womb of the soul.

Joseph von Hammer-Purgstall, a late-18th/early-19th century orientalist interpreted the name *Baphomet* to derive from the Greek *Baphe Metis* or *Baptism of Wisdom*. The indwelling of the divine is completed when the fire of Chokmah (Hebrew for "wisdom") fertilizes the womb of the Mother, Binah, by means of the Lion-Serpent or Baphomet.

---

13  *Liber* XV, part 3

# The Eighth Article

The eighth article reads:

> And I confess my life one, individual, and eternal that was, and is, and is
> to come.[14]

In the eighth article of our Creed, we are confessing our identity with this
adventuring god seeking full incarnation through us. For most of us, this is
a statement of faith, not certainty. The Gnostic Mass allows us to ritualistically participate in a world in which this is symbolically true. By doing the
steps and signs, by saying the words, and by taking communion we are participating in that higher reality beyond body and mind through our bodies
and minds—but this participation can only be effective when done with the
proper mindset, a mindset which is established by the Creed.

The purpose of the Gnostic Mass is to help us find ourselves in the world
we have just described in these eight articles. Its purpose is to lead us through
the motions of identifying with the solar-phallic deity at the center of our
being. This will lead to the process of incarnation being completed by the
Baptism of Wisdom, the result of which will be the god within us waking up
to the goddess all around Him.

# The Pranava

The Creed concludes:

> AUMGN, AUMGN, AUMGN.[15]

AUMGN is the Thelemic form of the Pranava, "Aum". According to Crowley "Aum" expressed the course of existence from immaterial breath or spirit,
represented by A or Aleph, into manifestation represented by U or Vau,
which then passes away into M or Mem, the silence of destruction.[16]

Crowley's dissatisfaction with AUM stems from his view that it makes
death seem like a catastrophe which later religions then had to "redeem"
with the formula of the dying god. He sought to modify AUM so that it
reflected the New Aeonic view that existence proceeds by means of undula-

---

14 Ibid.

15 Ibid.

16 For this and what follows, see *Magick in Theory and Practice*, ch 7.

tions or cycles and requires no sacrifices of atonement.

In his new formula, M is replaced by the 3-in-1 letter MGN. The total formula represents A, the Holy Spirit, present in the Gnostic Mass as the Secret Lord, expressing itself as U or V, the manifest individual, the celestial expression of which is the Sun or God. M or Mem now represents the withdrawal of phenomena back into unmanifest unity. This occurs with what we call death, but it also occurs with samadhi (the meditative state in which subject and object collapse into and annihilate one another). It also occurs in orgasm and is represented in the Gnostic Mass when the Priest sacrifices his life and his joy to the Sun-god, ON. In other words it represents the relinquishment of attachment to manifest existence, a process which does not entail catastrophe.

G or Gimel is the path on the Tree of Life to which The High Priestess and the Moon are attributed. The dark orb of the Moon does not generate light of its own; rather, it reflects the light of the Sun. Similarly, each incarnation we go through is merely the projection in space and time of the immortal, indestructible, adventuring god who is the true self.

N or Nun refers to Scorpio, represented by the eagle, the snake, and the scorpion. The Death card is attributed to this path, death being one description of the orgasm, the uniting of life and joy that produces a new incarnation. Nun also means serpent, which is the hieroglyph symbolizing the fire of the Holy Spirit that accomplishes the miracle of incarnation.

So in the total formula we have a recapitulation of many of the themes we have explored in other parts of the Creed, in particular the way the unmanifest and eternal expresses itself through the manifest and the perishable. This is shown in AUMGN to be a continuous, perhaps unending process.

## Conclusion

The Creed of the Gnostic Mass establishes the mindset Crowley intended us to carry into the ritual. What I have tried to impress upon you is that the Creed should be understood as expressing what Crowley termed the central truth of the philosophy of Thelema, namely, that all manifest existence results from the conjoining of Hadit with Nuit. They combine to give rise to manifest individuals. Manifest individuals or stars are changeless units that express themselves through constant change of appearance.

The Secret Lord and the cosmic Womb are Hadit and Nuit.

Their union in the heavens is the Sun. Their union in living beings is the generative principle or Chaos.

Their union represented as inanimate matter is the Earth—though the Earth is only apparently inanimate, as it contains the divine principle within itself, represented by its core. We also considered the way in which the Earth is also a representation of the human being in their natural state: their bodies and minds are like the matter of the Earth, concealing the fire of divinity within. We looked at how Babalon represents the very same soul purified, so as to become a passive medium between the divinity within and the divinity all around us.

The fire that leaps up into the soul, so as to unite that soul with its hidden god, is the Lion-Serpent or Baphomet. It impregnates the soul, transforming the individual into a 2-in-1 unity called the Saint.

We saw how E.G.C. embodies the exact same unity as a manifest individual, but now as a human institution. The church with its practices, procedures, and beliefs is the outer form, but it is animated by an inner form or inner church which is called the Communion of Saints in the Creed.

We considered how matter is transformed or transmuted into spiritual substance by means of the Miracle of the Mass. We saw how this more general process is exemplified in the Gnostic Mass by the consecration and consumption of the eucharist.

We looked at how the Baptism of Wisdom—the leaping up of the concealed fire into the womb of the soul—completes the Miracle of Incarnation and transforms the manifest individual into a Saint.

We considered how the Gnostic Mass is not just a dramatic portrayal of the truths we have just described. Rather, it allows us as congregants and ritualists to participate in those truths with our minds and our bodies, with the goal of eventually discovering within ourselves that very same principle of immortality described by the articles of our Creed.

The universe is not full of stuff. The universe is full of stars. It is stars all the way down.

The path of liberation in Thelema is the progressive realization of this truth, that the universe is alive: it is breathing, it is humming.

*AUMGN.*

# 12

# The Essence of O.T.O. Initiation

O.T.O. stands for *Ordo Templi Orientis*, which is Latin for *Order of the Temple of the East* or *Order of Oriental Templars*. The purpose of O.T.O. is to secure the liberty of the individual and his or her advancement in light, wisdom, understanding, knowledge, and power, through beauty, courage, and wit on the foundation of universal brotherhood.

All of the work of O.T.O. is based on and is informed by Thelema. *Thelema* is a Greek word which means *will*. It is a spiritual and religious philosophy, a spiritual path, or what I think of as a way of life which was created by Aleister Crowley.

The work of O.T.O. is carried out by means of our two component rites: Ecclesia Gnostica Catholica and Mysteria Mystica Maxima.

Ecclesia Gnostica Catholica—the Gnostic Catholic Church—or E.G.C. is our ecclesiastical rite. This part of O.T.O. is responsible for celebrating *Liber XV*, the Gnostic Mass, and for performing baptisms, confirmations, weddings, ordinations, and last rites. E.G.C. fulfills many of the functions of a church. E.G.C. will not be the focus of this lecture. Instead we will focus on our second component rite: Mysteria Mystica Maxima—Greatest Mystical Mysteries—or M∴M∴M∴.

Mysteria Mystica Maxima is a mystery school and an initiatory rite. In contrast with a religious rite, which is done publicly, the ceremonies of M∴M∴M∴ are carried out privately, and those who go through them are sworn never to share them with anyone who is not an initiate.

Our work in M∴M∴M∴ is in part based on the initiations of ancient mystery schools. In ancient mystery schools, a hierophant or an initiator would introduce a particular individual to a particular god or goddess, for example, Demeter, Persephone, or Dionysus. Our work in our initiatory rite in O.T.O. is similar in a lot of respects to those ancient mystery schools with one important exception: in O.T.O. the god or goddess that you are being introduced to is none other than yourself.

The motto of O.T.O. is *Deus est homo*: God is man or God is the human being—or as Crowley sometimes states it: *there is no god but man.*

In this statement, "there is no god but man," man is not sex-exclusive. It refers to the human being, the human individual.

That there is no god but the individual human being is one of the central mysteries, if not the essential mystery, of O.T.O. In part it's a mystery because, on the face of it, this statement makes no sense. It's a contradiction in terms.

This statement fuses two opposed terms. On the one hand, there is the concept of *God.* God is omnipotent, omniscient, and omnipresent. On the other hand, we have the human being who is weak, frail, vulnerable, embodied, subject to sickness, infirmity, aging, and ultimately death: a being that's blind from birth, that spends all of its life mired in ignorance. The human being is a limited being, a being which is restricted to a particular place and time, which is restricted to a particular culture, family, genetics, upbringing, socioeconomic status, and country of birth. In this statement we don't just see a union of opposed terms but a union of extremes, what Carl Jung would refer to as a *coniunctio.*

"There is no god but man" is not a statement of atheism. This statement does not say there is no god, full stop. It says there is no god but man. The word *God* here is not placed in scare quotes as if Crowley is somehow winking at us.

"There is no god but man" implies a dependence of the divine on the human. "There is no god but man" means that were there no individual human beings, there would be no God. There *could* be no God. As great, powerful, awesome, and terrifying as God is and can be, and no matter how much we are dwarfed in comparison, we are still needed for something. We are still necessary.

"There is no god but man" implies that God is revealed, at least to some degree. "There is no god but man" means that God is not completely withdrawn. God is not completely transcendent. This is not a purely mystical conception of God. We do not encounter God solely through a cloud of unknowing. God can be known at least in part by means of our senses, by means of our imaginations,  by means of our intellects. This is because God is flesh and blood. This mystery is a theme of the work of O.T.O. in all of its degrees, and its meaning is taught gradually throughout the degree ceremonies by means of allegory and symbol.

## The Man of Earth

There are 21 degrees in all in O.T.O. The first six degrees—0° through Perfect Initiate—are called the *Man of Earth* degrees. As in the case of the statement *Deus est homo*, *Man of Earth* is sex-inclusive. The Man of Earth is the run-of-the-mill individual. This is the natural individual, the individual who has not gone through initiation, who has not been spiritually awakened. Crowley represents this individual with the symbol of the inverted pentagram, which he tells us means spirit submerged in and dominated by matter. By representing the human being in their natural state with the inverted pentagram, Crowley is not saying that human beings are by nature evil. This is not a commentary on the sins of the flesh. Nor is there any notion in Thelema of original sin for which we have to atone. Nor is he saying that we are somehow cast off sparks of the divine that have fallen into and become trapped in matter. This is not Gnosticism. He's making a descriptive statement: we are spirits submerged in and dominated by matter.

The figure of the pentagram suggests the human body with its head, two arms, and two legs. When the figure is inverted, it suggests an individual who is upside-down. This is a person who does not know up from down or right from left. They lack orientation in life. To have orientation means having some reference point which orders all one's other experiences. Imagine I bring you blindfolded into a completely dark house you've never been in before. If I remove the blindfold and instruct you to find your way out, you can eventually do it by groping your way around. But if I briefly turn on the lights for even a second, you will make it out more quickly, because I have given you orientation. Likewise, if you're lost in the woods, you may make it out more quickly if you can figure out which way is north.

The inverted pentagram is the person without orientation. Their north star—the center of their being—is obscured, and so they are groping about in life. They are mistaken about what is most valuable in life, and so they're not capable of ordering the other things in their life hierarchically so they can pursue what is most worthy.

We understand ourselves by and large by the things that we experience and by the things that we desire. We identify with things of sense and with our physical bodies. We identify with our personalities, our tendencies, our memories, and our likes and dislikes. We identify with the things that we're trying to get in life: promotions, cars, some goal or other. But all of these things are subject to conditions far outside of our control, and so we find ourselves in a state of insecurity, of instability, and ceaseless fluctuation. We fear death.

The Man of Earth initiations are meant to teach this person who they truly are and to help them find their north star: the divine within them. The divine with them is not something of relative worth. It is something of infinite worth. Being thus oriented toward that thing of infinite worth, they are then able to arrange all the other things in life hierarchically and to know what's worth pursuing.

The person represented by the inverted pentagram has their real self, the real center of their being, hidden inside of them. This is the quintessence of spirit which we can think of as an aspect or a mode of ultimate reality, and Crowley tells us it's submerged in matter and submerged in the darkness, submerged under the earth. For the Man of Earth, this means that the solution to our ignorance, the solution to our weakness, the solution to our limitation is not to be sought somewhere else. It's not to be sought in heaven. It's not to be sought through a savior. It's not even to be sought in India or Tibet. It's to be sought right here, right now.

We find ourselves in a world of darkness. We are in search of light. Paradoxically, the light is to be found in the darkness. The light is not to be found in heaven. It is not to be found in the pleroma. It is not to be found in the blood of Christ. The light is to be found within the darkness of ourselves: those parts of reality and of ourselves rejected by other religions.

Similarly, our freedom is not to be sought by severing our relationships with other people or with our physical bodies. Freedom is to be found in and through conditions. Power is to be sought in and through vulnerability in embodiment, and immortality and eternity are to be found through our mortality, through our susceptibility to death.

The journey of the Man of Earth is a journey *underground*. We are not to travel up and away into heaven to escape all of this. We are to make the journey into Hell.

## Our Divine Inheritance

Although the divine is buried within us, it signals its presence to us in a variety of ways. It can express itself in dreams. It can express itself as a sense of lack, a sense that something is missing, a greater or lesser desire for something more than what this world seems even capable of offering. It expresses itself as a yearning to experience light, truth, wisdom, and peace.

Most individuals are probably only dimly aware of the sense that there could be something more than what our senses tell us is there, and when that feeling arises, thankfully there's no shortage of things at our disposal to get rid of that feeling: drink, drugs, gurus, and therapists. There are even spiritual teachers happy to tell you that you are already perfect. "Everyone is already enlightened! Striving after illumination will just further ensconce you in illusion. That will be $500, please."

Or perhaps it manifests itself in a more dramatic way at midlife: fear of mortality, a sense of dread, a sense of meaninglessness, a sense like something has been squandered or wasted.

But generally the more we acknowledge those promptings, the more we turn toward them instead of away from them, the more they grow. They turn into an unrelenting desire for meaning, a hunger for purpose that will not be satisfied by mere clichés, a desire for transcendence, beauty, and power. These desires drive us out into the world in search of spiritual experiences, drugs, gurus, spiritual philosophies, and practices of pretty much all kinds.

We tend to think that the solutions lie outside ourselves. All we have to do is find the right guru or master, the right practices. We have to "do the work," say the right barbarous invocation, join the most powerful wizard's Discord. That will bring about the appropriate life-changing experience, and the hunger and thirst will finally cease.

But there's another possibility, which is that the very sense of lack, the urge, the sense of urgency itself *is* the divine inside of us. If so, then all of the techniques, philosophies, and all the things from outside don't come in to fill it up but perhaps they can be food that causes it to germinate and to grow and to develop into something else.

We tend to think that we have the ability to somehow work with this desire, to apply it, to send it in a direction, and to ride it. But if this striving for the light is the divine within us, then we have no control over it. It is riding us. It is working on us. It is transforming us. We are the clay that it's working with. Schools, techniques, magical orders, and communities can help or hurt this process. Conditions are important. But the growth and development of the divine itself is a natural process. It unfolds naturally, and its growth is as much beyond our control as the growth of a tree.

The divine seed or drive within us is what Crowley refers to as the true will. The true will is what has the power to lead us from darkness into light.

# True Will and the Cosmos

True will is not your freedom of choice. It's not your style. It's not your personality. It's the true purpose of your sojourn—not just along the spiritual path, not just on Sundays, not just when you're in the temple or in the magical circle—but through this entire life, maybe even through multiple lives.

True will has its roots in the ancient ideas of macrocosm or cosmos. Ancient people did not see the world the way that we do now: as a mere mechanism. Instead they saw it as a living being. They saw it as a *zōon*. And like all living creatures, the cosmos has its own purpose, its own ends, its own metabolism, its own process of creation and procreation.

Societies, city-states, civilizations, and individuals were seen as the organs of this larger organism. Each contributed to the metabolism of the whole. Each person served a function in it. The work of civilization served human ends, but it also served divine ends. The magician played a special role in this scheme. The purpose of the magician was to go between worlds—between the world of the divine and the world of humans—and often this was conceived of as journeying underground. The magician had the power to journey underground and to bring back divine wisdom. They could plant it here for the benefit of human beings. The healing arts, astronomy, agriculture, mathematics, and laws came from the gods. While this was of benefit to human society, it was also part of a larger process whereby the divine was brought into this world and planted here and allowed to grow and to develop in its own right. To travel to the other world and to bring something back was seen as the continuation of a cycle which was larger than any one particular individual. It was larger than a generation or a culture or even a civilization. Magicians were chosen by the gods to fulfill this function. You could not become a magician by simply mastering a technique or taking a course.

Similarly, your true will is not something you choose. You do not create it. It is more like fate. You discover it. You can choose to live in alignment with it, and when you do, you are fulfilling the purpose which has been ordained for you. You find your place in this world. You serve something higher than yourself.

The problem that defines the Men of Earth is the ignorance of their true wills. The pentagram is inverted because the individual is oriented toward everything but their true purpose. To turn the pentagram around is to identify yourself with service to something higher. This higher part of yourself is your true self. It is the deepest part of your being. It is directly connected with the cosmological cycle, and therefore it never tastes death.

The more we serve the divine within ourselves and listen to and carry out its promptings, the clearer its voice becomes, and the greater it grows in strength within us.

The divine within us is like a seed. It is our divine inheritance. It knows the light, but it must seek it through the darkness of matter, particularly the darkness of our bodies and the darkness of this world. It uses our senses, our consciousness, our thoughts, and our personalities to do this. This means that the divine within us subjects itself to conditions: conditions of birth, genetics, family dynamics, upbringings, culture—things which to us seem like restrictions that hem us in, but in fact they are the means by which the divine within us can come to fruition.

We are the container and the soil for this divine growth. There is no god but man. The individual human being is the site of the fruition of the divine. God requires a body. God requires a personality and a mind in the same way that a seed requires food, air, water, and sunlight.

The divine needs our help in order to make its way through the darkness of the soil of our beings toward the light. This means that what we do matters. Where our intention goes, where our attention goes, how we align ourselves, and what actions we take matter to this divine being within us. This is not simply a path of "self-actualization," and it is not a path of "self-care". It is a path of gratitude to the divine inheritance with us, expressed as service to its growth.

To ignore the divine within ourselves—even to turn away from it—cannot hurt it. It is stainless. But without our consciousness, the divine never experiences the fullness of its own being, and we never experience ours. This is why how you live your life matters. To fail to do your true will is not a mere abstract moral failing. The being of God and the being of the individual are both on the line. The significance is cosmological.

## God and Relationality

There is no god apart from the individual human being, but that does not guarantee that there are individuals. Without our relationship to the divine within us, we may exist as biological beings. We are species of Great Apes. But we are not individual human beings. We are not living in the fullness of our divine inheritance. The relationship between the divine and the human is one of interdependence. We are the food of the divine within. It feeds on our attention and devotion. It swells in power as we live a life in accordance with it, as we heed the call, as we hear the word.

We are like the container in which it grows. The container has to have integrity. It can't be cracking on the sides and spilling out soil and water. This means maintaining self-discipline. It means maintaining the sense of orientation toward your true purpose in life and not allowing yourself to be pulled this way and that. Integrity means that you are the master of attraction and repulsion; they do not master you. Integrity means freedom from addiction.

The divine is not just vulnerable to our relationship with ourselves; it is also vulnerable to the relationships we have with other people. To what extent are your actions subject to the agendas of those around you? Are you oriented toward your intrinsic purpose, or are you merely the sum of the three or four strongest personalities around you?

Our relations with others can help or hinder the growth of the divine. They can also reflect the divine and embody the divine as well as obscure it. While being part of a community of spiritual practitioners does not guarantee that the divine within you will come to fruition, it can be of help if those individuals are also committed to cultivating the divine within themselves. Communities are notoriously tricky. While I will not make any promise for O.T.O. in particular, at its best, O.T.O. serves the purpose of approaching, encountering, and magnifying the divine through the yoga of our interpersonal relations.

What we are considering is a great deal larger than O.T.O. or any club or any magical fraternity. There is no god but the individual human being means that this world, this life that we inhabit right here, that we are in the middle of right now, right this moment—this world is the exclusive site of the divine. God is not God outside of this universe. God is only God in and through this universe.

But this universe is composed only of relations. It is a causally interconnected whole. There is no thing-in-itself in this universe. There is no thing that is not in causal interaction with something else—with everything else. This means that the development and the growth of the divine into a full being depends entirely on working with relations: the relationship with yourself, the relationship with the world, and the relationship with other human beings.

This is not a purely mystical path. This is not a path upward and outside of this world into the eighth sphere with the angels. This path is not fantasy. It's not a purely subjective path either. It's not purely personal. It's a path that necessarily involves the rest of the universe.

In other words it's a *magical* path.

## Divinity and Magic

When I say *magic*, I do not mean sitting in a closed room with incense burning all around while you badly pronounce Hebrew at the walls of your apart-
ment. I'm talking about a path in life. I'm talking about a complete way of
living and being. I'm talking about walking a path with the divine as the
divine. I'm talking about embodying the divine in everything we say and in
everything that we do.

Rather than worrying about how to pronounce Hebrew or Greek, we
ought to think first about what it means to live with *dignity*. Dignity means
the state or quality of being worthy of honor or respect. In other words by
your own standard, can you respect the way that you act in challenging situations? Are you the sort of person that you yourself would look up to when
you're facing a really hard challenge? When the shit hits the fan, are you the
sort of person that you would turn to for help or that you'd want around?

In this world misfortune is guaranteed. You can't control everything. Because we exist in a vast, causally interconnected universe, a lack of vaccines
on the other side of the world can lead a virus to mutate, to become more
infectious and more deadly. It can then circle the globe, get your mother sick,
and kill her. There is no individual solution to that problem. That is not a
problem you alone can prevent. But almost any terrible situation can be made
worse through dishonorable, undignified behavior. If you can't rely upon
yourself in a difficult situation, then it's unlikely other people can either.

Aleister Crowley taught that it's when we're most at unity with ourselves that the divine within us is able to shine through. You can take that
all the way out as far as you can go into mystical experience, but if you can
only experience yourself as God in states of mystical bliss, then that's a pretty
self-limiting concept of divinity. If you lose your divinity—or let's say if you
lose your dignity—as soon as you're low on money, have a fight with your
spouse, lose your job, get sick, or just do the banishing to close your temple
and walk out the door, is that really divinity worthy of the name?

Dignity does not exhaust the meaning of divinity. But it is an easily accessible point of entry into it. And it is also a useful point of orientation—a place
to return to again and again—as you deal with life's ups and downs.

As we grow in relationship to the god within, the god within grows in relationship to us. It's been said that for every step we take toward God, God takes two toward us. The human and the divine meet face to face and are joined in the House of the Sun. But the Sun isn't in heaven. The Sun is under the earth. It's in the most unlikely place. It's in the dark. The chariot to the underworld is driven by the Daughters of the Sun. As it is said in the Greek Magical Papyri, Helios is the Lord of Hell. Within us, the Lord of Hell is Hadit. His number is 666.

The House of the Sun is in our hearts. It's where the Rose and the Cross are joined. It's where the square of consciousness is joined to the circle of the all. It's where the *hieros gamos* or the mystical marriage occurs. It's where we're permanently wedded to the god within: a god who consummates His union with us as His bride and becomes flesh and blood as a result.

This culminates in a state of surrender which is called *spiritual death*. Spiritual death is not biological death, nor is it catastrophic ego loss, despite Crowley's occasionally hysterical descriptions. To undergo spiritual death does not mean losing your personality. You do not suddenly begin speaking in a low, even tone all the time like an NPR host. That's what people do when they are trying to convince themselves and others they are enlightened.

Spiritual death means losing our grip on what is inessential. It's about learning what's of infinite worth and having all those other things fall into their right places. Spiritual death is about a change in perspective and a shift in identity. It does not mean losing the personality but no longer being identified with it. It means no longer confusing ourselves with our circumstances or what we are trying to achieve right at this moment. It's about realizing that the god within which has been growing is the essential part of ourselves. It was never ours; rather we belonged to it. It was the other way around the whole time.

Each of us has a part of ourselves which is beyond death. When we undergo biological death, all that goes away is the particular manifestation, what's called the magical garment of the god, but as long as there remain those in this world who serve the divine, who have the sensitivity to the divine and the humility to listen and to serve that divine within, then the divine cycle continues. The divine will continue to come into this world, both for its benefit and for ours, and the cycle of existence will continue.

## Conclusion

Allegedly the last words of the Neoplatonic philosopher Plotinus were, "Try to bring back the god in you to the divine in the All." Plotinus was not a Thelemite, and Thelema is not Neoplatonism. But it is important to remember that this process I've been speaking about this evening is larger than O.T.O., and it is not the property of Thelema or any particular religion. It can be encountered through many different traditions. It can even be encountered on your own, through the religion of the senses and of nature. But it does not belong to you or to any of those traditions. It belongs to the cosmos.

The function of traditions with their initiations, their practices, and their teachings is not to make the divine grow within you. Initiations, practices, and teachings are food, air, water, and sunlight for what is ultimately a natural process. Thelema offers resources for feeding the divine within you. Those resources are our Holy Books, the mystical and magical practices Crowley prescribed to his students, as well as the structured relations he established in A∴A∴ and O.T.O.

The initiation rituals of O.T.O. are secret, but I have attempted to give you a sense of the theory motivating them. Nearly every idea I have conveyed to you is taught in O.T.O.'s initiation rituals by means of allegory and drama. The purpose of going through the initiation is to introduce you to these ideas in a highly charged, sacred context. The initiation rituals allow you to do more than read or hear these ideas. They allow you to physically interact with them through your body and through all of your senses. In many cases—though not all—this provides a powerful catalyst for the growth of the divine within.

# Bibliography

Aberth, Susan L., Bransford, Jesse, Breeze, William. "Panel on 'Language of the Birds: Occult and Art' at 80WSE Gallery, New York,." Recorded February 10, 2016. Accessed June 7, 2023. https://www.artforum.com/video/panel-on-language-of-the-birds-occult-and-art-at-80wse-gallery-new-york-58280

Acher, Frater. *The Everyday Path to Your Holy Guardian Angel*. Frater Acher, 2011.

Churton, Tobias. *Aleister Crowley, The Beast in Berlin: Art, Sex, and Magick in the Weimar Republic*. Rochester Vermont: Inner Traditions, 2014.

Copenhaver, Brian P. *Hermetica: The Greek Corpus Hermeticum and the Latin Asclepius in a new English translation with notes and introduction*. Cambridge: Cambridge University Press, 1992.

Crowley, Aleister, Desti, Mary, and Waddell, Leila. *Magick Liber ABA Book Four Parts I-IV, Second Revised Edition*. Boston: Weiser Books, 2002.

Emerson, Ralph Waldo. "Compensation," https://archive.vcu.edu/english/engweb/transcendentalism/authors/emerson/essays/compensation.html

Greenberg, Clement. *Forum Lectures*. Washington, D.C.: Voice of America, 1960.

IAO131. "3 Definitions of True Will in Thelema." Accessed June 7, 2023. https://thelemicunion.com/3-definitions-true-will-thelema/

Kim, Juensung. "The Science of Magic & Transformation." Accessed June 7, 2023. https://youtu.be/jlbwdKvS_Zo

Kingsley, Peter. *Ancient Philosophy, Mystery and Magic: Empedocles and Pythagorean Tradition.* Oxford: Clarendon Press, 1995.

Kraig, Donald Michael. *Modern Magick, Second Edition, Eleven Lessons in the High Magickal Arts.* St. Paul, Minnesota: Llewellyn Publications, 2001.

Lao-Tzu, *Tao Te Ching: A New English Version, with Forward and Notes.* Translated by Stephen Mitchell. New York: Harper Perennial Modern Classics, 1988.

Lemley, Brad. "Why is There Life?" *Discover.* November 2000.

Levi, Eliphas. *The Doctrine and Ritual of High Magic: A New Translation, translated by John Michael Greer and Mark Anthony Mikituk.* New York: Penguin Random House LLC, 2017.

Meyer, M., & Robinson, J. *The Nag Hammadi Scriptures.* HarperCollins. Retrieved from https://www.perlego.com/book/596472/the-nag-hammadi-scriptures-pdf (Original work published 2010)

Nietzsche, Friedrich. *Beyond Good and Evil.* London: Penguin Books, 1990.

Sabazius X° and Tau Helena. *Mystery of Mystery: A Primer of Thelemic Ecclesiastical Gnosticism.* Berkeley, CA: Conjoined Creation, 2015.

Schiller, Friedrich. *On the Aesthetic Education of Man in a Series of Letters.* Oxford: Oxford University Press, 1982.

Seligmann, Kurt. *The Mirror of Magic or Magic, Supernaturalism and Religion.* New York: Grosset and Dunlap, 1968.

Vervaeke, John. "Awakening from the Meaning Crisis, episode 1." Accessed

June 7, 2023. https://youtu.be/54l8_ewcOlY

White, Manon Hedenborg. *The Eloquent Blood.* New York: Oxford University Press, 2020.

Wittgenstein, Ludwig. *Philosophical Investigations.* Oxford: Blackwell Publishing, 1999.